Heinz-Dietrich Fischer

American Public Figures Communicate Through Memoirs

Pulitzer Prize Panorama

edited by

Prof. Dr. Heinz-Dietrich Fischer
(Bochum)

Volume 22

LIT

Heinz-Dietrich Fischer

American Public Figures Communicate Through Memoirs

Pulitzer Prize Winning Autobiographies

LIT

Gefördert durch Mittel der Pressestiftung RWV, Essen

Cover image:
The Computer Graphic on the front-cover, entitled "Return to Square", was created by Masao Koomura and Kunio Yamanaka of the Computer Technique Group, Tokyo.

This book is printed on acid-free paper.

Bibliographic information published by the Deutsche Nationalbibliothek
The Deutsche Nationalbibliothek lists this publication in the Deutsche Nationalbibliografie; detailed bibliographic data are available in the Internet at http://dnb.dnb.de.

ISBN 978-3-643-91295-4 (pb)
ISBN 978-3-643-96295-9 (PDF)

A catalogue record for this book is available from the British Library.

Flössergasse 10
CH-8001 Zürich
Tel. +41 (0) 76-632 84 35
E-Mail: zuerich@lit-verlag.ch http://www.lit-verlag.ch

Distribution:

In the UK: Global Book Marketing, e-mail: mo@centralbooks.com
In North America: Independent Publishers Group, e-mail: orders@ipgbook.com
In Germany: LIT Verlag Fresnostr. 2, D-48159 Münster
Tel. +49 (0) 2 51-620 32 22, Fax +49 (0) 2 51-922 60 99, e-mail: vertrieb@lit-verlag.de

e-books are available at www.litwebshop.de

Preface

When Joseph Pulitzer (1847-1911) designed the prizes named after him, he not only thought about awards for outstanding achievements in various journalism fields but he also cared for distinguished book publications in fictional and nonfictional areas. Two nonfictional award categories were called „History“ and „Biography or Autobiography.“ In 1962, a third prize of that kind was added to the existing award groups, entitled „General Nonfiction.“

With regard to the „Biography or Autobiography“ prizes it can be said that over the span of more than one-hundred years of existence about 90 percent of the awards went to biographical works, leaving only a small rest to autobiographical volumes. While primarely research-based biographies of public figures from different fields intend to be - to some extent - objective descriptions of the lives and merits of persons, autobiographies on the other hand may be called partly subjective reflections of their authors, textual self-fashioning.

„Notoriously difficult to define,“ the 'Living Handbook of Narratology' states, „autobiography in the broader sense of the word is used almost synonymously with 'life writing' and denotes all modes and genres of telling one's own life. More specifically, autobiography as a literary genre signifies a retrospective narrative that undertakes to tell the author's own life, or a substantial part of it, seeking (at least in its classic version) to reconstruct his/her personal development within a given historical, social and cultural framework.“

The volume at hand contains small excerpts from a dozen Pulitzer Prize-winning autobiographies of very different kind, in each case based on the first editions of the works. The texts are reprinted with reference to the 'Doctrine of Fair Use' as embodied in the United States Copyright Act. According to this doctrine, excerpts of copyrighted works may be reprinted when their use does not encompass a substantial portion of these works. So it is in each of these cases.

To realize this scholarly volume, it was necessary to use the award-winning autobiographical books as located in the Pulitzer Prize Collection at the Rare Book and Manuscript Library at Columbia University in New York City. In addition to the text sources, thanks to the Pulitzer Prize administrators Dana Canedy and Edward M. Kliment at Columbia's Graduate School of Journalism, the unpublished and confidential reports of the Pulitzer Prize juries could be consulted. I am also thankful to Dr. Jörg Kurzeja of RWV at Essen, Germany.

Ruhr University,
Bochum, Germany
August 2020

H.-D. Fischer

This Volume
is dedicated to

Prof. Dr. Joan M. H. J. Hemels

Distinguished International
Journalism and Mass Media Researcher,
a true European Scientist

Contents

HISTORIAN TRAVELS TO EUROPE AS A YOUNG MAN

by *Henry B. Adams*

He was born on February 16, 1838, in Boston, Massachusetts, and died on March 27, 1918, in Washington, D. C. Henry Brooks Adams was born into one of the country's most prominent families. Both his paternal grandfather, John Quincy Adams, and great grandfather, one of the most famous among the Founding Fathers of the U.S., had been Presidents. After his graduation from Harvard University in 1858, Henry B. Adams embarked on a grand tour of Europe, during which he also attended lectures in civil law at the University of Berlin.

Adams returned home from Europe in the midst of the heated presidential election of 1860, which also was the year his father, Charles Francis Adams Sr., sought re-election to the U.S. House of Representatives. Henry tried his hand again at law, taking employment with a Boston firm, but this was short-lived. After his successful re-eleetion, Charles Francis asked Henry to be his private secretary. Henry shouldered the responsibility reluctantly and with some self-doubt. During this time, Henry was the anonymous Washington Correspondent of the *Boston Daily Advertiser*.

On March 19, 1861, President Abraham Lincoln appointed Charles Francis Adams Sr. United States Ambassador to the United Kingdom. Henry accompanied his father to London as his private secretary. He also became the anonymous London correspondent of the *New York Times*. The two Adamses were kept very busy, moderating Confederate diplomatic intrigues and trying to obstruct the construction of 'Confederate commerce raiders by British shipyards. Henry's writings for the *New York Times* argued that Americans should be patient with the British.

While in Britain, Henry was befriended by many noted men, including Charles Lyell and Frances T. Palgrave. He worked to introduce the young Henry James to English society, with his closest and livelong friend Charles Milnes Gaskell. While still in Britain, Henry read and was taken with the works of John Stuart Mill. For Adams, Mill's 'Considerations on Representative Government' showed the necessity of an enlightened, moral, and intelligent elite to provide leadership to a government elected by the masses and subject to demagoguery, ignorance, and corruption.

In 1868, Adams returned to the United States and settled in Washington, D.C., where he began working as a journalist. Adams saw himself as a traditionalist longing for the democratic ideal of the 17th and 18th centuries. Accordingly, he was keen on exposing political corruption in his journalism. In 1870, Adams was appointed professor of medieval history at Harvard, a position he held until his early retirement in 1877 at age 39. As an academic historien, Adams is considered to have been the first to conduct historical seminar work in the United States. Among his students was Henry Cabot Lodge, who worked closely with Adams as a graduate student. In 1894, Adams was elected president of the American Historical Association.

In 1904, Adams privately published a copy of his book 'Mont Saint Michel and Chartres', a pastiche of history, travel, and poetry that celebrated the unity of medieval society, especially as represented in the great cathedrals of France. In 1907 he published his memories of his early years in a small private edition for selected friends, called 'The Education of Henry Adams'. During his lifetime, he was best known for his 'History of the United States During the Administrations of Thomas Jefferson and James Madison', a nine-volume work, praised for its literary style. In 1912, Adams suffered a stroke, perhaps brought on by news of the sinking of the 'Titanic', for which he had return tickets to Europe. Six years later Henry Adams died at age 80.

Only following Henry Adam's death, 'The Education of Henry Adams' was posthumously published and made available to the general public, in an edition issued by the Massachusetts Historical Society. The work came out in September 1918 and sold more than 12,000 copies within six months in the United States, achieving greater success than any other book of Henry Adams and retaining its popularity as a classic American literature. Jean Gooder who edited the volume, mentioned that the work was „in western tradition of autographical writing."

Shortly after its publication, T. S. Eliot had reviewed the book in *Atheneum* on May 23, 1919, in a scant two pages. „If Henry Adams wrote as his own historian, or as a historian of himself," Eliot stated, „it is doubtful, whether the book ought to be called autobiography, for there is far too little of the author in it." Nevertheless, the Pulitzer Prize jurors in their report of February 8, 1919, had „come easily to the unanimous decision, that the award this year for biography should go to 'The Education of Henry Adams', published by Houghton Mifflin Co." Since the Advisory Board of the Pulitzer Prizes did not object, Adams posthumously earned the award in the „Biography or Autobiography" prize category. Following now are parts from the book about the author's first travel to Europe, told in a third-person style:

»The boy Henry wanted to go to Europe; he seemed well behaved, when anyone was looking at him; he observed conventions, when he could not escape them; he was never quarrelsome, towards a superior; his morals were apparently good, and his moral principles, if he had any, were not known to be bad. Above all, he was timid and showed a certain sense of self-respect, when in public view. What he was at heart, no one could say; least of all himself; but he was probably human, and no worse than some others. Therefore, when he presented to an exceedingly indulgent father and mother his request to begin at a German University the study of the Civil Law - although neither he nor they knew what the Civil Law was, or any reason for his studying it-the parents dutifully consented, and walked with him down to the railwaystation at Quincy to bid him good-bye, with a smile which he almost thought a tear.

Whether the boy deserved such indulgence, or was worth it, he knew no more than they, or than a Professor at Harvard College; but whether worthy or not, he began his third or fourth attempt at education in November, 1858, by sailing on the steamer Persia, the pride of Captain Judkins and the Cunard Line; the newest, largest and fastest steamship afloat. He was not alone. Several of his college companions sailed with him, and the world looked cheerful enough until on the third day, the world-as far as concerned the young man-ran into a heavy storm. He learned then a lesson that stood by him better than any University teaching ever did-the meaning of a November gale on the mid-Atlantic - which, for mere physical misery, passed endurance. The subject offered him material for none but serious treatment; he could never see the humor of sea-sickness; but it united itself with a great variety of other impressions which made the first month of travel altogether the rapidest school of education he had yet found. The stride in knowledge seemed gigantic. One began at last to see that a great many impressions were needed to make a very little education, but how many could be crowded into one day without making any education at all, became the *pons asinorum* of tourist mathematics. How many could turn out to be wrong, or whether any would turn out right, was ultimate wisdom.

The ocean, the Persia, Captain Judkins, and Mr. C.P.R. James, the most distinguished passenger, vanished one Sunday morning in a furious gale in the Mersey, to make place for the drearier picture of a Liverpool street as seen from the Adelphi coffee-room in November murk, followed instantly by the passionate delights of Chester and the romance of red-sandstone architecture. Millions of Americans have felt this succession of emotions. Possibly very young and ingenuous tourists feel them still, but in days before tourists, when the romance was a reality, not a picture, they were overwhelming. When the boys went out to Eaton Hall, they were awed, as Thackeray or Dickens would have felt in the presence of a Duke. The very name of Grosvenor struck a note of grandeur. The long suite of lofty, gilded rooms with their gilded furniture; the portraits; the terraces; the gardens; the landscape; the sense of superiority in the England of the fifties, actually set the rich nobleman apart, above Americans and shopkeepers. Aristocracy was real. So was the England of Dickens. Oliver Twist and Little Nell lurked in every church-yard shadow, not as shadow but alive. Even Charles the First was not very shadowy, standing on the tower to see his army defeated. Nothing thereabouts had very much changed since he lost his battle and his head. An eighteenth-century American boy fresh from Boston naturally took it all for education, and was amused at this sort of lesson. At least he thought he felt it.

Then came the journey up to London through Birmingham and the Black District, another lesson, which needed much more to be rightly felt. The plunge into darkness lurid with flames; the sense of unknown horror in this weird gloom which then existed nowhere else, and never had existed before, except in volcanic craters; the violent contrast between this dense, smoky, impenetrable darkness, and the soft green charm that one glided into, as one emerged - the revelation of an unknown society of the pit - made a boy uncomfortable, though he had no idea that Karl Marx was standing there waiting for him, and that sooner or later the process of education would have to deal with Karl Marx much more than with Professor Bowen of Harvard College or his Satanic free trade majesty John Stuart Mill. The Black District was a practical education, but it was infinitely far in the distance. The boy ran away from it, as he ran away from everything he disliked.

Had he known enough to know where to begin he would have seen something to study, more vital than the Civil Law, in the long, muddy, dirty, sordid, gas-lit dreariness of Oxford Street as his dingy four-wheeler dragged its weary way to Charing Cross. He did notice one peculiarity about it worth remembering. London was still London. A certain style dignified its grime; heavy, clumsy, arrogant, purse-proud, but not cheap; insular but large; barely tolerant of an outside world, and absolutely selffconfident. The boys in the streets made such free comments on the American clothes and figures, that the travellers hurried to put on tall hats and long overcoats to escape criticism. No stranger had rights even in the Strand. The eighteenth century held its own. History muttered down Fleet Street, like Dr. Johnson, in Adams's ear; Vanity Fair was alive on Piccadilly in yellow chariots with coachmen in wigs, on hammer-cloths; footmen with canes, on the footboard, and a shrivelled old woman inside; half the great houses, black with London smoke, bore large funereal hatchments; everyone seemed insolent and the most insolent structure in the world was the Royal Exchange and the Bank of England. In November,

1858, London was still vast, but it was the London of the eighteenth century that an American felt and hated.

Education went backward. Adams, still a boy, could not guess how intensely intimate this London grime was to become to him as a man, but he could still less conceive himself returning to it fifty years afterwards, noting at each return how the great city grew smaller as it doubled in size; cheaper as it quadrupled its wealth; less imperial as its empire widened; less dignified as it tried to be civil. He liked it best when he hated it. Education began at the end, or perhaps would end at the beginning. Thus far it had remained in the eighteenth century, and the next step took it back to the sixteenth. He crossed to Antwerp. As the 'Baron Osy' steamed up the Scheldt in the morning mists, a travelling-band on deck began to play, and groups of peasants, working along the fields, dropped their tools to join in dancing. Ostade and Teniers were as much alive as they ever were, and even the Duke of Alva was still at home. The thirteenth-century Cathedral towered above a sixteenth-century mass of tiled roofs, ending abruptly in walls and a landscape that had not changed.

The taste of the town was thick, rich, ripe, like a sweet wine; it was mediaeval, so that Rubens seemed modern; it was one of the strongest and fullest flavors that ever touched the young man's palate; but he might as well have drunk out his excitement in old Malmsey, for all the education he got from it. Even in art, one can hardly begin with Antwerp Cathedral and the Descent from the Cross. He merely got drunk on his emotions, and had then to get sober as he best could. He was terribly sober when he saw Antwerp half a century afterwards. One lesson he did learn without suspecting that he must immediately lose it. He felt his middle ages and the sixteenth century alive. He was young enough, and the towns were dirty enough - unimproved, unrestored, untouristed - to retain the sense of reality. As a taste or a smell, it was education, especially because it lasted barely ten years longer; but it was education only sensual. He never dreamed of trying to educate himself to the Descent from the Cross. He was only too happy to feel himself kneeling at the foot of the Cross; he learned only to loath the sordid necessity of getting up again, and going about his stupid business.

This was one of the foreseen dangers of Europe, but it vanished rapidly enough to reassure the most anxious of parents. Dropped into Berlin one morning without guide or direction, the young man in search of education floundered in a mere mess of misunderstandings. He could never recall what he expected to find, but whatever he expected, it had no relation with what it turned out to be. A student at twenty takes easily to anything, even to Berlin, and he would have accepted the thirteenth century pure and simple since his guides assured him that this was his right path; but a week's experience left him dazzled and dull. Faith held out, but the paths grew dim. Berlin astonished him, but he had no lack of friends to show him all the amusement it had to offer. Within a day or two he was running about with the rest to beer-cellars and music-halls and dance-rooms, smoking bad toobacco, drinking poor beer, and eating sauerkraut and sausages as though he knew no better. This was easy. One can always descend the social ladder. The trouble came when he asked for the education he was promised. His friends took him to be registered as a student of the University; they selected his professors and courses; they showed him where to buy the Institutes of Caius and several German works on the Civil Law in nunlerous vol urnes; and they led him to his first lecture.

His first lecture was his last. The young man was not very quick, and he had almost religious respect for his guides and advisers; but he needed no more than one hour to satisfy him that he had made another failure in education, and this time a fatal one. That the language would require at least three months' hard work before he could touch the Law was an annoying discovery; but the shock that upset him was the discovery of the university itself. He had thought Harvard College a torpid school, but it was instinct with life compared with all that he could see of the. University of Berlin. The German students were strange animals, but their professors were beyond pay: The mental attitude of the university was not of an American world. What sort of instruction prevailed in other branches, or in science, Adams had no occasion to ask, but in the Civil Law he found only the lecture system in its deadliest form as it flourished in the thirteenth century.

The professor mumbled his comments; the students made, or seemed to make, notes; they could have learned from books or discussion in a day more than they could learn from him in a month, but they must pay his fees, follow his course, and be his scholars, if they wanted a degree. To an American the result was worthless. He could make no use of the Civil Law without some previous notion of the Common Law; but the student who knew enough of the Common Law to understand what he wanted, had only to read the Pandects or the commentators at his ease in America, and be his own professor. Neither the method nor the matter nor the manner could profit an American education.

This discovery seemed to shock none of the students. They went to the lectures, made notes, and read textbooks, but never pretended to take their professor seriously. They were much more serious in reading Heine. They knew no more than Heine what good they were getting beyond the Berlin accent-which was bad; and the beer - which was not to compare with Munich; and the dancing-which was better at Vienna. They enjoyed the beer and music,

Königl. Friedrich-Wilhelms-Universität

zu Berlin.

Verzeichniss

der

Studirenden.

Namen der Studirenden.	Ostern.	Michaelis.	Geburtsort oder Vaterland.	Studium.	Wohnung. Hausnummer.	Wohnung. Namen der Straßen.
A.						
Ackermann, E.	—	57	Holstein	Med.	51	Louisen
Adam, F.	—	58	Schlesien	Phil.	31	Kronen
Adams, F.	—	58	Rheinpreußen	Med.	52	Louisen
Adams, H. B.	—	58	Amerika	Rechte	21	Dorotheen
Adelung, W.	—	56	Prov. Brandenburg	Med.	40	Tauben
Aeplinius, O. F.	58	—	Prov. Sachsen	Theol.	14	Spittelmarkt
Ahlhorn, A.	—	58	Oldenburg	Rechte	49	Kronen
Albert, M.	—	58	Siebenbürgen	Theol.	1	Kalkscheunen
Alba, J.	58	—	Frankfurt a. M.	Med.	27	Rosen
Alt, L.	—	58	Hamburg	Rechte	35	Leipziger
Anderson, N.	—	58	Nordamerika	„	2	Charlotten
Andrea, F. W. R.	—	58	Prov. Sachsen	Phil.	229	Friedrichs
Ansell, G.	56	—	London	Med.	63	Louisen
Anspach, M.	—	58	Westpreußen	„	12	N. Wilhelms
Appelius, H.	—	57	Berlin	Rechte	53	Holzmarkt
Arendt, C. J. H. E.	56	—	„	Phil.	17	Unt. d. Linden
Arndt, F.	58	—	Meckl. Strelitz	Med.	17	Gips
Arndt, W.	—	58	Westpreußen	Phil.	14	Mühlendamm
Arndt, K.	—	58	Hamburg	Rechte	33	Dorotheen
Arnold, W.	—	57	Pommern	„	16	Schiffbauerd.
Aschenborn, J.	—	58	Berlin	„	25	Chaussée
Ascher, E.	—	58	„	Med.	15	Münz
Aschoff, L.	—	58	Westphalen	„	74	Krausen

Henry B. Adams' registration as a law student at Berlin University during the Winter Term 1858/59 but they refused to be responsible for the education. Anyway, as they defended themselves, they were learning the language. So the young man fell back on the language, and being slow at languages, he found himself falling behind all his friends, which depressed his spirits the more because the gloom of a Berlin winter and of Berlin architecture seemed to him a particular sort of gloom never attained elsewhere.

One day on the Linden he caught sight of Charles Sumner in a cab, and ran after him. Sumner was then recovering from the blows of the South Carolinian cane or club, and he was pleased to find a young worshipper in the remote Prussian wilderness. They dined together and went to hear *William Tell* at the Opera. Sumner tried to encourage his friend about his difficulties of language: „I came to Berlin,“ or Rome, or whatever place it was, as he said with his grand air of mastery -“ came to Berlin, unable to say a word in the language; and three months later when I went away, I talked it to my cabman.“ Adams felt himself quite unable to attain in so short a time such social advantages, and one day complained of his trials to Mr. Robert Apthorp of Boston who was passing the winter in Berlin for the sake of its music.

Mr. Apthorp told of his own similar struggle, and how he had entered a public school and sat for months with ten-year-old boys, reciting their lessons and catching their phrases. The idea suited Adams's desperate frame of mind. At least it ridded him of the University and the Civil Law and American associations in beer-cellars. Mr. Apthorp took the trouble to negotiate with the head-master of the Friedrichs-Wilhelm- Werdersches Gymnasium for permission to Henry Adams to attend the“ school as a member of the Obertertia, a class of boys twelve or thirteen years old, and there Adams went for three months as though he had not always avoided high schools with singular antipathy. He never did anyything else so foolish, but he was given a bit of education which served him some purpose in life.

It was not merely the language, though three months passed in such fashion would teach a poodle enough to talk with a cabman, and this was all that foreign students could expect to do, for they never by any chance would come in contact with German society, if German society existed, about which they knew nothing. Adams never learned to talk German well, but the same might be said of his English, if he could believe Englishmen. He learned not to annoy himself on this account. His difficulties with the language gradually ceased. He thought himself quite Germanized in 1859. He even deluded himself with the idea that he read it as though it were English, which proved that he knew little about it; but whatever success he had in his own experiment, interested him less than his contact with German education.

Main building of Berlin University where Adams studied Law

He had revolted at the American school and university; he had instantly rejected the German university; and as his last experiience of education he tried the German high-school. The experiment was hazardous. In 1858 Berlin was a poor, keen-witted, provincial town, simple, dirty, uncivilized, and in most respects disgusting. Life was primitive beyond what an American boy could have imagined. Overridden by military methods and buureaucratic pettiness, Prussia was only beginning to free her hands from internal bonds. Apart from discipline, activity scarcely existed. The future Kaiser Wilhelm I, regent for his insane brother King Friedrich Wilhelm IV, seemed to pass his time looking at the passers-by from the window of his modest palace on the Linden.

German manners, even at Court, were sometimes brutal, and German thoroughness at school was apt to be routine. Bismarck himself was then struggling to begin a career against the inertia of the German system. The condition of Germany was a scandal and nuisance to every earnest German, all whose energies were turned to reforming it from top to bottom; and Adams walked into a great public school to get educated, at precisely the time when the Germans wanted most to get rid of the education they were forced to follow. As an episode in the search for education, this adventure smacked of Heine.

The school-system has doubtless changed, and at all events the schoolmasters are probably long ago dead; the story has no longer a practical value, and had very little even at the time; one could at least say in defence of the German school that it was neither very brutal nor very imrnoral. The headmaster was excellent in his Prussian way, and the other instructors were not worse than in other schools; it was their system that struck the systemless American with horror. The arbitrary training given to the memory was stupefying; the strain that the memory endured was a form of torture; and the feats that the boys performed, without complaint, were pitiable. No other faculty than the memory seemed to be recognized. Least of all was any use made of reason, either analytic, synthetic or dogmatic. The German government did not encourage reasoning.

All State-education is a sort of dynamo machine for polarizing the popular mind; for turning and holding its lines of force in the direction supposed to be most effective for State-purposes. The German machine was terribly efficient. Its effect on the children was pathetic. The Friedrich-Wilhelm-Werdersches Gymnasium was an old building in the heart of Berlin which served the educational needs of the small tradesmen or bourgeoisie of the neighborhood - the children were Berliner-kinder if ever there were such, and of a class suspected of sympathy and concern in the troubles of 1848. None was noble or connected with good society. Personally they were rather sympathetic than not, but as the objects of education they were proofs of nearly all the evils that a bad system could give. Apparently Adams, in his rigidly illogical pursuit, had at least reached his ideal of a viciously logical education. The boys' physique showed it first, but their physique could not be wholly charged to the school.

German food was bad at best, and a diet of sauerkraut, sausage and beer could never be good; but it was not the food alone that made their faces white and their flesh flabby. They never breathed fresh air; they had never heard of a playground; in all Berlin not a cubic inch of oxygen was admitted in winter into an inhabited building; in the school every room was tightly closed and had no ventilation; the air was foul beyond all decency; but when the American opened a window in the five minutes between hours, he violated the rules and was invariably rebuked. As long as cold weather lasted, the windows were shut. If the boys had a holiday, they were apt to be taken on long tramps in the Tiergarten or elsewhere, always ending in over-fatigue, tobacco-smoke, sausages and beer. With this, they were required to prepare daily lessons that would have quickly broken down strong men of a healthy habit, and which they could learn only because their minds were morbid. The German university had seemed a failure, but the German high-school was something very near an indictable nuisance.

Before the month of April arrived, the experiment of German education had reached this point. Nothing was left of it except the ghost of the Civil Law shut up in the darkest of closets, never to gibber again before anyone who could repeat the story. The derisive Jew laughter of Heine ran through the university and everything else in Berlin. Of course, when one is twenty years old, life is bound to be full, if only of Berlin beer, although German student life was on the whole the thinnest of beer, as an American looked on it, but though nothing except small fragments remained of the education that had been so promising - or promised - this is only what most often happens in life, when by-products turn out to be more valuable than staples. The German university and German law were failures; German society, in an American sense, did not exist, or if it existed, never showed itself to an American; the German theatre, on the other hand, was excellent, and German opera, with the ballet, was almost worth a journey to Berlin; but the curious and perplexing result of the total failure of German education was that the student's only clear gain-his single step to a higher life-came from time wasted; studies neglected; vices indulged; education reversed-it came from the despised beer-garden and music-hall; and it was accidental, uninntended, unforeseen.

When his companions insisted on passing two or three afternoons in the week at music halls, drinking beer, smoking German tobacco, and looking at fat German women knitting, while an orchestra played dull music, Adams went with them for the sake of the company, but with no pretence of enjoyment; and when Mr Apthorp gently protested that he exaggerated his indifference, for of course he enjoyed Beethoven, Adams replied simply that he loathed Beethoven; and felt a slight surprise when Mr. Apthorp and the others laughed as though they thought it humor. He saw no humor in it. He supposed that, except mUSICIans, everyone thought Beethoven a bore, as everyone except mathematicians thought mathematics a bore. Sitting thus at his beer-table, menntally impassive, he was one day surprised to notice that his mind followed the movement of a Sinfonie. He could not have been more astonished had he suddenly read a new language. Among the marvels of education, this was the most marvellous. A prisonnwall that barred his senses on one great side of life, suddenly fell, of its own accord, without so much as his knowing when it happend.

Amid the fumes of coarse tobacco and poor beer, surrounded by the commonest of German Hausfrauen, a new sense burst out like a flower in his life, so superior to the old senses, so bewildering, so astonished at its own existence, that he could not credit it, and watched it as something apart, accidental and not to be trusted. He slowly came to admit that Beethoven had partly become intelligible to him, but he was the more inclined to think that Beethoven must be much overrated as a musician, to be so easily followed. This could not be called education, for he had never so much as listened to the music. He had been thinking of other things. Mere mechanical repetition of certain sounds had stuck to his unconscious mind. Beethoven might have this power, but not Wagner, or at all events not the Wagner later than *Tannhäuser*. Near forty years passed before he reached the *Götterdämmerung*.

One might talk of the revival of an atrophied sense - the mechanical reaction of a sleeping consciousness - but no other sense awoke. His sense of line and color remained as dull as ever, and as far as ever below the level of an artist. His metaphysical sense did not spring into life, so that his mind could leap the bars of German expression into sympathy with the idealities of Kant and Hegel. Although he insisted that his faith in German thought and literature was exalted, he failed to approach German thought, and he shed never a tear of emotion over the pages of Goethe and Schiller. When his father rashly ventured from time to time to write him a word of common sense, the young man would listen to no sense at all, but insisted that Berlin was the best of educations in the best of Germanies; yet, when, at last, April came, and some genius suggested a tramp in Thuringen, his heart sang like a bird; he realized what a nightmare he had suffered, and he made up his mind that, wherever else he might, in the infinities of space and time, seek for education, it should not be again in Berlin.

The tramp in Thüringen lasted four-and-twenty hours. By the end of the first walk, his three companions - John Bancroft, James J. Higginson and B.W. Crowninshield, all Boston and Harvard College like himself - were satisfied with what they had seen, and when they sat down to rest on the spot where Goethe had written: „Warte nur, balde ruhest du auch!“ The profoundness of the thought and the wisdom of the advice affected them so strongly that they hired a wagon and drove to Weimar the same night. They were all quite happy and lighthearted in the first fresh breath of leafless spring, and the beer was better than at Berlin, but they were all equally in doubt why they had come to Germany, and not one of them could say why they stayed. Adams stayed because he did not want to go home, and he had fears that his father's patience might be exhausted if he asked to waste time elsewhere.

They could not think that their education required a return to Berlin. A few days at Dresden in the spring weather satisfied them that Dresden was a better spot for general education than Berlin, and equally good for reading Civil Law. They were possibly right. There was nothing to study in Dresden, and no education to be gained, but the Sistine Madonna and the Correggios were famous; the Theatre and Opera were sometimes excelllent, and the Elbe was prettier than the Spree. They could always fall back on the language. So he took a room in the household of the usual small government clerk with the usual plain daughters, and continued the study of the language. Possibly one might learn something more by accident, as one had learned something of Beethoven. For the next eighteen months the young man pursued accidental education, since he could pursue no other; and by great good fortune, Europe and America were too busy with their own affairs to give much attention to his. Accidenntal education had every chance in its favor, especially because nothing came amiss.

Perhaps the chief obstacle to the youth's education, now that he had come of age, was his honesty; his simple-minded faith in his intentions. Even after Berlin had become a nightmare, he still persuaded himself that his German education was a success. He loved, or thought he loved the people, but the Germany he loved was the eighteenth-century which the Germans were ashamed of, and were destroying as fast as they could. Of the Germany to come, he knew nothing. Military Germany was his abhorrence. What he liked was the simple character; the good-natured sentiment; the musical and metaphysical abstraction; the blundering incapacity of the German for practical affairs. At that time everyone looked on Germany as incapable of competing with France, England or America in any sort of organized energy. Germany had no confidence in herself, and no reason to feel it. She had no unity, and no reason to want it. She never had unity. Her religious and social history, her economical interests, her military geography, her political convenience, had always tended to eccentric rather than concentric motion. Until coal-power and railways were created, she was mediaeval by nature and geography, and this was what Adams liked.«

PHYSICIST TELLS THE STORY OF HIS ACADEMIC CAREER

by *Michael I. Pupin*

He was born on October 4, 1858, in Idvor, the region of Banat in today's Serbia, he died on March 12, 1935, in New York City. Michael Idvorsky Pupin went to elementary school in his birthplace, to Serbian Orthodox school, and later to German elementary school in Perlez. He enrolled in high school in Panĉevo, and later in the Real Gymnasium. He was one of the best students there; a local archpriest saw his enormous potential and talent, and influenced the authorities to give Pupin a scholarship.

Because of his activity in the 'Serbian Youth' movement, which at that time had many problems with Austro-Hungarian police authorities, Pupin had to leave Panĉevo. In 1872 he went to Prague, where he continued the sixth and first half of the seventh school year. After his father died in 1874, the sixteen-year-old Pupin decided to cancel his education in Prague due to financial problems and to move to the United States. For the next five years in the U.S., Pupin worked as a manual laborer, while he learned English, Greek and Latin.

After three years of various courses, in the autumn of 1879 he successfully finished his tests and entered Columbia College, where he became known as an exceptional athlete and scholar. Pupin graduated with honors in 1883 and became an American citizen at the same time. After he completed his studies, with emphasis in the fields of physics and mathematics, Pupin returned to Europe, initially the United Kingdom, where he continued his schooling at the University of Cambridge from 1883-1885. He obtained his PhD at the University of Berlin in 1889.

Pupin returned to the United States to become a lecturer of mathematical physics in the newly formed Department of Electrical Engeneering at Columbia University in New York City. His research pioneered carrier wave detection and current analysis. He was an early investigator into X-ray imaging. He learned of Röntgen's discovery of unknown rays passing through wood, paper, isulators, and thin metal leaving traces on a photographic plate, and attempted this himself. Using a vacuum tube, which he had previously used to study the passage of electricity through rarefied gases, he made successful images on January 2, 1896. Edison provided Pupin with a calcium tungstate fluoroscopic screen.

In 1899 Pupin received his patent for loading coils, archaically called 'Pupin Coils'. The importance of the patent was made clear when the American rights to it were aquired by 'American Telephone and Telegraph' company (AT&T), making Pupin wealthy. For AT&T the invention was immensely valuable due to its ability to greatly extend the range of long distance telephones and especially submarine ones. When the United States joined the First World War in 1917, Pupin was working at Columbia University, organizing a research group for submarine detection techniques. During the war Pupin was a member of the state council for research and state advisory board for aeronautics. For his work he received a laudative from U.S. president Warren G. Harding.

After World War I, Pupin was already a well-known and acclaimed scientist, as well as a politically influential figure in America. He influenced the final decisions of the Paris Peace Conference when the borders of the future kingdom of Serbst, Croats and Slovenians were drawn. Pupin stayed in Paris for two months during the peace talks in April and May 1919 on the insistence of the U. S. government. In a difficult situation during the negotiations on the borders of Yugoslavia, Pupin personally had written a memorandum on March 19, 1919, to American president Woodrow Wilson, who, based on the data received from Pupin, negotiated about the historical and ethnic characteristics of the border areas of Dalmatia, Slovenia, Istria, Banat, Medimurje, Baranja and Macedonia.

Besides of Pupin's 34 patents in course of his career, he published several dozen scientific disputes, articles and reviews. Since the early 1920s he also worked on his memoirs that came out in 1923, entitled „From Immigrant to Inventor." When the book came to the attention of next year's Pulitzer Prize jurors, they praised the volume, according to their report of February 25, 1924, when the jury chairman stated: „I can tell ... how strongly I feel about Pupin. There is a first rate example of Americanism, of the Americanizing process, of a man getting thoroughly adjusted to the genius of the country and paying back a debt, so to say, by putting it all on record. It is well written and interesting. It seems to fill our bill completely as a bit of American achievement, both in living the life and in recording it." Since the Advisory Board did not object, Michael Pupin earned the 1924 Pulitzer Prize for „Biography or Autobiography". Following now are some passages from the work, dealing with Pupin's research and teaching position at Columbia University:

»Shortly after earning my PhD at Berlin University, I was offered a position at New York's Columbia University which should start by the end of September 1889. As the ship which carried me back to the United States entered New York Harbor I saw on my right Castle Garden; it looked the same as it did fifteen years before, when I first entered on the immigrant ship, and it reminded me of that earlier day. I said to my bride, who was standing by my side, that I did not carry much more money into New York Harbor than I did fifteen years before, when I first looked upon Castle Garden, and yet I felt as rich as a Croesus, I felt, I told her, that I owned the whole of the United States, because I was sure that the United States owned me; that I had an ideal American bride, who had assured me that I had Iived up to the standards of an ideal American bridegroom; and that I had a fine position in a great American institution and strong hopes, of filling it to everybody's satisfaction.

The new „Department of Electrical Engineering in the School of Mines of Columbia College" had announced its courses of instruction quite a number of months before I arrived in New York. The late Francis Bacon Cracker, at that time the newly appointed instructor in electrical engineering and my future colleague and lifelong friend, had been consulted with regard to these courses, and he was most liberal to the theoretical side, which was to be my share of the instruction. He attached much importance to the fundamental theory, although he was a practical engineer. The new department was to be independent of the other scientific departments. We had some difficulty, however, in maintaining that independence; the older departments of engineering showed a disposition to claim some right of guardianship over the new infant department. For instance, many chemists thought that electrical engineering was largely chemistry on account of the storage batteries, the galvanic cells, and the eIectrochemical processes which formed an important part of the eIectrical operations in the early history of applied eIectricity. Others asserted that, since mechanical engineering attended to the design and the construction of electromagnetie generators and to the power plant which furnished the driving power, electrical engineering was, therefore, largely mechanical engineering.

Crocker and I maintained that there is an electrical science which is the real soul of electrical engineering, and that every other abstract science or its application was an incident only in electrical engineering. We won out in spite of the fact that at other institutions of higher learning in the United States electrical engineering was taught in the departments of physics or of mechanical engineering. But it was not an easy matter in those days to persuade people that the electrical science with its applications was then, or that it ever would be, big enough to need a department of its own, like, for instance, civil engineering.

A small brick shed, a temporary structure, had been built at Columbia College to accommodate the new department. The students called it the „cowshed," and the boy who invented the name did not indulge in any stretching of his imagination. It certainly looked like a cowshed. The laboratory equipment consisted of a dynamo, a motor, and an alternator, with some so-called practical measuring instruments. When I compared the facilities of the new „Department of Electrical Engineering at Columbia College“ with that of the Polytechnic School in Berlin, I felt somewhat humbled, but not discouraged. I said to Crocker: „Our guns are small and few in number; the men behind the guns will have to expand much beyond their present size if this department is to make any impression upon the electrical art.“ „Pupin,“ said Crocker, „you have no idea how rapidly a young fellow grows when he tries to teach a new subject to poorly prepared beginners.“

Crocker and I were given to understand that any additional equipment during the first year would have to be bought from contributions outside of the university. We raised some money by giving a course of twelve popular lectures for which we charged ten dollars per person. Each lecture lasted two hours; we were somewhat dubious about their quality, and so we provided a generous quantity. We raised in this manner three hundred dollars and bought additional equipment, but no two young scientists ever worked harder to earn three hundred dollars. The experience, however, was worth many times that amount. Our audience consisted of businessmen and lawyers, who were either interested in the electrical industries, or expected to become interested. They had hardly any previous scientific training. It took much judgment and skill to talk science to these people without shooting much above their heads. Every one of them believed that the electrical science was in its infancy, and that most of its useful applications were obtained empirically by a rule of thumb. When we told them that the electrical scicnce was one of the most exact of all physical sciences, some shook their heads and exhibited considerable scepticism. One of them asked me: „Doctor, do you know what electricity is?“ „No,“ said I, and he added another question: „Then how can you have an exact science of electricity when you do not even know what electricity is?“ To this I retorted: „Do you know what matter is? Of course you do not, nor does anybody else know it, and yet who will deny that there are exact sciences relating to material things? Do you deny that astronomy is an exact science?“ It is a difficult thing to make unscientific people understand that science studies first and foremost the activities of things and not their ultimate nature.

In that first course of public lectures I found it necessary to devote much of my exposition to the correction of erroneous notions lodged in the minds of my audience. When I told that audience that no electrical generator generates electricity, because electricity was made by God and, according to Faraday, its quantity in the universe is constant, and that for every positive charge there is an equal negative one, most members of my audience were inclined to think that I was talking metaphysics. „Then what does it generate ?“ asked one of my hearers. I answered: „It generates motion of electricity, and by that motion it furnishes us with means of doing useful work like telegraphy, telephony, and electrical lighting.“ Then I added: „The electrical science studies the forces which make electricity move against the reactions of the bodies through which it moves; in the overcoming of these reactions the moving electricity does useful work.“ Illustrations from dynamics of material bodies did not help very mueh, because my audience had hardly any knowledge of even the elements of Newton's great work, although Newton considered these elements obvious truths. All they knew about Newton was that he had „discovered gravitation.“ When I told them that Newton had discovered the law of gravitational action and not gravitation itself, they thought that I was splitting hairs. I was never quite sure that those good people had carried away much knowledge from my lectures, but I was quite sure that they had left much knowledge with me. In trying to straighten out their notions I straightened out my own very considerably. Crocker was right when he said: „You have no idea how rapidly a young fellow grows when he tries to teach a new subject to poorly prepared beginners.“ That was the real profit from our first course of public lectures.

Every cultured person is expected to have an intelligent view of literature, of the fine arts, and of the social sciences, which is as it should be. But who has ever thought of suggesting that culture demands an intelligent view of the primary concepts in fundamental sciences? If cultured people had it, there would be no need to renew periodically the tiresome topic of the alleged clash between science and religion, and there would be much more straight thinking about things in general. Every child in the public schools should be made perfectly familiar with the simple experiments which illustrate the fundamental elements of Newton's divine philosophy, as Milton calls science. Barnard, Joseph Henry, Andrew White, and the other leaders of scientific thought in the United States, who started the great movement in favor of higher scientific research and of a better scientific education, had a difficult up-hill pull, beeause people in high places lacked an intelligent view of science. A famous lawyer, a trustee of a great educational institution, looked surprised when I told him, over thirty years ago, that one cannot teach science without laboratories both for the elementary and for the advanced instruction. He actually believed that graduate schools in science needed only a lot of blackboards, chalk, and sponges, and a lecturer who could prepare his lectures by reading books. He believed what he thought would suit him best, namely, that a university should be built on the top of a heap of chalk, sponges, and books. These instrumentalities are cheaper than laboratories, and that appeals to many university trustees. The teacher who can lecture from books and not from his experience in the laboratory is also much cheaper. But heaven help the country which trusts its destiny to cheap men operating with cheap instrumentalities. I gave that trustee a lecture by reciting the sermon which Tyndall preached in the „Summary and Conclusions“ of his famous lectures of 1872-1873. I was bold enough to deliver several of these lectures to men in high places. Some liked them and some did not, but they all agreed, that I had my own opinions upon the subject and was not afraid to express them.

The American Institute of Electrical Engineers had heard of my somewhat novel opinions regarding the teaching of the electrical science in its bearing upon electrical engineering, and it invited me to give an address upon the subject at its annual meeting in Boston, in the summer of 1890. The address was entitled „Practical Aspects of the Alternating Current Theory.“ It was a eulogy of the electrical science, and particularly of Faraday, Maxwell, and Joseph Henry on the purely scientific side, and of the technical men who were developing the system of electrical power distribution by alternating electrical forces. I noticed that my audience was divided into two distinct groups; one group was cordial and appreciative, but the other was as cold as ice. The famous electrical engineer and inventor, Elihu Thomson, was in the friendly group, and he looked me up after the address and congratulated me cordially. That was a great encouragement and I felt happy. Another man, a well-known physicist and engineer, also looked me up, and asked me whether I really expected that students of electrical engineering could ever be trusted to swallow and digest all the mathematical stuff which I had presented in my address. The „mathematical stuff“ to which he referred was a very elementary theoretical illustration. I thought of my chums, the tripos youngsters at Cambridge, and of their wonderful capacity for swallowing and digesting „mathematical stuff,“ but said nothing; the man who was addressing me was one of those people who had a small opinion of the capacity and willingness of our American boys to „swallow and digest“ just as much „mathematical stuff“ as their English cousins do.

A short time prior to my return to Columbia College, in 1889, a bitter polemic had been carried on in the New York newspapers concerning the two methods of electrical power distribution, the direct and the alternating current method. The New York interests favored the first, and another group, including the Westinghouse Company, supported the alternating current method. The opponents of the latter method called it the „deadly alternating current,“ and did their best to discredit it. They actually succeeded, I was told, in persuading the State authorities to install an alternating current machine at the Sing Sing prison, to be used in electrocution. When in my addrcss at Boston I recited my eulogy of the alternating current system I did not know of this bitter polemic, but when I heard of it I understood the chilliness among a part of my audience.

In the following autumn I was made to understand that my address in Boston had made a bad impression, and that it had offended the feelings of some big men who were interested in the electrical industries. I could not help seeing the glaring hint that the new „Department of Electrical Engineering at Columbia College" was to suffer from the fact that one of its two instructors was accused of an unpardonable „electrical heresy." The great and mighty person who broached this matter to me suggested that perhaps the easiest way out of this difficulty was my resignation. „Very well," said I, „I will certainly resign if the trustees of Columbia College, who appointed me, find me guilty of a scientific heresy." The trustees never heard of this incident, but my colleague Crocker did, and he said in his characteristic manner: „There are many persons to-day who would not hesitate to burn the witch of Salem, but no persons of that kind are on the board of trustees of Columbia College." Crocker was a Cape Cod man and he had a very soft spot for the witch of Salem.

The notion among many captains of industry that the electrical science was in its infancy, and that it worked by the rule of thumb, made it possible to launch an opposition of that kind against the introduction of the alternating current system of electrical distribution of power. Tesla's alternating current motor and Bradley's rotary transformer for changing alternating currents into direct were available at that time. The electrical art was ready then to do many of the things which it is doing to-day so well, if it had not been for the opposition of people who were afraid that they would have to scrap some of their direct current apparatus and the plants for manufacturing it, if the alternating current system received any support. A most un-American mental attitude! It was clear to every impartial and intelligent expert that the two systems supplemented each other in a most admirable manner, and that the advancement of one would also advance the other. Men like Elihu Thomson and my colleague Crocker knew that, but ignorance and false notions prevailed in the early nineties, because the captains of electrical industries paid small attention to highly trained electrical scientists. That explains why in those days the barbarous steel cables were still employed to drag ears along Third Avenue, New York, and why in 1893 I saw the preparatory work on Columbus Avenue, New York, for installing additional barbarous steel ropes to drag street-cars. But, fortunately, electrical traction came to the rescue of Columbus Avenue.

During the summer of 1893 I had the good fortune to meet, quite often, William Barclay Parsons, the distinguished engineer, the future builder of the first New York subway, and to-day the distinguished chairman of the Board of Trustees of Columbia University. He passed the summer vacation at Atlantic Highlands, and I at Monmouth Beach, and we used the same steamboat in our occasional trips to New York. His head was full of schemes for the solution of the New York rapid-transit problem, but I observed that his ideas were not quite clear on the question of the electrical power transmission to be employed. A very few years later his ideas had cleared wonderfully. He had visited Budapest in 1894 and had seen there surface cars operated electrically and most satisfactorily by an underground trolley. It was a most instructive object-lesson, but how humiliating it was to the engineering pride of the great United States to consult little Hungary in electrical engineering! The electrical power transmission system employed to-day in the New York subways is practically the same which had been proposed to and accepted by Parsons, the chief engineer, not so many years after our trips to New York, in 1893; it is the electrical power transmission consisting of a combination of the alternating and direct current systems. No fundamentally novel methods were employed which did not exist at the time when the alternating current machine was installed at Sing Sing for the purpese of electrocuting people by the „deadly alternating current." In less than five years a radical change in popular notions had taken place about a matter which was well understood from the very first by men of higher scientific training, like Stillwell, the chief engineer of the Niagara Power Company, and Sprague, the well-known pioneer in electrical traction, the inventor of the multiple unit system, without which our subway would be practicably impossible.

Four historical events, very important in the annals of the electrical science in the United States, had happened in rapid succession between 1890 and 1894. The first was the successful electrical transmission of power between Lauffen and Frankfurt, in Germany, in 1891; it employed the alternating current system. The second was the decision of the Niagara Falls Power and Construction Company to employ the alternating current system for the transmission of its electrical power; Professor Henry Augustus Rowland, of Johns Hopkins University, as consulting expert of the company, favored this system; another consulting scientific expert, the famous Lord Kelvin, favored the direct current system. The third historical event was the consolidation of the Edison General Electric Company with the Thomson-Houston Company of Lynn, Massachu-setts. This consolidation meant the end of the opposition to the alternating current system on the part of people who were most influential in the electrical industries. No such opposition could exist in an electrical corporation where Elihu Thomson's expert opinion had any weight. The fourth

Pupin's residence at Norfolk, Conn., with adjoining farm buildings

historical event was the Electrical Congress at the World Exposition in Chicago, in 1893. Helmholtz came over as an official delegate of the German Empire, and was elected honorary president of the congress. The subjects discussed at that congress, and the men who discussed them, showed that the electrical science was not in its infancy, and that electrical things were not done by the rule of thumb.

Once I asked Professor Rowland whether anybody had ever suggested to him resigning from Johns Hopkins University on the ground that in favoring the alternating current system for the Niagara Falls Power Transmission plant he had made himself liable to a charge of heresy. „Heresy?“ said he; „I thought that my heresy was worth a big fee, and when the company attempted to cut it down the courts sustained my claim.“ An interesting bit of history is attached to this. When the Niagara Power and Construction Company objected to the size of the fee which Rowland charged for his services as scientific adviser, and asked for a reduction, the matter was referred to the court. During Rowland's cross-examination the defendant's lawyer, the late Joseph Choate, asked him the question: „Who, in your opinion, is the greatest physicist in the United States?“ Rowland answered without a moment's hesitation: „I am.“ The judge smiled, but agreed with the witness, and his agreement was in harmony with the opinion of all scientific men. Rowland justified his apparently egotistical answer by the fact that as a witness on the stand he was under oath to speak the truth; he certainly spoke the truth when he testified that he was the leading physicist in the United States.

Rowland's interest in the electrical science and its technical applications helped much to dissipate the notion, entertained by many, that it was empirical and still in its infancy. Bogus inventors always encouraged this superstition. The attention which Rowland and his former pupil, the late Doctor Louis Duncan, devoted to electrical engineering at Johns Hopkins University helped much to raise the status of electrical engineering. When the new General Electric Company was organized by the consolidation of the Edison General Electric Company and the Thomson-Houston Company, Elihu Thomson became the chief scientific adviser of the new corporation, and its highest court of appeals in scientific matters. I remember telling my colleague, Crocker, that if the Thomson-Houston Company had contributed nothing else than Elihu Thomson to the new corporation it would have contributed more than enough. Thomson, in my opinion, was the American Siemens, and Rowland was the American Helmholtz, of the new era in the history of American industries - the era of close co-operation between abstract science and engineering. With these two men among the leaders of the electrical science and the electrical industry in the United States, the senseless opposition to the alternating current system of power distribution began to wane. It vanished quickly after the Electrical Congress of 1893. The first visible result of the co-operation between abstract science and the technical arts was the splendid power plant at Niagara Falls, and later the electrical power distribution system in the New York subways, in which the alternating and the direct current systems supplemented each other most admirably.

The scientific spirit of Rowland's laboratory and lecture-room was felt everywhere in the electrical industries; it was felt also in our educational institutions. His and his students' researches in solar spectra and in other problems of higher physics made that spirit the dominating influence among the rising generation of physieal science in America. It was universally acknowledged that Johns Hopkins was a real university. The intellectual movement in favor of high er scientific research, first inaugurated by Joseph Henry, President Barnard of Columbia College, and Doctor John William Draper, in the early seventies, was marching on steadily under the leadership of Rowland when I started my academic career at Columbia, thirty-four years ago, and he led on like a „doughty knight of Troy," as Maxwell used to call him. It was the spirit of Johns Hopkins which inspired the generation of the early nineties in its encouragement of the movement for the development of the American university. Some enthusiasts at Columbia College went even so far as to advocate the abolition of the college curriculum and the substitution of a Columbia University for Columbia College; I was not among these enthusiasts, because I knew only too well the historical value of Columbia College and of other American colleges. What would the University of Cambridge be without its ancient colleges? College lays the foundation for higher citizenship; the university lays the foundation for higher learning.

Speaking for physical sciences I can say that in those days there was no lack of trained scientists who could easily have extended the work of the American college, and added to it a field of advanced work resembling closely the activity of the European universities. Most of these men had received their higher academic training in European universities, and quite a number of them came from Johns Hopkins. But there were two obstacles: first, lack of experimental-research facilities; second, lack of leisure for scientific research. Rowland and his followers recognized the existence of these obstacles, and demanded reform. Most of the energy of the teachers of physical sciences was consumed in the lecture-room; they were pedagogues, „pouring information into passive recipients," as Barnard described it. My own case was a typical one. How could I do any research as long as I had at my disposal a dynamo, a

THE WHITE HOUSE
WASHINGTON

October 14, 1922.

My dear Doctor Pupin:

I accept with regret your resignation as a member of the National Advisory Committee for Aeronautics. In doing so I want to express to you the thanks of the Government and people of the United States of your services as a member of the National Advisory Committee for Aeronautics since its organization in 1915.

I take this occasion to record recognition and appreciation of the fact that, as Chairman of the Sub-committee on Aircraft Communications, during the World War you undertook to develop a reliable means of communication between aircraft in flight, and that, by virtue of experiments conducted and directed in your own laboratory, you were successful in contributing in an important respect to the development of one of the great marvels of our age, the radio telephone.

I regret that you cannot continue to devote your talents to the scientific study of the problems of flight as a member of the National Advisory Committee for Aeronautics.

Most sincerely yours,

Warren G Harding

Dr. Michael I. Pupin,
Columbia University,
New York City.

Facsimile of a letter from U.S. President Warren G. Harding motor, an alternator, and a few crude measuring instruments only, all intended to be used every day for the instruction of electrical-engineering students? When the professor of engineering died, in the summer of 1891, apart of his work, theory of heat and hydraulics, was assigned to me. The professor of dynamics died a little later, and his work also was transferred to me. I was to carry the additional load of lecture-room work temporarily, but was relieved from it, in part only, after several years. As a reward my title was advanced to adjunct professor, with an advance of salary to two thousand five hundred dollars per annum. But in return for this royal salary I had to lecture three to four hours each forenoon, and help in the electrical laboratory instruction in the afternoons.

While this pedagogic load was on my back scientific research could not be seriously thought of. My young colleagues in other colleges were similarly situated. This overloading of young scientists with pedagogic work threatened to stunt, and often did stunt, their growth and also the growth of the rising American university. „Let chairs be founded, sufficiently but not Iuxuriously endowed, which shall have original research for their main object and ambition,“ was the historie warning which Tyndall addressed to the American people in 1873, but in 1893 there was little evidence that it was heeded anywhere outside of Johns Hopkins University. But there they had Rowland and a number of other stars of the first magnitude who had succeeded Joseph Henry, Barnard, and Draper as leaders of the great movement in favor of higher scientific research. In 1883 Rowland delivered a memorable address as vice-president of one of the sections of the American Association for the Advancement of Science. It was entitled, „A Plea for Pure Science,“ and described the spirit not only of Johns Hopkins of those days but also of all friends of higher learning in science. That spirit was advocated here by Tyndall in 1872-1873, and under Rowland's leadership it was bound to win our battle for higher ideals in science. The people of the United States owe a great debt of gratitude to Johns Hopkins for the leadership in that great movement which, as we see today, has produced a most remarkable intellectual advancement in this country. Nearly thirty years ago I heard Rowland say in a public address: „They always say in Baltimore that no man in that city should die without leaving something to Johns Hopkins.“ When he said it he knew that Johns Hopkins was very poor. It is poorer today than ever, and no rich man in the United States should die without leaving something to Johns Hopkins, the pioneer university of the United States.

Rowland said once that lack of experimental facilities and of time was not a valid excuse for neglecting entirely scientific research. I agreed with that opinion; neglect breeds indifference, and indifference degenerates into atrophy of the spirit of inquiry. The alternating current machine of the electrical engineering laboratory at Columbia was free in the evenings, and so was my time; that is, if my wife should not object, and, being a noble and unselfish woman, she did not object. With the assistance of several enthusiastic students, among them Gano Dunn, to-day one of the most distinguished engineers in the United States, I started investigating the passage of electricity through various gases at low pressures, and published two papers in the American Journal of Science. I soon discovered that most of my results had been anticipated by Professor J. J. Thomson, of Cambridge, who, in all probability, had received his inspiration from the same source from which I had received mine. He not only had anticipated me but, moreover, he showed a much better grasp of the subject than I had, and had much better experimental facilities. I decided to leave the field to him, and to watch his beautiful work from the outside. It was a wise decision, because it prepared me to understand the epoch-making discoveries in this field which were soon to be announced, one in Germany and one in France, I turned my attention to another field.

I must mention, however, one of the results which Thomson had not anticipated and which created quite an impression among astronomers. I noticed a peculiar appearance in the electrical discharge proceeding from a small metal sphere which was located in the centre of a large glass sphere containing air at Iow pressure. The discharges looked very much like the luminous corona of the sun which astronomers observe during eclipses, and which was always a mysterious puzzle in solar physics. Pasting a tin-foil disk on the glass sphere, so as to hide the metal sphere and see only the discharge proceeding from it, I photographed the appearance of the discharge.

In a communication read later before the New York Academy of Sciences I was much bolder, having previously discussed the subject with my friends at Johns Hopkins and with the late Professor Young, the famous astronomer at Princeton. I soon found myself advocating strongly the electromagnetic theory of solar phenomena. A German professor, Ebert by name, a wellknown authority on electrical discharges in gases, took me very seriously indeed, which was very flattering, but he claimed priority. I had no difficulty in establishing my priority through the columns of Astronomy and Astro Physics, one of whose editors was George Ellery Hale, to-day the distinguished director of Mount Wilson Observatory. I was indeed fortunate to make his acquaintance during that period when both he and I were very young men. His influence prevented me from running wild with my electromagnetic theory of solar phenomena.«

GENERAL COMMANDS U.S. TROOPS DURING WORLD WAR I

by *John J. Pershing*

He was born on a farm near Laclede, Missouri, on September 13, 1860, he died on July 15, 1948, in Washington, D.C. John Joseph Pershing attended a school in Laclede that was reserved for precocious students who were also the children of prominent citizens. Completing high school in 1878, he became a teacher of local African-American children. While pursuing his teaching career, Pershing also studied at the State Normal School, later named Truman State University, in Kirksville, Missouri, from which he graduated in 1880 with a bachelor of science degree in scientific didactics.

Two years later, he applied to the United States Military Academy. Pershing was sworn in as a West Point cadet in the fall of 1882. He was selected early for leadership positions and became successively First Corporal, First Sergeant, First Lieutenant, and First Captain. Pershing commanded, ex officio, the honor guard that saluted the funeral train of President Ulysses S. Grant as it passed West Point in August 1885. He graduated in the summer of 1886 and was commissioned a second lieutenant. Pershing briefly considered petitioning the Army to let him study law, but he was in favor of active Army duty.

He reported for active duty on September 30, 1886, and was assigned to a cavalry troop stationed at Fort Bayard, in the New Mexico Territory. While serving at the 6th Cavalry, Pershing participated in several Indian campaigns and was cited for bravery for actions against the Apache. Between 1887 and 1890, he served with the 6th Cavalry at various postings in California, Arizona and North Dakota. On December 9, 1890, Pershing and his troop arrived at Sioux City, Iowa, where Pershing played a role in suppressing the last uprisings of the Lakota (Sioux) Indians.

In September 1891 Pershing was assigned as the Professor of Military Science and Tactics at the University of Nebraska-Lincoln, a position he held for four years. While carrying out this assignment, he attended the university's College of Law, from which he received his LL.B. degree. In 1895, Pershing took command of a troop of the 10th Cavalry Regiment, one of the original Buffalo Soldier regiments composed of African-American soldiers under white officers. In 1897 he was appointed to the West Point tactical staff as an instructor, where he was assigned to Cadet Company A.

At the start of the Spanish-American War on April 23, 1898, Pershing was the regimental quartermaster for the 10th Cavalry and fought on Kettle and San Juan Hills in Cuba. In March 1899, after suffering from malaria, Pershing was put in charge of the Office of Customs and Insular Affairs which oversaw occupation forces in territories gained in the Spanish-American War, including Cuba, Puerto Rico, the Philippines, and Guam. When the Philippin-American War began, Pershing reported to Manila on August 17, 1899, was assigned to the Department of Mindanao and Jolo, and commanded efforts to suppress the Filipino Insurrection. On November 27, 1900, he was appointed Adjutant General of his department and served in this posting until March 1, 1901.

He served in the Philippines, and in June 1903, he was ordered to return to the United States. President Theodore Roosevelt, taken by Pershing's ability, petitioned the Army General Staff to promote Pershing to Colonel. In 1904 he was assigned as the Assistant Chief of Staff of the Southwest Army Division stationed in Oklahoma City. Pershing was stationed as military attaché in Tokyo in 1905. After serving as an observer in the Russo-Japanese War, he returned to the United States in the fall of 1905. President Roosevelt nominated Pershing as Brigadier General, a move which U.S. Congress approved.

In 1908, Pershing briefly served as a U.S. military observer in the Balkans, an assignment which was based in Paris. Upon returning to the United States in 1909, Pershing was assigned once again to the Philippines, an assignment in which he served until 1913. On December 20, 1913, he received orders to take command of the 8th Brigade at the Presidio in San Francisco. With tensions running high on the border between the United States and Mexio, the brigade was deployed to Fort Bliff, Texas, in April 1914. On March 15, 1916, Pershing led an expedition into Mexico to capture Pancho Villa. They routed Villa's revolutionaries, but failed to capture him.

At the start of the United States' involvement in World War I President Woodrow Wilson considered mobilizing an army to join the fight. Following America's entrance into the war in May 1917, Wilson briefly interviewed Pershing, and then selected him for the command. Pershing exercised significant control over his command, with a full delegation of authority from Wilson and the Secretary of War. After departing from New York Harbor under top secrecy in May, Pershing arrived in France in June 1917. American forces were deployed in France in the autumn of 1917. It was Pershing's most famous post when he served as the commander of the American Expeditionary Forces on the Western Front in 1917-18, where he also founded the military magazine *Stars and Stripes* on February 8, 1918.

Pershing rejected British and French demands that American forces be integrated with their armies. His soldiers first saw serious battle at Cantigny,

Chateau-Thierry, Belleau Wood, and Soissons. To speed up the arrival of American troops, they embarked for France leaving heavy equipment behind, and used British and French tanks, artillery, airplanes and other munitions. In September 1918 at St. Mihiel, the First Army was directly under Persing's comrnand; it overwhelmed - the encroachment into Allied territory - that the German Army had held for three years. For the Meuse-Argonne Offensive, Pershing shifted roughly 600,000 American soldiers to the heavily defended forest of the Argonne. The Allied Hundred Days Offensive, which the Argonne fighting was part of, contributed to Germany calling for an armistice.

After the war, during the 1920s, Pershing held several high-rank positions in the U.S. Army. During the 1930s, he largely retreated to private life, but returned to the public eye with publication of his two-volume memoirs, 'My Experiences in the World War,' that came out in 1931. When the work came to the attention of the Pulitzer Prize jurors of the following year, they stated in their report of March 22, 1932: „We are of the opinion, that General Pershing's 'My Experience in the World War' is the best work of the year and the one which should receive the award."

Then, the jury members stated about the book's content: „We are of the opinion that Pershing has not only written the most authoritative, the most penetrating and the most decisive account of our own part in the war but that he has presented a finer spirit in narration than any of the others, more objectivity, more fullness, and more balance... Pershing's book is epic in the sense that it is a great national story, displaying the American character in its finest aspects. It has drama, too, for we constantly feel two motives working in antagonism - the determination of European Powers that America should play no decisive part in the war and the determination of Pershing that it should ..., a great chapter in American history." For the Advisory Board it was no question that Pershing earned the 1932 Pulitzer Prize in the „History" award category. Following now are the author's memories from the end of the First World War and Germany' s armistice:

»On November 7, 1918, the enemy's main line of communications was now within range of the machine guns of the First Army, which had driven him twenty-four miles since the 1st of November. His position on the Western Front was no longer tenable and he urged immediate consideration of an armistice. Late on November 9th Marshal Foch, then in conference with German representatives regarding the terms of the Armistice, sent telegraphic instructions to all Commanders-in-Chief from which it might be inferred that he was uncertain regarding the outcome of negotiations and wished to let the enemy know that there could be no further delay.

The following was the message received: „The enemy, disorganized by our repeated attack, retreats along the entire front. It is important to coordinate and expedite our movements. I appeal to the energy and the initiative of the Commanders-in-Chief and of their armies to make decisive the results obtained.“ Orders in response to this appeal were immediately issued and their execution by the First Army was under way on November 10th and 11th.

In the First Army, the V Corps advanced rapidly the morning of the 11th. Elements of the 89th Division occupied Stenay and established a line on the hill to the north. Pouilly-sur-Meuse was mopped up early in the morning and Autreville was occupied. The 2d Division advanced to the ridge west of Moulins; while the 77th Division held its line of the 10th. In the III Corps, on the morning of the 11th, the 90th Division entered Baâlon, and the 5th and 32d Divisions were preparing to attack.

On Monday, November 11, 1918, at 6 o'clock A.M. I received a message from French Marshal Foch, through Colonel Mott, that hostilities would cease at 11 A.M. I had information on tentative plans for following up Germans. I sent congratulations to the King of Belgium by Comte d'Oultremont on glorious outcome of the war. Assistant Secretary of War F. P. Keppel came to dine. I left on my train for Paris at 11 P.M., taking General McAndrew, Colonels Boyd and Quekemeyer, Lieutenant Colonel Griscom, and Captain Hughes.

As the conference between Marshal Foch and the German delegates proceeded, and in anticipation of advices regarding the Armistice, telephone lines were kept constantly open between my headquarters and those of the First and Second Armies. When word came to me at 6 A.M. that hostilities would cease at 11 A.M., directions to that effect were immediately sent to our armies. Our troops had been advancing rapidly during the preceding two days and although every effort was made to reach them promptly a few could not be overtaken before the prescribed hour.

Between September 26th and November 11th, twenty-two American and six French divisions, with an approximate fighting strength of 500,000 men, on a front extending from southeast of Verdun to the Argonne Forest, had engaged and decisively beaten forty-three different German divisions, with an estimated fighting strength of 470,000. Of the twenty-two American divisions, four had at different times during this period been in action on fronts other than our own.

The enemy suffered an estimated loss of over 100,000 casualties in this battle and the First Army about 117,000. The total strength of the First Army, including 135,000 French troops, reached 1,031,000 men. It captured 26,000 prisoners, 874 cannon, 3,000 machine guns and large quantities of material.

The transportation and supply of divisions to and from our front during this battle was a gigantic task. There were twenty-six American and seven French divisions, besides hundreds of thousands of corps and army troops, moved in and out of the American zone. A total of 173,000 men were evacuated to the rear and more than 100,000 replacements were received.

It need hardly be restated that our entry into the war gave the Allies the preponderance of force vitally necessary to outweigh the tremendous increase in the strength of the Germans on the Western Front, due to the collapse of Russia and the consequent release of German divisions employed against her. From the military point of view, we began to aid the Allies early in 1918, when our divisions with insufficient training to take an active part in battle were sent to the inactive front to relieve French divisions, in order that they might be used where needed in the fighting line.

The assistance we gave the Allies in combat began in May with the successful attack of one of our divisions at Cantigny. This was followed early in June by the entrance into battle of the two divisions that stopped the German advance on Paris near Château-Thierry, and by three others that were put in the defensive line. In July two American divisions, with one Moroccan division,

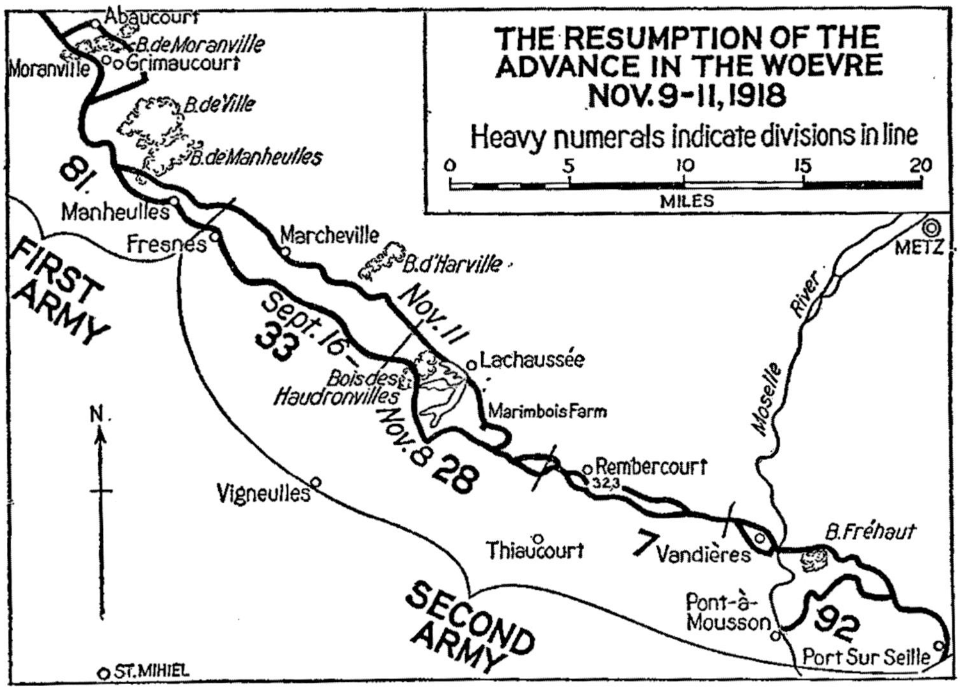

formed the spearhead of the counterattack against the Château-Thierry salient, in which nine of our divisions participated. There was a total of approximately 300,000 American troops engaged in this Second Battle of the Marne, which involved very severe fighting, and was not completed until the Germans were driven beyond the Vesle in August.

In the middle of September an army of 550,000 Americans reduced the St. Mihiel salient. The latter part of September our great battle of the Meuse-Argonne was begun, lasting through forty-seven days of intense fighting and ending brilliantly for our First and Second Armies on November 11th, after more than 1,200,000 American soldiers had participated. It was a time to forget the hardships and the difficulties, except to record them with the glorious history of our achievements. In praise and thanks for the decisive victories of our armies and in guidance for the future, the following order was issued:

G. H. Q.
American Expeditionary Forces.

General Orders
No. 203. France, Nov. 12, 1918.

„The enemy has capitulated. It is fitting that I address myself in thanks directly to the officers and soldiers of the Ameriean Expeditionary Forces who by their heroic efforts have made possible this glorious result. Our armies, hurriedly raised and hastily trained, met a veteran enemy, and by courage, discipline and skill always defeated him. Without eomplaint you have endured incessant toil, privation and danger. You have seen many of your comrades make the supreme sacrifice that freedom may live. I thank you for the patience and courage with which you have endured. I congratulate you upon the splendid fruits of victory which your heroism and the blood of our gallant dead are now presenting to our nation. Your deeds will live forever on the most glorious pages of America's history.

These things you have done. There remains now a harder task which will test your soldierly qualities to the utmost. Succeed in this and little note will be taken and few praises will be sung; fail, and the light of your glorious achievements of the past will sadly be dimmed. But you will not fail. Every natural tendeney may urge towards relaxation in discipline, in conduct, in appearance, in everything that marks the soldier. Yet you will remember that each officer and each soldier is the representative in Europe of his people and that his brilliant deeds of yesterday permit no action of today to pass unnoticed by friend or by foe. You will meet this test as gallantly as you have met the tests of the battlefield. Sustained by your high ideals and inspired by the heroic part you have played, you will carry back to our people the proud consciousness of a new Americanism born of sacrifice. Whether you stand on hostile territory or on the friendly soil of France, you will so bear yourself in diseipline, appearance and respect for all civil rights that you will confirm for all time the pride and love which every American feels for your uniform and for you.

John J. Pershing,
General, Commander-in-Chief."

The experience of the World War only confirmed the lessons of the past. The divisions with little training, while aggressive and courageous, were lacking in the ready skill of habit. They were capable of powerful blows, but their blows were apt to be awkward-teamwork was often not well understood. Flexible and resourceful divisions cannot be created by a few maneuvers or by a few months' association of their elements. On the other hand, without the keen intelligence, the endurance, the willingness, and the enthusiasm displayed in the training areas and on the battlefields, the decisive results obtained would have been impossible.

The Meuse-Argonne battle presented numerous difficulties, seemingly insurmountable. The success stands out as one of the great achievements in the history of American arms. Suddenly conceived and hurried in plan and preparation; complicated by close association with a preceding major operation; directed against stubborn defense of the vital point of the Western Front; attended by cold and inclement weather; and fought largely by partially trained troops; this battle was prosecuted with an unselfish and heroic spirit of courage and fortitude which demanded eventual victory. Physically strong, virile, and aggressive, the morale of the American soldier during this most trying period was superb.

Upon the young commanders of platoons, companies, and battalions fell the heaviest burden. They not only suffered all the dangers and rigors of battle but carried the responsibility of caring for and directing their men, often newly arrived and with but little training. Where these leaders lacked practical knowledge of tactics, they supplied the deficiency by fearless onslaughts against the enemy's line. Yet, quick to learn, they soon developed on the field into skilled leaders who inspired their men with increasing confidence.

To the higher commanders and their staffs great credit is due for the successful performance of an exceptionally complicated and arduous task. The problems born of inexperience multiply with each increase of strength, and the division, corps, and particularly the army headquarters were confronted by questions of superlative difficulty. The importance of their work is rarely realized or appreciated.The army staff at one time was involved in serving a front of ninety-four miles and a force of approximately one million men. With typical American directness of action and intensity of purpose, each member carried out his duties despite all obstacles.

Deeds of daring were legion. It is not intended to discriminate in favor of those whose heroic services have been recognized. There were thousands of others who bore themselves with equal gallantry but whose deeds are known only by the victorious results they helped to achieve. However, as typifying the spirit of the rank and file of our great army, I would mention Lieutenant Samuel Woodfill, 5th Division, who attacked single-handed a series of German machine gun nests near Cunel and dispatched the crews of each in turn until reduced to the necessity of assaulting the last detachment with a pick; Sergeant Alvin C. York, of the 82d Division, who stood off and captured 132 Germans after his patrol was literally surrounded and outnumbered ten to one; and Major Charles W. Whittlesey and his men of the 77th Division, who, when their battalion was cut off in the Argonne, refused to surrender and held out until finally relieved.

There is little to add in praise of the spirit of determination that stimulated each individual soldier to overcome the hardships and difficulties that fell to his lot. With fortitude and perseverance he gave his every energy to the accomplishment of his task, whether it required him to charge the enemy's guns or play the less conspicuous role of forwarding supplies. In their devotion, their valor, and in the loyal fulfillment of their obligations, the officers and men of the American Expeditionary Forces have left a heritage of which those who follow may ever be proud.

While we extol the virtues of the men who had the privilege of serving America in the ranks of her armies, it must be remembered that they received their inspiration of loyalty and of devotion to the country's cause from those at home. They were but the chosen representatives of the American people, whose resolute spirit they transformed into victory on the field of honor. We who were in France were conscious always of the indefatigable efforts made to supply us with the men and materials necessary for our success. Individual officers and men, no matter what their position or their duty, were inspired by patriotic determination to respond to the fullest extent possible to our calls. We became, in fact, a nation in arms, a nation imbued with and expressing the will to victory.

My diary of Tuesday, November, 12, 1918, contains this information: „Arrived in Paris this morning. Colonel Mott was here with instructions from

The Official Newspaper of the A. E. F.

The Stars and Stripes

By and For the Soldiers of the A. E. F.

VOL. 1—NO. 1. FRANCE, FRIDAY, FEBRUARY 8, 1918. PRICE: 50 CENTIMES.

MEN ON LEAVE NOT TO BE LED ROUND BY HAND

Impression That They Will Be Chaperoned Wholly Erroneous.

A MESSAGE FROM OUR CHIEF

IN this initial number of THE STARS AND STRIPES, published by the men of the Overseas Command, the Commander-in-Chief of the American Expeditionary Forces extends his greetings through the editing staff to the readers from the first line trenches to the base ports.

These readers are mainly the men who have been honored by being the first contingent of Americans to fight on European soil for the honor of their country. It is an honor and privilege which makes them fortunate above the millions of their fellow citizens at home. Commensurate with their privilege in being here, is the duty which is laid before them, and this duty will be performed by them as by Americans of the past, eager, determined, and unyielding to the last.

The paper, written by the men in the service, should speak the thoughts of the new American Army and the American people from whom the Army has been drawn. It is your paper. Good luck to it.

(Signed) JOHN J. PERSHING, Commander-in-Chief, A. E. F.

TOOTH YANKING CAR IS TOURING FRANCE

Red Cross Dentist's Office Lacks Nothing but the Lady Assistant

ARMY MEN BUILD AN OVER-SEAS PITTSBURGH

Mammoth Warehouses and the World's Largest Cold Storage Plant Spring Up in Three Months.

FORESTERS AND ENGINEERS DOING THE WORK.

Pershing on the front page of the first issue of the U.S. military magazine *The Stars and Stripes*, February 8, 1918

Marshal Foch about following up the Germans. Held brief conference on subject with McAndrew and Harbord, and left immediately with Boyd and Quekemeyer for Marshal Foch's headquarters at Senlis. Met Marshal Foch for the first time since victory and the meeting was one to be remembered. By direction of the President, bestowed on him the Distinguished Service Medal. We returned to Paris in the afternoon to find pandemonium."

When I saw Marshal Foch he was in high spirits and said a great many complimentary things about the splendid work of the American Army, my cordial cooperation, and how he appreciated my straightforward methods. He said that he had always known my attitude on every question, because I stated it frankly and clearly and then lived up to it. I was equally enthusiastic in praise of his leadership. What was said and the realization that the victory was won and the war actually over affected us both deeply and for some moments we were speechless. Both of us were rather overcome by emotion as we embraced and each gave the other the time-honored French „accolade."

We pulled ourselves together shortly, as one of the objects of my visit was to decorate him with the Distinguished Service Medal, this being the first to be presented to any officer other than an American. He had directed a small guard of some fifteen or twenty territorial orderlies, under the command of a sergeant, to be formed in the yard in rear of his quarters, with two trumpeters to furnish the music. Standing in front of this command and facing him, I made a short speech in French and pinned on his blouse the token of our country's esteem and appreciation of his distinguished services. My aide handed one of his aides a signed copy of what I said. The Marshal spoke somewhat at length on how he valued the honor and how brilliantly the Americans had fought beside the Allies and was so moved that he could hardly finish what he had to say. He shook hands with me very cordially and stood holding my hand with both of his as he ordered the flourish of trumpets to close the ceremony.

I had luncheon with him, during which Weygand gave a brief account of the conference with the German delegates regarding the terms of the Armistice. He said that the Germans came across the line by automobile on the afternoon of November 7th and boarded a special railway coach sent by the French to meet them. During the night this car and the Marshal's were placed side by side in the forest between Compiègne and Soissons. The emissaries were ushered into the Marshal's presence and after producing their credentials were asked the object of their visit. They replied that they had come to discuss the terms of an armistice. The Marshal then made it clear that he, himself, was not requesting an armistice and did not care to have one. When asked if they wished an armistice, they replied that they did. The Marshal said if that was the case, here were the terms, a copy of which he handed them. The severity of the demands seemed to surprise them and they appeared very much depressed. They had no power to sign an armistice, they said, without the consent of the Chancellor, and after some little discussion they started an officer to the German capital with the terms.

They did not seem to object to turning over 5,000 cannon, but deplored the condition which required them to surrender 30,000 machine guns. They finally succeeded in getting this reduced to 25,000 machine guns on the ground that they might have some left for riot duty. In speaking of the danger of riots, the delegates were asked why they did not send some of their reserve divisions to maintain order in the interior. Their reply was that they had no divisions in reserve, as *every division that they had was actually in line*. Then they complained about the short time allowed for evacuation, stating that the German Army was in no condition to move, either forward or backward.

During the 9th and 1oth, while waiting for instructions from their Government, the delegates talked very freely with Weygand about conditions in Germany and spoke particularly of the lack of food and the fear that there would be famine in places because of the bad transportation service.

A wireless message from the German Government authorizing the delegates to sign the Armistice was received about 11:00 P.M. on the 1oth. It took until 5:00 A.M. the 11th to decode the message, complete the discussion and draw up the terms in the rough. In order to stop bloodshed, the last page of the conditions was written first, and this was signed a few minutes after 5:00 A.M. on the 11th. At that hour word was sent out to the armies that fighting would cease at 11:00 A.M.

After luncheon we drove back to Paris and everybody was still celebrating. It looked as though the whole population had gone entirely out of their minds. The city was turned into pandemonium. The streets and boulevards were packed with people singing and dancing and wearing all sorts of odd costumes. The crowds were doing the most clownish things. One could hardly hear his own voice, it was such a bedlam.

It was next to impossible for our automobile to make any headway through the mass of humanity. We were two hours in crossing the Place de la Concorde, the crowd was so dense and so riotous. It happened that I was recognized before we had gone very far and French men and women boarded the car, climbed on top of it and got inside, and no amount of persuasion would prevail upon them to let us pass. Finally a group of American soldiers, who were enjoying the hilarity, came along and seeing our helpless condition took charge and succeeded in making an opening sufficiently large to permit the car to be moved a yard or so at a time until we got free. If all the ridiculous things done during those two or three days by dignified American and French men and women were recorded the reader would scarcely believe the story. But this was Paris and the war was over.

I went to the Ecole de Guerre, where Marshal Joffre had his quarters, and in a very simple ceremony that took place in his office I pinned our Distinguished Service Medal on his breast. Only a few staff officers were present, among them the Marshal's faithful Chief of Staff, Colonel Fabre, while the officers who accompanied me were Harbord, Boyd, and Quekemeyer. This grand old French Commander-in-Chief was very proud of this recognition by our Government, but expressed himself in few words. It gave me the greatest pleasure to make this presentation.

We next motored to Provins to confer the same decoration on General Pétain. After luncheon, together with several of his generals and staff officers, we repaired to the front court, where a guard of about twenty soldiers was already formed. Facing General Pétain, who stood in front of the command, I spoke a few words regarding his exceptional service to his country and thanked him for his uniform consideration and great assistance to our armies and pinned on the medal. It was especially gratifying to me to decorate Pétain, as my relations with him were always closer than with any of the other Allied officers and we had become fast friends. He made some complimentary remarks about our Army and seemed much pleased and deeply appreciative of the recognition shown by our Government of his great abilities.

At Cambrai, where I went to decorate Field Marshal Sir Douglas Haig, a brigade of Highlanders, which included some of the most distinguished units of the British Army, was assembled for the occasion. The ceremony was very impressive. Marshal Haig stood opposite the center of the line, the very picture of the ideal soldier that he was. The band of bagpipes swung down the line playing a medley of Scottish airs in thrilling fashion. As the command stood at „Present Arms," I approached the Field Marshal and after a few words pinned our decoration on him. The march-past of the troops completed a memorable event.

Upon my arrival in Paris that afternoon, I hastened over to call on M. Clemenceau. To my mind, he was the greatest of French civil officials. Though some seventy-six years of age, he had the vigor, the fire, and the determination of a man of fifty. He will live long in history. I had not seen him since the cessation of hostilities and when we met he was much affected, and indeed demonstrative. We fell into each other's arms, choked up and had to wipe our eyes. We had no differences to discuss that day.«

IMMIGRANT STARTS TO EDIT THE LADIES' HOME JOURNAL

by *Edward W. Bok*

He was born as Eduard Willem Gerard Cesar Bok on October 9, 1863, in Den Helder, Netherlands, and died on January 9, 1930, in Lake Wales, Florida. At the age of six, he immigrated to Brooklyn, New York, where he washed the windows of a bakery shop after school to help support his family. His people were so poor that in addition he used to go out in the street with a basket every day and collect stray bits of coal that had fallen in the gutter where the coal wagons had delivered fuel.

Thirteen years old, Bok quit school to be an office boy. About this time he proposed a new writing project, which was the preparation of one-hundred-word biographies to appear on the back of souvenir cards. He promptly received his first comrnission, which was followed by a second and third one. While continuing his job as office boy, Bok spent his evenings writing theatrical reviews for the *Brooklyn Eagle*, publishing theatre programs and editing the *Philomathean Review* for Brooklyn's Plymouth Church.

When he became a stenographer, Edward Bok began work with the publishing house of Henry Holt and Company in 1882. Two years later he became involved with the book publisher Charles Scribner's Sons, where he eventually became its advertising manager. From 1884 until 1887 Bok was the editor of the *Brooklyn Magazine*, and in 1886 he founded the Bok Syndicate Press. After moving to Philadelphia in 1889, he obtained the editorship of the *Ladies' Home Journal*. During his editorship, the *Journal* became the first magazine in the world to have one million subscribers. In September 1919 Bok relinquished editorship of the *Ladies' Home Journal*, completing thirty years of service.

Afterwards he wanted to tell his uncommon life in a book of memories. „This book“, he explained in the preface, „was to have been written in 1914, when I foresaw some leisure to write it, for I then intended to retire from active editorship. But the war came, an entirely new set of duties commanded, and the project was laid aside.“ But in September 1920 the work was published in New York, entitled „The Americanization of Edward Bok - The Autobiography of a Dutch Boy Fifty Years after.“ The book, written in third person style, fascinated the Pulitzer Prize jurors of the „Biography / Autobiography“ award category in April 1921 and they declared him the winner. Following now are small passages from Bok's memoirs, dealing with his early years as editor of the *Ladies' Home Journal*:

»Cyrus H. K. Curtis, the owner and publisher of *The Ladies' Home Journal*, in April 1889 had decided that he needed an editor for his magazine, in order to relieve his wife, who was then editing it. Edward Bok got the offer, but first he hesitated a little bit to accept it. His instinct was strongly in favor of an acceptance. A natural impulse moved him, without reasoning, to action. Reasoning led only to a cautious mental state, and caution is a strong factor in the Dutch character. The longer he pursued a conscious process of reasoning, the farther he got from the position. But the instinct remained strong.

Bok stopped in Philadelphia to consult his friend, George W. Childs; and here he found the only person who was ready to encourage him to make the change. Bok now Iaid the matter before his mother, in whose feminine instinct he had supreme confidence. With her, he met with instant discouragement. But in subsequent talks he found that her opposition was based not upon the possibilities inherent in the position, but on a mother's natural disinclination to be separated from one of her sons.

Bok now consulted his business associates, and, to a man, they discouraged the step, but almost invariably upon the argument that it was suicidal to leave New York. He had now a glimpse of the truth that there is no man so provincially narrow as the untravelled New Yorker who believes in his heart that the sun rises in the East River and sets in the North River.

He realized more keenly than ever before that the decision rested with him alone. On September 1, 1889, Bok wrote to Mr. Curtis, accepting the position in Philadelphia; and on October 13 following he left the Scribners, where he had been so fortunate and so happy, and, after a week's vacation, followed where his instinet so strongly led, but where his reason wavered. On October 20, 1889, Edward Bok became the editor of *The Ladies' Home Journal*.

There is a popular notion that the editor of a woman's magazine should be a woman. At first thought, perhaps, this sounds logical. But it is a curious fact that by far the larger number of periodicals for women, the world over, are edited by men; and where, as in some cases, a woman is the proclaimed editor, the direction of the editorial policy is generally in the hands of a man, or group of men, in the background. Why this is so has never been explained, any more than why the majority of women's dressmakers are men; why music, with its larger appeal to women, has been and is still being composed, largely, by men, and why its greatest instrumental performers are likewise men; and why the church, with its larger membership of women, still has, as it always has had, men for its greatest preachers.

In fact, we may well ponder whether the full editorial authority and direction of a modern magazine, either essentially feminine in its appeal or not, can safely be entrusted to a woman when one considers how largely executive is the nature of such a position, and how thoroughly sensitive the modern editor must be to the hundred and one practical business matters which today enter into and form so large apart of the editorial duties. We may question whether women have as yet had sufficient experience in the world of business to cope successfully with the material questions of a pivotal editorial position. Then, again, it is absolutely essential in the conduct of a magazine with a feminine or home appeal to have on the editorial staff women who are experts in their line; and the truth is that women will work infinitely better under the direction of a man than of a woman.

It would seem from the present outlook that, for some time, at least, the so-called woman's magazine of large purpose and wide vision is very likely to be edited by a man. It is a question, however, whether the day of the woman's magazine,as we have known it, is not passing, Already the day has gone for the woman's magazine built on the old lines which now seem so grotesque and feeble in the light of modern growth. The interests of women and of men are being brought closer with the years, and it will not be long before they will entirely merge. This means a constantly diminishing necessity for the distinctly feminine magazine.

Naturally, there will always be a field in the essentially feminine pursuits which have no place in the life of a man, but these are rapidly being cared for by books, gratuitously distributed, issued by the manufacturers of distinctly feminine and domestic wares; for such publications the best talent is being employed, and the results are placed within easy access of women, by rneans of newspaper advertisement, the store-counter, or the mails. These will sooner or later - and much sooner than later - supplant the practical portions of the woman's magazine, leaving only the general contents, which are equally interesting to men and to women. Hence the field for the magazine with the essentially feminine appeal is contracting rather than broadening, and it is likely to contract much more rapidly in the future.

The field was altogether different when Edward Bok entered it in 1889. It was not only wide open, but fairly crying out to be filled. The day of *Godey's Lady's Book* had passed; *Peterson's Magazine* was breathing its last; and the home or women's magazines that had attempted to take their place were sorry affairs. It was this consciousness of a void ready to be filled that made the Philadelphia experiment so attractive to the embryo editor. He looked over the field and reasoned that if such magazines as did exist could be fairly successful, if women were ready to buy such, how much greater response would there be to a magazine of higher standards, of larger initiative - a magazine that would be an authoritative clearing-house for all the problems confronting women in the home, that brought itself closely into contact with those problems and tried to solve them in an entertaining and efficient way; and yet a magazine of uplift and inspiration: a magazine, in other words, that would give light and leading in the woman's world.

The method of editorial expression in the magazines of 1889 was also distinctly vague and prohibitively impersonal. The public knew the name of scarcely a single editor of a magazine: there was no personality that stood out in the mind: the accepted editorial expression was the indefinite „we"; no one ventured to use the first person singular and talk intimately to the reader. Edward Bok's biographical reading had taught him that the American public loved a personality: that it was always ready to recognize and follow a leader, provided, of course, that the qualities of leadership were demonstrated. He felt the time had come - the reference here and elsewhere is always to the realm of popular magazine literature appealing to a very wide audience - for the editor of some magazine to project his personality through the printed page and to convince the public that he was not an oracle removed from the people, but a real human being who could talk and not merely write on paper.

He saw, too, that the average popular magazine of 1889 failed of large success because it wrote down to the public - a grievous mistake that so many editors have made and still make. No one wants to be told, either directly or indirectly, that he knows less than he does, or even that he knows as little as he does: every one is benefited by the opposite implication, and the public will always follow the leader who comprehends this bit of psychology. There is always a happy medium between shooting over the public's head and shooting too far under it. And it is because of the latter aim that we find the modern popular magazine the worthless thing that, in so many instances, it is to-day.

It is the rare editor who rightly gauges his public psychology. Perhaps that is why, in the enormous growth of the modern magazine, there have been produced so few successful editors. The average editor is obsessed with the idea of „giving the public what it wants," whereas, in fact, the public, while it knows what it wants when it sees it, cannot clearly express its wants, and never wants the thing that it does ask for, although it thinks it does at the time. But woe to the editor and his periodical if he heeds that siren voice!

The editor has, therefore, no means of finding it out aforehand by putting his ear to the ground. Only by the simplest rules of psychology can he edit rightly so that he may lead, and to the average editor of to-day, it is to be

THE LADIES' HOME JOURNAL
OCTOBER
1895
TEN CENTS
THE CURTIS
PUBLISHING
COMPANY
PHILADELPHIA
THE CENTRAL NEWS COMPANY, PHILADELPHIA,
GENERAL AGENTS

feared, psychology is a closed book. His mind is all too often focussed on the circulation and advertising, and all too little on the intangibles that will bring to his periodical the results essential in these respects.

The editor is the pivot of a magazine. On him everything turns. If his gauge of the public is correct, readers will come: they cannot help coming to the man who has something to say himself, or who presents writers who have. And if the reader comes, the advertiser must come. He must go where his largest market is: where the buyers are. The advertiser, instead of being the most difficult factor in a magazine proposition, as is so often mistakenly thought, is, in reality, the simplest. He has no choice hut to advertise in the successful periodical. He must come along. The editor need never worry about him. If the advertiser shuns the periodical's pages, the fault is rarely that of the advertiser: the editor can generally look for the reason nearer home.

One of Edward Bok's first acts as editor was to offer a series of prizes for the best answers to three questions he put to his readers: what in the magazine did they like least and why; what did they like best and why; and what omitted feature or department would they like to see installed? Thousands of answers came, and these the editor personally read carefully and classified. Then he gave his readers' suggestions back to them in articles and departments, but never on the level suggested by them. He gave them the subjects they asked for, but invariably on a slightly higher plane; and each year he raised the standard a notch. He always kept „a huckleberry or two" ahead of his readers. His psychology was simple: come down to the level which the public sets and it will leave you at the moment you do it. It always expects of its leaders that they shall keep a notch above or a step ahead. The American public always wants something a little better than it asks for, and the successful man, in catering to it, is he who follows this golden rule.

Edward Bok has often been referred to as the one „who made *The Ladies' Home Journal* out of nothing," who „built it from the ground up," or, in similar terms, implying that when he became its editor in 1889 the magazine was practically non-existent. This is far from the fact. The magazine was begun in 1883, and had been edited by Mrs. Cyrus H. K. Curtis, for six years, under her maiden name of Louisa Knapp, before Bok undertook its editorship. Mrs. Curtis had laid a solid foundation of principle and policy for the magazine: it had achieved a circulation of 440,000 copies a month when she transferred the editorship, and it had already acquired such a standing in the periodical world as to attract the advertisements of Charles Scribner's Sons, which Mr. Doubleday, and later Bok himself, gave to the Philadelphia magazine - advertising which was never given lightly, or without the most careful investigation of the worth of the circulation of a periodical.

What every magazine publisher knows as the most troublous years in the establishment of a periodical, the first half-dozen years of its existence, had already been weathered by the editor and publisher. The wife as editor and the husband as publisher had combined to lay a solid basis upon which Bok had only to build: his task was simply to rear a structure upon the foundation already laid. It is to the vision and to the genius of the first editor of *The Ladies' Home Journal* that the unprecedented success of the magazine is primarily due. It was the purpose and the policy of making a magazine of authoritative service for the womanhood of America, a service which would visualize for womanhood its highest domestic estate, that had won success for the periodical from its inception. It is difficult to believe, in the multiplicity of similar magazines to-day, that such a purpose was new; that *The Ladies' Home Journal* was a path-finder; but the convincing proof is found in the fact that all the later magazines of this class have followed in the wake of the periodical conceived by Mrs. Curtis, and have ever since been its imitators.

When Edward Bok succeeded Mrs. Curtis, he immediately encountered another popular misconception of a woman's magazine - the conviction that if a man is the editor of a periodical with a distinctly feminine appeal, he must, as the term goes, „understand women." If Bok had believed this to be true, he would never have assumed the position. How deeply rooted is this belief was brought home to him on every hand when his decision to accept the Philadelphia position was announced. His mother, knowing her son better than did any one else, looked at him with amazement. She could not believe that he was serious in his decision to cater to women's needs when he knew so little about them. His friends, too, were intensely amused, and took no pains to hide their amusement from him. They knew him to be the very opposite of „a lady's man," and when they were not convulsed with hilarity they were incredulous and marvelled.

No man, perhaps, could have been chosen for the position who had a less intimate knowledge of women. Bok had no sister, no women confidantes: he had lived with and for his mother. She was the only woman he really knew or who really knew him. His boyhood days had been too full of poverty and struggle to permit him to mingle with the opposite sex. And it is a curious fact that Edward Bok's instinctive attitude toward women was that of avoidance. He did not dislike women, but it could not be said that he liked them. They had never interested him. Of women, therefore, he knew little; of their needs less. Nor had he the slightest desire, even as an editor, to know them better, or to seek to understand them. Even at that age, he knew that, as a man, he could not, no matter what effort he might make, and he let it go at that.

What he saw in the position was not the need to know women; he could employ women for that purpose. He perceived clearly that the editor of a magazine was largely an executive: his was principally the work of direction; of studying currents and movements, watching their formation, their tendency, their efficacy if advocated or translated into actuality; and then selecting from the horizon those that were for the best interests of the home. For a home was something Edward Bok did understand. He had always lived in one; had struggled to keep it together, and he knew every inch of the hard road that makes for domestic permanence amid adverse financial conditions. And at the home he aimed rather than at the woman in it.

To enlarge the contents of his magazine, Edward Bok developed an idea of adding a new department of *The Ladies' Home Journal*, called „Side Talks with Girls", written by a certain „Ruth Ashmed". Bok had devined the fact that in thousands of cases the American mother was not the confidante of her daughter, and reasoned if an inviting human personality could be created on the printed page that would supply this lamentable lack of American family life, girls would flock to such a figure. But all depended on the confidence which the written word could inspire. He tried several writers, but in each case the particular touch that he was sought for was lacking. So Bok tried it himself as the author.

He changed the name to Ruth Ashmore, and decided to let the manuscript go into the magazine. He reasoned that he would then have a month in which to see the writer he had in mind, and he would show her the proof. But a month filled itself with other duties, and before the editor was aware of it, the composition-room wanted „copy" for the second instalment of „Side Talks with Girls." Once more the editor furnished the copy!

Within two weeks after the second article had been written, the magazine containing the first instalment of the new department appeared, and the next day two hundred letters were received for „Ruth Ashmore," with the mail-clerk asking where they should be sent. „Leave them with me, please," replied the editor. On the following day the mail-clerk handed him five hundred more.

The editor now took two letters from the top and opened them. He never opened the third! That evening he took the bundle home, and told his mother of his predicament. She read the letters and looked at her son. „You have no right to read these," she said. The son readily agreed. His instinct had correctly interpreted the need, but he never dreamed how far the feminine nature would reveal itself on paper.

The next morning the editor, with his letters, took the train for New York and sought his friend, Mrs. Isabel A. Mallon, the „Bab" of his popular syndicate

Edward Bok as editor of „The Ladies' Home Journal“ in his Philadelphia office

letter. „Have you read this department?" he asked, pointing to the page in the magazine. „I have," answered Mrs. Mallon. „Very well done, too, it is. Who is 'Ruth Ashmore'?" „You are," answered Edward Bok.

And while it took considerable persuasion, from that time on Mrs. Mallon became Ruth Ashmore, the most ridiculed writer in the magazine world, and yet the most helpful editor that ever conducted a department in periodical literature. For sixteen years she conducted the department, until she passed away, her last act being to dictate a letter to a correspondent. In those sixteen years she had received one hundred and fifty-eight thousand letters: she kept three stenographers busy, and the number of girls who to-day bless the name of Ruth Ashmore is legion. But the newspaper humorists who insisted that Ruth Ashmore was none other than Edward Bok never knew the partial truth of their joke!

The editor soon supplemented this department with one dealing with the spiritual needs of the mature woman. „The King's Daughters „ was then an organization at the summit of its usefulness, with Margaret Bottome its president. Edward Bok had heard Mrs. Bottome speak, had met her personally, and decided that she was the editor for the department he had in mind. "I want it written in an intimate way as if there were only two persons in the world, you and the person reading. I want heart to speak to heart. We will make that the title," said the editor, and unconsciously he thus created the title that has since become familiar wherever English is spoken: „Heart to Heart Talks." The title gave the department an instantaneous hearing; the material in it carried out its spirit, and soon Mrs. Bottome's department rivalled, in popularity, the page by Ruth Ashmore.

These two departments more than anything else, and the irresistible picture of a man editing a woman's magazine, brought forth an era of newspaper paragraphing and a flood of so-called „humorous" references to the magazine and editor. It became the vogue to poke fun at both. The humorous papers took it up, the cartoonists helped it along, and actors introduced the name of the magazine on the stage in plays and skits. Never did a periodical receive such an amount of gratuitous advertising. Much of the wit was absolutely without malice: some of it was written by Edward Bok's best friends, who volunteered to „let up" would he but raise a finger.

But he did not raise the finger. No one enjoyed the „paragraphs" more heartily when the wit was good, and in that case, if the writer was unknown to him, he sought him out and induced him to write for him. In this way, George Fitch was found on the Peoria, Illinois, *Transcript* and introduced to his larger public in the magazine and book world through *The Ladies' Home Journal*, whose editor he believed he had „most unmercifully roasted"; - but he had done it so cleverly that the editor at once saw his possibilities.

When all his friends begged Bok to begin proceedings against the *New York Evening Sun* because of the libellous (?) articles written about him by „The Woman About Town," the editor admired the style rather than the contents, made her acquaintanee, and secured her as a regular writer: she contributed to the magazine some of the best things published in its pages. But she did not abate her opinions of Bok and his magazine in her articles in the newspaper, and Bok did not ask it of her: he felt that she had a right to her opinions - those he was not buying; but he was eager to buy her direct style in treating subjects he knew no other woman could so effectively handle.

And with his own limited knowledge of the sex, he needed, and none knew it better than did he, the ablest woman he eould obtain to help him realize his ideals. Their personal opinions of him did not matter so long as he could command their best work. Sooner or later, when his purposes were better understood, they might alter those opinions. For that he could afford to wait. But he could not wait to get their work. By this time the editor had come to see that the power of a magazine might lie more securely behind the printed page than in it. He had begun to accustom his readers to writing to his editors upon all conceivable problems.

This he decided to encourage. He employed an expert in each line of feminine endeavor, upon the distinct understanding that the most scrupulous attention should be given to her correspondence: that every letter, no matter how inconsequential, should be answered quickly, fully, and courteously, with the questioner always encouraged to come again if any problem of whatever nature came to her. He told his editors that ignorance on any question was a misfortune, not a crime; and he wished their correspondence treated in the most courteous and helpful spirit.

Step by step, the editor built up this service behind the magazine until he had a staff of thirty-five editors on the monthly pay-roll; in each issue, he proclaimed the willingness of these editors to answer immediately any questions by mail, he encouraged and cajoled his readers to form the habit of looking upon his magazine as a great clearing-house of information. Before long, the letters streamed in by the tens of thousands during a year. The editor still encouraged, and the total ran into the hundreds of thousands, until during the last year, before the service was finally stopped by the Great War of 1917-18, the yearly correspondence totalled nearly a million letters.

The work of some of these editors never reached the printed page, and yet was vastly more important than any published matter could possibly be. Out of the work of Ruth Ashmore, for instance, there grew a class of cases of the most confidential nature. These cases, distributed all over the country, called for special investigation and personal contact. Bok selected Mrs. Lyman Abbott for this piece of delicate work, and, through the wide acquaintance of her husband, she was enabled to reach, personally, every case in every locality, and bring personal help to bear on it. These cases mounted into the hundreds, and the good accomplished through this quiet channel cannot be overestimated.

The lack of opportunity for an education in Bok's own life led him to cast about for some plan whereby an education might be obtained without expense by any one who desired. He finally hit upon the simple plan of substituting free scholarships for the premiums then so frequently offered by periodicals for subscriptions secured. Free musical education at the leading conservatories was first offered to any girl who would secure a certain number of subscriptions to *The Ladies' Home Journal*, the complete offer being a year's free tuition, with free room, free board, free piano in her own room, and all travelling expenses paid. The plan was an immediate success: the solicitation of a subscription by a girl desirous of educating herself made an irresistible appeal.

This plan was soon extended, so as to include all the girls' colleges, and finally all the men's colleges, so that a free education might be possible at any educational institution. So comprehensive it became that to the close of 1919, one thousand four hundred and fiftyfive free scholarships had been awarded. The plan has now been in operation long enough to have produced some of the leading singers and instrumental artists of the day, whose names are familiar to all, as well as instructors in colleges and scores of teachers; and to have sent several score of men into conspicuous positions in the business and professional world.

Edward Bok has always felt that but for his own inability to secure an education, and his consequent desire for self-improvement, the realization of the need in others might not have been so strongly felt by him, and that his plan whereby thousands of others were benefited might never have been realized. The editor's correspondence was revealing, among other deficiencies, the wide-spread unpreparedness of the average American girl for motherhood, and her desperate ignorance when a new life was given her. On the theory that with the realization of a vital need there is always the person to meet it, Bok consulted the authorities of the Babies' Hospital of New York, and found Doctor Emelyn L. Coolidge

To the authorities in the world of babies, Bok's discovery was, of course, a known and serious fact. Doctor Coolidge proposed that the magazine create a department of questions and answers devoted to the problems of young mothers. This was done, and from the publication of the first issue the questions began to come in. Within five years the department had grown to such proportions that Doctor Coolidge proposed a plan whereby mothers might be instructed, by mail, in the rearing of babies - in their general care, their feeding, and the complete hygiene of the nursery.

Bok had already learned, in his editorial experience, carefully to weigh a woman's instinct against a man's judgment, but the idea of raising babies by mail floored him. He reasoned, however, that a woman, and more particularly one who had been in a babies' hospital for years, knew more about babies than he could possibly know. He consulted baby-specialists in New York and Philadelphia, and, with one accord, they declared the plan not only absolutely impracticable but positively dangerous. Bok's confidence in woman's instinct, however, persisted, and he asked Doctor Coolidge to map out a plan.

This called for the services of two physicians: Miss Marianna Wheeler, for many years superintendent of the Babies' Hospital, was to look after the prospective mother before the baby's birth; and Doctor Coolidge, when the baby was born, would immediately send to the young mother a printed list of comprehensive questions, which, when answered, would be immediately followed by a full set of directions as to the care of the child, including carefully prepared food formulae. At the end of the first month, another set of questions was to be forwarded for answer by the mother, and this monthly service was to be continued until the child reached the age of two years. The contact with the mother would then become intermittent, dependent upon the condition of mother and child. All the directions and formulae were to be used only under the direction of the mother's attendant physician, so that the fullest cooperation might be established between the physician on the case and the advisory department of the magazine.

Despite advice to the contrary, Bok decided, after consulting a number of mothers, to establish the system. It was understood that the greatest care was to be exercised: the most expert advice, if needed, was to be sought and given, and the thousands of cases at the Babies' Hospital were to be laid under contribution. There was then begun a magazine department which was to be classed among the most clear-cut pieces of successful work achieved by *The Ladies' Home Journal*.

Step by step, the new departure won its way, and was welcomed eagerly by thousands of young mothers. It was not long before the warmest commendation from physicians all over the country was received. Promptness of response and thoroughness of diagnosis were, of course, the keynotes of the service: where the cases were urgent, the special delivery post and, later, the nightletter telegraph service were used.

So intimate had become this relation, so efficient was the service rendered, that its readers could not be pried loose from it; where women were willing and ready, when the domestic pinch came, to let go of other reading matter, they explained to their husbands or fathers that *The Ladies' Home Journal* was a necessity - they did not feel that they could do without it. The very quality for which the magazine had been held up to ridicule by the unknowing and unthinking had become, with hundreds of thousands of women, its source of power and the bulwark of its success.

Bok was beginning to realize the vision which had lured him from New York: that of putting into the field of American magazines a periodical that should become such a clearing-house as virtually to make it an institution.«

JOURNALIST PURCHASES A NEWSPAPER IN KANSAS

by *William A. White*

The journalist was born on February 10, 1868, in Emporia, Kansas, and died in his hometown on January 29, 1944. William Allen White moved to El Dorado, Kansas, with his parents, where he spent the majority of his childhood. He loved animals and reading various books. He attended the College of Emporia and the University of Kansas, and in 1889 started work at the *Kansas City Star* as an editorial writer. White married Sallie Lindsay in 1893, and in 1895 he bought the *Emporia Gazette* for $ 3,000 from William Yoast Morgan and became its editor.

White was a political conservative at this early stage of his career. In 1896 a White editorial titled „What's the Matter with Kansas" attracted national attention with a scathing attack on William Jennings Bryan, the Democrats, and the Populists. White sharply ridiculed Populist leaders for letting Kansas slip into economic stagnation and not keeping up economically with neighboring states because their anti-business policies frightened away economic capital from the state. The Republicans sent out hundreds of thousands of copies of the editorial in support of William Mc Kinley during the intensely fought presidential election 1896, providing White with national exposure.

With his warm sense of humor, articulate editorial pen, and common sense approach to life, White soon became known throughout the country. His *Gazette* editorials were widely reprinted; he wrote stories on politics, published numerous books, including biographies of presidents Woodrow Wilson and Calvin Coolidge. Locally he was known as the greatest booster for Emporia. White became a leader of the Progressive movement in Kansas, forming the Kansas Republican League in 1912 to oppose railroads. He helped Theodore Roosevelt form the Progressive Party in 1912 in opposition to the conservative forces surrounding incumbent Republican president William Howard Taft.

White was a reporter at the Versailles Conference in 1919 and a strong supporter of Woodrow Wilson's proposal for the League of Nations. The League went into operation but the United States never joint. During the 1920s, White was critical of both the isolationism and the conservatism of the Republican Party. White's finest hour came in his vigorous assault, beginning with *Gazette* editorials in 1921, on the KuKluxKlan - a crusade that led him to run for governor of Kansas years later so that his anti-Klan message would reach a broader state and national audience. As expected, White did not win the election, but he was widely crediced with deflating Klan intentions in Kansas.

One of White‘s editorials, titled „To an Ancious Friend“ and published in the *Emporia Gazette* on July 27, 1922, earned William Allen White the 1923 Pulitzer Prize for Editorial Writing. The jury’s decision, as stated in the report of April 13, 1923, based on the original description of the award as being given „for distinguished editorial writing in a United States newspaper, published daily, Sunday, or at least once a week, during the year, the test of excellence being clearness of style, moral purpose, sound reasoning, and power to influence public opinion in the right direction.“

White’s award-winning editorial had been written after being arrested in a dispute over free speech following objections to the way the state of Kansas handled the men who participated in the Great Railroad Strike of 1922. In the 1930s White was an early supporter of the Republican presidential nominees, Alf Landon of Kansas in 1936 and Wendell Willkie in 1940. However, White was on the liberal wing of the Republican Party and wrote many editorials praising the New Deal of Franklin D. Roosevelt.

The last quarter century of White’s life was spent as an unofficial national spokesman for Middle America. This led President Franklin Roosevelt to ask White to help generate public support for the Allies before America’s entry into World War II. In 1940 White was fundamental in the formation of the Committee to Defend America by Aiding the Allies, sometimes known as the White Committee. He had to fight the powerful America First faction, which believed, like most other Republicans, that the U.S. should stay out of the war. White spent much of his last three years involved with this committee.

Beside of his journalistic merits, White also was an author of many books of nonfiction and fiction. So he served for many years as juror in various Pulitzer Prize award categories. He also was member of the Pulitzer Prize Advisory Board from 1937 until 1943. After his death the following year, White’s family tried to bring out his unpublished memoirs that finally came out in 1946, entitled „The Autobiography of William Allen White.“ The volume posthumously received the 1947 Pulitzer Prize in the „Biography or Autobiography“ award category, after the jury report of March 12, 1947, had praised the work. „William Allen White had a rich experience both on the personal and the active side,“ the jurors said, „he knew intimately most of the influential characters of his time and had a part in many of the most important political happenings. He gives a first hand picture, which students of history will always find indispensable ..., each one a masterpiece of characterization and description. In the opinion of the committee, this Autobiography is destined to survival, for it is American to the core in spirit and is genuine literature in execution.“

Following now are some passages of the award-winning book, dealing with the time when White bought the *Emporia Gazette*:

»As I look back on those years in Kansas City when I was on the Star, and try to patch together some picture of that youth in his mid-twenties, his chief characteristic seems to have been an eager ardor - like that of a friendly pup. Probably that is why the old Colonel sent him to represent the paper on one of those chamber of commerce good-will excursions which cities used to give in those days. The chamber of commerce hired a special train and sent it south to the Ozarks and east almost to St. Louis, skirting eastern Kansas, northern Arkansas, and passing through west and central Missouri. We were on the train a week or ten days, and I came to know some of the businessmen of Kansas City as I knew those of Lawrence and Eldorado. We had our dining car, and because the train was fairly hilarious some one of the twoscore passengers was tight most of the time, giving us a continual source of uproarious delight. And we ate where chambers of commerce in other towns would invite us.

I was taking on fat. We lived well. We started the day with the old-fashioned, mid Victorian breakfast in the winter, buckwheat cakes, bacon and eggs, fried potatoes, some kind of fruit, generally apple sauce; and in the six warm months, pancakes or toast and jam, I had a streetcar pass and came home for lunch. Always we sat down to our meals - there was no nonsense about eating in the kitchen; and once a day we had a square meal of some dimensions, usually three courses. We all enjoyed it. Because I enjoyed my meals, took them with gusto, and regarded the table as a place of high emprise, Sallie, a Kentuckian by birth, made an adventure out of cooking. Her mother cooked well, and my mother had learned cooking before her marriage in the school of hard knocks, So Sallie had good instruction, really enthusiastic support, in her culinary quest, and she made of her table areal adventure. But I suppose we gave the same thought and delight to making our home, as we quested through Kansas City secondhand stores for old mahogany. Each piece of furniture that we brought in was bought after we had saved the money for it.

We still have around the house pieces which we bought in those days. We are eating at the mahogany table that we bought when we started housekeeping, and the cherry chairs that came with it are still brought out when we have extra company. We are bound to our idols. Home meant much to me. It always has meant much more than any other part of my life. I approached it at noon and night with warm anticipation always, I liked to think in those days that I was quite somebody downtown. At the office I was, in the vernacular, „a hell of a fellow.“ There I knew all of the reporters, all of the men in the telegraph room, and most of the advertising salesmen. The circulation man was a dear friend. On the streets of Kansas City I spoke to many people. It pleased me to dress as well as I could afford to. Sallie and I liked to go out always to the Saturday matinees, sometimes to dinner and to public gatherings; but I had no nonsense in my head about going downtown at night. The happiest place I knew was home.

It was in those days in the early 1890s, that I began to hunt for a Kansas newspaper, one that I could afford to buy. I talked it over with my wife Sallie - and, at the proper time, with my mother. She had a little property at Eldorado. She had hung onto the real estate my father had left her - the big house where we lived, the farm near town, another good residence on a fashionable street. These brought her a little income. She could have lived on it. With that capital in the back of my head, Sallie and I began to talk over various locations. And we were this smart: we knew we had to live in a college town. Whatever talent we had, whatever freedom I yearned for, could thrive and take root only in a town where there was a considerable dependable minority of intelligent people, intellectually upper middle class. These I could write for. These, I felt, understood what I was trying to do. These people, being in the leadership in a college community, would afford me an insurance which instinctively, even then, I felt that I must have. So I tried to buy the Lawrence Journal. It cost too much, I tried the Manhattan Mercury. It was not for sale. I tried an Ottawa paper. It was making too much money and was beyond my reach. So it narrowed down to Emporia.

Two papers were slowly starving to death in Emporia in the hard times of the middle nineties, the Daily Republican, which had absorbed the Daily News, and the Gazette. The News had been established in 1857 with the founding of the town; the Republican, in 1880. It was a staunch, rock-ribbed party paper. Its rival - the Gazette - had been established in 1890 by the Populists, who could not get advertising support nor much cash from circulation. So they sold it to W. Y. Morgan, who had helped me with my first job on the Lawrence Journal as he was retiring from the university. Morgan was financed by Major Calvin Hood of the Emporia National Bank, and after much dickering we agreed on a price of three thousand dollars. Offering my mother's property as security, I borrowed a thousand from Governor Morrill, who was a banker, and a thousand dollars from the Plumb estate - somewhat because my father and Senator Plumb had been friends, and somewhat because his oldest son, A. H. Plumb, and I had been fraternity brothers. And each of them had good security. George Plumb, a brother of the senator, lent me two hundred fifty dollars on my personal note, and Major Hood transferred to me a seven-hundred-fifty-dollar note which Morgan had carried. I was three months making the deal, at odd times when I could get away from the Star.

Sallie and I had a hundred dollars or so in the bank, which was spent mostly on moving and thc thousand little incidentals that come at such times. I only know this: Sallie and my mother did not comc with me to Emporia when I took charge of the Gazette; and after I bought my ticket on the afternoon train, the Saturday before June 1, I had a dollar and twenty-five cents in my pocket. It seemed ample at thc time. I was happy. I still can remember with what joy I rode across Kansas into the sunset and through the long twilight. The train went by way of Ottawa, and I still retain the picture of the ride through the Marais des Cygnes Valley.The grass was lush. The trees were in first foliage. The prairie flowers were abloom in the pastures and in the wood lots. Mostly blue flowers, they were.The streams were full. The ponds were full. The hour filled me with a delight that I have held through nearly fifty years. I have forgotten what visions of conquest I had; they were probably lively enough. I only remember that the road across eastern Kansas into the sunset and through the twilight was ineffably beautiful and gave me a deep joy.

This also I remember: when I stepped off the train at Emporia it was into a considerable crowd of idlers who in that day came to the station to see the two plug trains come in from Kansas City. The announcement had been made that I had bought the Gazette. I was a fairly familiar figure on the streets of Emporia - from my student days and my occasional sorties into the town as a gay young blade who danced in Jay's Opera House. Also I was spotted when I made the many visits to Emporia completing the deal with Morgan to buy the Gazette. I knew many of the faces that greeted me. I had a moment's indecision: Should I lug my heavy baggage uptown to the boarding house where I was expected, and establish a reputation as a frugal, thrifty young publisher, or should I establish my credit in the community by going in a hack? The hack was a quarter. I decided, as a credit-strengthening act, to take the hack. I piled in. I never regretted it. I was never the kind who could have made my money by saving it. But if the crowd had known that when I paid the hackman I had j ust a dollar left (a fact which was nobody's business) the opinion of the town would have been divided about me. As it was, no question arose in the mind of the town about my financial ability. A good front is rather to be chosen than great riches.

I was twenty-seven years old. Just ten years before that May evening that landed me in Emporia, I had left Emporia to take a job in a printing office. In those ten years I had learned the printer's trade and had made a living at it. I had become a reporter, I had been in charge of the circulation of a small daily. I had earned my way through college, at least partially, by writing. I had managed a weekly newspaper, the Weekly Eldorado Republican, hired and fired the help, solicited the advertising, written most of the editorials and all of the locals. I had taken charge of the bank account, and had made twenty-five hundred dollars a year, for Mr. Murdock and left his credit A Number I.

I had written for the Kansas City Journal and for the Star, and had published a book which had sold out in sixty days. My stuff - prose or verse - had been copied across the country. I had had a little nibble of fame. I was not afraid of the Emporia Gazette. I was not uneasy about the mortgages on my mother's property.I had fitted myself to do everything, from sweeping out to writing the editorials and keeping the bank account, that I could ask any other man to do. So I was not afraid to plank down twenty-five cents to the hackman and go on a dollar over Sunday until the money from the Gazette began to come in. Which is another way of saying that I was a brash youth with a lot of assurance,who took considerable satisfaction, even pleasurable delight, in getting in a tight place and wiggling out. I never played poker but I did enjoy throwing dice with Fate that May evening as I rode regally through Emporia with the top of the hack down, a dollar in my pocket, and in my heart the sense that I had the world by the tail with a downhill pull.

I had crossed the Rubicon - that border line in this world between the hired man and the boss. I waked the next morning, which was Sunday, scared. t had the key to the office in my pocket. After breakfast I went to look at it, all alone. Here's what I saw: a room twenty-five by sixty with a smaller cubbyhole ten by fifteen, subtracted from that floor space. In the cubbyhole were three chairs and a pine-board table built into the wall. There land the two reporters were supposed to do our writing, to keep the books and get out the copy generally for the paper. It opened into the street. The walls of the cubbyhole were covered with theatrical posters, campaign pictures of statesmen pasted on the wallpaper; and a few photographs of local celebrities and crooks were tacked above the desk. There was a swivel chair - presumably mine. A second chair had a large cane bottom and arms, and the third was a common kitchen chair. The oilcloth on the floor had been scuffed into holes beneath each chair. So much for the editorial department.

The rest of the sixty-by-twenty-five floor space was the composing room and printing office. In the middle stood the cylinder press on which the Gazette was printed: a Cottrell equipped with a water motor which in drouthy seasons was disconnected and replaced by a colored man who turned a crank. Half a dozen racks for type cases were strung along the walls of the room, and three composing stones stood in the center of the floor. A heavy lead roller, weighing seventy-five pounds, stood on one end of the largest composing stone. That was the proof press. And that was all of the machinery that went with the Emporia Gazette.

I wonder if God has yet forgiven me for my sinful pride in it all. I knew what everything was - how good it was, or how bad from misuse or wear and tear. As a printer, I looked over the various cases and was pleased to find they were full. There had been much thrift in the organization of the shop. The floors were swept, and everything was in order, which was another good omen. But I fear that the tidiness was for the new boss. I must have spent an hour in there, gloating over my treasure. The foreman, Jack McGinley, a six-foot, two-hundred-forty-pound, curly-headed, blackeyed Irishman, with a goatee and mustache, showed up in midmorning, and he and I talked until noon about the paper, the pay roll, and business prospects generally. Jack was a dozen years older than I and was a good printer; he had at one time owned his own paper. I did not know it then, but he was a periodical drinker and had sacrificed his position on the right-hand bank of the Rubicon to his lip for liquor. He took me in hand like a father, and I have never had a wiser, more loyal friend than he. He came to be my refuge in many a storm. Why he liked me, I do not know. He had every reason to dislike me; for I was younger than he, and was the boss. I seemed to have smart city ways; very likely I was most opinionated. But he realized early how much I trusted him.

The paper was supposed to have between seven and eight hundred subscribers. Jack told me that there were only four hundred and eighty-five in the town of Emporia and fewer than a hundred in the county, and that the county collections were far in arrears. Jack seemed to have helped Mr. Morgan with the books. In the seesawing and horse trading, Mr. Morgan bad given me certain of the May bills and the arrears in certain other collections. It was a fair trade. Jack knew about it and helped me to straighten out the accounts. He and I, being somewhat of the same blood and of an ardent nature, dropped our guards in that hour alone in the office, and when noon came we stood at the front door. I offered him my hand. He looked me over from head to foot, quite formally, a heavy-set young fellow whose pudgy hands had never known toil heavier than typesetting, a youth with evident, even maybe a little conspicuous, modesty in his voice and mien to hide an inner self-esteem. Jack surveyed that figure with intuitive Irish appraisal, then smiled a beaming, possessive, fatherly smile and said: „You'll do. I guess we'll make it!“ I hope I blushed when I thanked him, and we shook hands warmly. The binding tie was welded.

Sallie and my mother did not come to Emporia until the end of the first week. Sunday afternoon I wrote my salutatory editorial. Reading it the other day, after nearly half a century, I am amazed to find that it stands up. It still represcnts my ideals, realized with such a sad and heavy discount in approximate. But what I wrote I tried to do. Here it is:

„ENTIRELY PERSONAL

June 3, 1895: To the gentle reader who may, through the coming years during which we are spared to one another, follow the course of this paper, a word of personal address from the new editor of the GAZETTE is due. In the first place, the new editor hopes to live here until he is the old editor, until some of the visions which rise before him as he dreams shall have come true. He hopes always to sign „from Emporia" after his name when he is abroad, and he trusts that he may so endear himself to the people that they will be as proud of the first words of the signature as he is of the last words. He expects to perform all the kind offices of the country editor in this community for a generation to come. It is likely that he will write the wedding notices of the boys and girls in the schools; that he will announce the birth of the children who will some day honor Emporia, and that he will say the final words over those of middle age who read these lines.

His relations with the people of this town and country are to be close and personal. He hopes that they may be kindly and just. The new editor of the GAZETTE is a young man now, full of high purposes and high ideals. But he needs the close touch of older hands. His endeavor will be to make a paper for the best people of the city. But to do that he must have their help. They must counsel with him, be his friends, often show him what their sentiment is. On them rests the responsibility somewhat. The „other fellows" will be around. They will give advice. They will attempt to show what the public sentiment is. They will try to work their schemes, which might dishonor the town. If the best people stay away from the editor's office, if they neglect to stand by the editor, they must not blame him for mistakes. An editor is not all wise. He judges only by what he sees and hears. Public sentiment is the only sentiment that prevails. Good sentiment, so long as it does not assert itself, so long as it is a silent majority, is only private sentiment. If the good, honest, upright, God-fearing, law-abiding people of any community desire to be reflected to the world, they must see that their private opinion is public opinion. They must stand by the editors who believe as they do.

It is a plain business proposition. The new editor of the GAZETTE desires to make a clean, honest local paper. He is a Republican and will support Republican nominees first, last, and all the time. There will be no bolting, no sulking, no „holier than thou“ business about his politics - but politics is so little. Not one man in ten cares for politics more than two weeks in a year. In this paper, while the politics will be straight, it will not be obtrusive. It will be confined to the editorial page - where the gentle reader may venture at his peril. The main thing is to have this paper represent the average thought of the best people of Emporia and Lyon County in all their varied interests. The editor will do his best. He has no axes to grind. He is not running the paper for a political pull. If he could get an office he wouldn't have it. He is in the newspaper business as he would be in the drygoods business - to make an honest living and to leave an honest name behind. If the good people care for a fair, honest home paper, that will stand for the best that is in the town - here it is.

In the meantime, I shall hustle advertising, job work and subscriptions, and write editorials and „telegraph“ twelve hours a day in spite of my ideals. The path of glory is barred hog-tight for the man who does not labor while he waits.

William A. White

I slammed that editorial on the copy hook when left the office that Sunday night, and the next morning came down to take charge. Nothing new confronted me except the sense that I was actually boss, not a sub-boss for someone else, which was more frightening than exhilarating. But I had this comfort that first day. I met scores of my father's old friends who had known him twenty-five years before in Emporia. They were mostly substantial citizens, many of them old-line, anti-Populist, silk-stocking Democrats. And they heartened me. Mr. Morgan, my predecessor, took me up and down Commercial Street, introduced me to all thc merchants and most of the lawyers and some of the doctors. I pickedup local items as I went, talked advertising to advertisers, and did a good day's work. We had two reporters, one of whom helped keep the books, and we all solicited advertising. The total pay roll of the office was forty-five dollars. I had to find that much money before the next Saturday night.

The ravens brought it. It may be well to give the reader something of the economic picture of the times, to set down what the wages of skilled labor were in Emporia in 1895. Jack, the foreman, got twelve dollars; later a raise to fifteen. The best printer got eight dollars a week, and four girls set type at from two-fifty to four dollars a week, according to their skill. The office devil got two-fifty, and Mr. Morgan told me he was entitled to a raise to three dollars the first of July. The reporters got eight and ten dollars each.

But living costs were low. A frying chicken cost fifteen cents, steak ten cents a pound, bacon eight and nine cents, flour two dollars a hundred, sugar twenty pounds for a dollar.Sallie and I paid eighteen dollars a month for a six-room house. It did not have a sign of a pipe or a wire in it, either for water or for light. We laid aside five dollars, and no more, for our grocery and incidental budget, and lived within it. We kept no maid, but we could have gotten one for from a dollar and a half to three dollars a week. Those wages and those commodity prices represented a hangover from the old days when communities, even homes, and certainly farms, were selfsufficient, when craftsmen in many trades set their wages on the basis of a self-sufficient home, a smaIl farm and garden, cows and chickens and pigs as one of the props of every family.

But the world had moved on in the quarter of a century before 1895. Railroads and other machines had wiped out all but the skeleton of the old self-subsistent civilization, and the catastrophic maladjustment between the two epochs was evident all around Emporia, and particularly on the farms. Unemplovment had beaten down the price of corn, wheat, hay, hogs, and livestock until farming was unprofitable. The protest of Populism was the political phase of the unpainted farm houses and barns one saw all over the midwestern country, the run-down fences, the fallow, weedy fields; and in towns, the vacant stores and bankruptcy sales. One of the town banks, though I did not know it at first, was slowly sinking into insolvency. It was not Major Hood's bank.

Yet in the big houses, ten or twenty of them, people lived well. The bankers and some of the doctors and lawyers drove spanking teams to carriages that cost as much as three hundred dollars. The Whist and High Five clubs, attended by the best people, had gay parties. Dances were given with some style and éclat, perhaps in the third-floor garrets of the baronial rococo mansions built in the seventies, or maybe in the skating rink or the hall of some fraternal insurance society. People who had money were living well in Emporia; others, hanging on by their eyebrows. And Populism was raging across the state, across the Missouri Valley, and through the South.

I did not realize during those first days in Emporia why our town was divided, as were most towns in the western world, into bank factions, deeply divided, bitterly feudal. But now I see across the years that those two factions in Emporia - the faction gathered about Major Hood and his bank and the faction gathered around Charley Cross and William Martindale and their banks - arose and thrived as local clans bound by purely monetary interests, and somewhat made necessary by the fact that storekeepers, professional people, and the owners of the little industries around the town could not live without

W. A. White (top center), aged thirty, with his staff of ten wrote, edited, set up in hand type, and printed the Emporia Gazette in 1898.

credit. This, the banks furnished. The use of credit was made widely necessary by this transition from a simple self-supporting and self-sufficient economy to the new economy in the machine age. Capital, as represented by the banks, was still tribal, feudal, competitive. The banks fought for business. Their customers lined up behind the banks, and all over this part of the world in the nineties as the economic scenery of the world was changing. Factions, feuds, internal bitternesses, wicked and sometimes bloody rivalries were fostered at the front doors of the banks in towns and cities across the land - at least across our western land. I only know about that.

So when Mr. Morgan took me up and down Commercial Street and Fifth and Sixth avenues, calling on our friends and customers, I went unwittingly wearing the collar of the Emporia National Bank, Major Hood's bank, the bank which Plumb and Hood had founded twenty-five years before. This civic brawl, typical of the day and time, was a sad reality in the life of a young editor who took his pen in hand that Sunday afternoon to write his salutatory to the town of his birth. That night, in the Emporia Republican, „our loathed but esteemed contemporary," a two-line item appeare thus: „Will A. White, of Kansas City, has bought the Gazette from W. Y. Morgan. Next!" The editor of the Republican was a man in his sixties who had served the town in the legislature, who had secured the location of the State Teachers College in Emporia, who was an acknowledged leader of the Republican party in Kansas, and vicegerent of the Santa Fe Railroad, which named a town for him on one of its branches in an adjoining county. He was a dignified man with a rather large head who covered the bald frontal area of his skull with long hair from the side and dyed it, and who always wrote the resolutions at the Republican county convention.

He was of the samurai caste in Kansas Republicanism, receiving remuneration from the Santa Fe as needed for his paper's pay roll, and was a spokesman of the other bank, the Cross-Martindale bank. When it was closed, a few years later, a sheaf of the old editor's blank notes, accommodation paper, was found in the bank which they slipped into the note case to polish up the record for the national bank inspector. He did not realize it, but I was the young bull who had come to horn the old one out of the herd. Toward the end of his career, as was the fashion of the day, he devoted much space to abusing me. The Gazette never replied. Not a line in our paper indicated that we even knew he was on earth; and that - his reporters told ours - galled him more deeply than anything we could say. He was used to every form of abuse but contempt.

Sallie and my mother came to Emporia the weekend after I arrived. Sallie came down to the office daily, and we worked together - she on society items and other local items, I writing the editorial, soliciting advertising, taking care of the bank account. Soon we invited Lew Schmucker to quit his job as a railway postal clerk and come to the Gazette as bookkeeper, reporter, and advertising salesman. To him, it was a dream come true, for he had always wanted to be a newspaperman. So we jogged along six months or so, with nothing more serious to cloud our happy lives than a weekly overdraft at the bank Monday morning, which was wiped out by Wednesday evening.

It is a lovely thing in youth to have „the valor of ignorance," to have no other cares than a weekly overdraft at the bank and to have hold of a lever - the Archimedean lever that moves your world - and to be overwhelmingly in love and be able to laugh at the accidents of fate and turn the barbs of misfortune with the armor of an invulnerable self-confidence. We two - Sallie and I - walked to and from work every day, chattering, honking our laughter, billing and cooing like birds - perhaps equally brainless, which was a good thing also, for we did not realize how precarious was our lot. Times were unbelievably hard that first summer. The overdraft began to mount Friday, sank into a dark abysm Saturday night, and, strain as we would Monday, Tuesday, and Wednesday, we rarely got it entirely wiped out. Once in a while Major Hood at the bank would call me in and remonstrate. Twice that summer we had to give our note for fifty or a hundred dollars to cover the deepening overdraft. But we went on cutting our paper dolls at the office most happily. I printed two stories in the Gazette for filler which Richardson, the Sunday editor, had rejected on the Star. One story was called „The Court of Boyville"; the other was the story of „Aqua Pura." Both appeared later in a book, as you shall see. But from the Gazette they were copied and got around the country.

So, in the winter or early spring of 1896, we had two offers from legitimate book publishers, asking if we had any other stories like that, enough to make a book. We had! We chose Way & Williams, Chicago publishers, largely because they were western; and we turned down Henry Holt & Company chiefly because they were eastern. We were loyal westerners without much sense. So we began gathering up our stories for The Book. A fivehundred-dollar advance came from the publishers with the contract, and we slapped that advance on one of the mortgages. Which made us still happier, and carefree. We screamed our delight like jays as we went about our work and through the town. That five hundred dollars seemed to cheer the old Major up. At least it strengthened our credit so that we could deepen the overdraft a little when we had to; but we could not get rid of it. Major Hood, known in the city as Little Major, was our friend and banker.

Editorially, from the very first week the Gazette was a conservative Republican newspaper. I had no use for the protective tariff, but I tolerated it because I wished to advocate the gold standard. Kansas was sadly bitten by the fiat money theory. Senator Plumb, who had bossed the state and led it politically in the seventies and eighties, had been for the free coinage of silver. He owned silver mines in Colorado. Most of our Kansas statesmen toyed with the free-silver idea. They hoped to beat the Populists by making fun of pure fiat money, and at the same time advocate the free coinage of silver which was 40 per cent fiat. So, when the Gazette advocated the single gold standard, it was politically a pariah in Kansas. It is not unlikely that occasional editorials in the files of the Gazette, speaking well of the theory of proteetion, were my defense weapons against attack upon my gold-standard flank. But I set no great store by the editorial page. I believed that local news, if honestly and energetically presented, would do more for subscriptions and more for the Gazette's standing in the community than its editorial page. Indeed I believed then and believe now that a newspaper that prints the news - all of it - that is fit to print, can take any editorial position it desires without loss of prestige or patronage. People choose their paper not because of its politics but because of its integrity, its enterprise, and its intelligence. They want an honest paper, well written, where they can find all the news to which they are entitled.

Except for occasional boycotts, which were noisy, but highly incompetent, our editorials never got us in trouble. It was the news items that brought in irate subscribers. Our policy, for instance, was to drop the word „lady" and substitute the word „woman." A lady who had paid a fine for streetwalking came in to protest not the publication of the news of her fine, but the fact that we called her a woman, and she assured us that she was as much of a lady as any of the other girls in this town. And from that hour to this, the Gazette has referred to all females as women except that police-court characters were always to be designated as „ladies."«

STATESMAN FACES OUTBREAK OF THE KOREAN WAR

by *Dean G. Acheson*

The politician was born on April 11, 1893, in Middletown, Connecticut, and died on October 12, 1971 in Sandy Spring, Maryland. Dean Gooderham Acheson attended Groton School and Yale College from 1912 to 1915, where he joined Scroll and Key Society, was elected to Phi Beta Kappa and was brother of the Delta Kappa Epsilon fraternity. At Groton and Yale he had the reputation of a partier and prankster; he was somewhat aloof but still popular with his classmates. Kennan earned his Bachelor of Arts degree in 1915.

Thereafter, he enrolled at the Harvard University Law School, but his studies were interrupted, when he served with the United States Navy during World War I. He completed his law course in 1918 and was granted his LL.B. degree. From 1919 to 1921 he worked as private secretary for Supreme Court justice Louis Brandeis. From this post Acheson went to the Washington law firm of Covington, Burling and Rublee, where he practiced corporate and international law from 1921 to 1933.

In March 1933 President Franklin Delano Roosevelt appointed him Undersecretary of the Treasury. When Secretary Willim H. Woodin fell ill, Acheson suddenly found himself acting secretary despite his ignorance of finance. Because of his opposition to Roosevelt's plan to deflate the Dollar by controlling gold prices (thus creating inflation), Acheson was forced to resign in November 1933. In 1934 he returned to his law firm, now called Burling, Rublee, Acheson and Schorb. In 1939-1940 he headed a committee to study the operation of administrative bureaus in the federal government.

It was in 1941, that Roosevelt requested Acheson to return to government service as Assistant Secretary of State. Acheson implemented much of United States economic policy aiding Great Britain and harming the Axis Powers. In 1944, Acheson attended the Bretton Woods Conference as the head delegate from the State Department. At this conference,the post-war economic structure was designed. The conference was the birthplace of the International Monetary Fund, the World Bank, and the General Agreement on Tariffs and Trade, the last of which would evolve into the World Trade Organization.

Later, in 1945, President Harry S. Truman selected Acheson as his Undersecretary of United States Department of State; he retained this position working under Secretaries of State Edward Stettenius, James F. Burns and George

Marshall. And, as late as 1945/46 Acheson sought détente with the Soviet Union. In 1945, as chairman of a special committee to prepare a plan for the international control of atomic energy, he wrote the famous Acheson-Lilienthal report. At first Acheson was conciliatory towards Joseph Stalin. The Soviet Union's attempts at regional hegemony in Eastern Europe and in Southwest Asia, however, changed Acheson's thinking, and he became a primary architect of the Cold War strategies.

After six and a half years in the State Department, he resigned in 1947 to return to private practice. At that time President Truman bestowed on him the Medal of Merit for his services. Two years later, on January 7, 1949, Acheson was recalled to active duty when President Truman announced his nomination as Secretary of State. In this position he built a working framework for containment. Acheson became the main designer of the military Alliance NATO, and signed the part for the United States. The formation of NATO was a dramatic departure from historie American foreign policy goals of avoiding any 'entangling alliances.'

During the summer of 1949, Acheson had the State Department produce a study of recent Sino-American relations, including aspects about the future of the Korean Peninsula. With the Communist takeover of mainland China in 1949, that country switched from a close friend of the U.S. to a bitter enemy. The two powers became heavy opponents during the Korean War which started in June 1950. Critics blamed Acheson for what they called the 'loss of China' and launched several years of organized opposition to Acheson's tenure.

Finally, Acheson retired from his position as Secretary of State on January 20, 1953, the last day of the Truman administration. Acheson returned to his private law practice and served on Yale University's Board of Trustees. He was elected a Fellow of the American Academy of Arts and Sciences in 1955. Although his official governmental career was over, his influence was not. He was ignored by the Eisenhower administration but headed up Democratic Policy Groups in the late 1950s. Much of President John F. Kennedy's flexible response policies came from the position papers drawn up by this group.

Acheson's law offices were strategically located a few blocks from the White House and he accomplished much out of office. He became an unofficial advisor to the Kennedy and Johnson admininistrations. During the Cuban Missile Crisis, for example, he was dispatched by Kennedy to France to brief French President Charles de Gaulle and gain his support for the United States blockade. During the 1960s, Acheson was a leading member of a bipartisan group of establishing elders known as 'The Wise Men', who initially supported the Vietnam War. President Johnson asked Acheson to reassess American military policy, and he decided that military victory was impossible. He advised Johnson to pull out of Vietnam as quickly as possible. In later years, Acheson first supported Richard Nixon for president in 1968 but broke with him with the incursion into Cambodia in 1970.

In 1969 Acheson brought out a book entitled „Present at the Creation - My years in the state Department", covering the period from 1941 through 1952/53. The author's Apologia calls it „a tale of large conceptions, great achievements and some failures." The work received much praise, one critic confirmed „Dean Acheson's place as the clearest thinking, most effective Secretary of State of the Twentieth Century." The Modern Library placed the volume at No. 42 on its top 100 nonfiction-books of the 20th Century. When the Pulitzer Prize jurors of the History award category made their list of finalists, Acheson's memoirs were called their first choice.

„Acheson's prodigious memory one feels is due to the passionate interest in the men and events he knew and experienced," the jury report of January 6, 1970, stated and then added: „Here is a notable literary distinction, also an honesty that is not hidden by the irony, the sophistication, and truly elegant wit. There is about Acheson a quality patently American, as there was about the colleagues he so much admired: Harry Truman and George Marshall. And there is about these memoirs of a great public figure, written in the classic manner, an air of gallantry and high emprise, of magnanimity, too, which even those who disagreed with him on great issues then (and for that matter now) cannot fail to recognize and respond to." The Advisory Board agreed and so Dean G. Acheson earned the 1970 Pulitzer Prize for History, just one year before his death. Following now are parts of the award-winning work, dealing with Acheson's role during the early phases of the Korean War:

»After the Governors' Conference on Tuesday, June 20, 1950, a Harvard commencement speech on Thursday, a Cabinet meeting, press conference, and preparation for a military assistance appearance on the Hill on Friday, we escaped Washington the next day, June 24, for a quiet weekend at Harewood Farm. As quiet, that is, as that haven could then be. The white telephone tied into the White House switchboard was used sparingly by considerate associates, but it was used. Even when evening came and the busy world was hushed and the fever of day was over, the movements of the security officers changing guard during the night echoed through that small house. The crank mail, which Senator McCarthy's attentions had increased, led to the undesired innovation of night as well as day shifts of guards around me, a regimen not conducive to relaxation. However, the weekend began well. After some hours of gardening and a good dinner 1 had turned in to read myself to sleep.

Saturday, June 24: About ten o'clock the White House telephone had me up again. John Hickerson, Assistant Secretary for United Nations Affairs, Dean Rusk, Assistant Secretary for Far Eastern Affairs, and Philip C. Jessup, Ambassador at Large, had been called to the Department by a cable from our Ambassador in Seoul, Korea, John Muccio, an experienced and level-headed officer, reporting an attack from the north across the 38th parallel on South Korean forces. It described a heavy attack, different from patrol forays that had occurred in the past, and in Muccio's opinion was an all-out offensive against the Republic of Korea.

This cable had crossed an inquiry from the Department stimulated by disturbing press rumors out of Seoul. Hickerson and the others were in touch with Frank Pace, Secretary of the Army. Louis Johnson, Secretary of Defense, and General Bradley, Chairman of the Joint Chiefs of Staff, were in Tokyo. Other Chiefs of Staff had not yet been located, and former Senator Warren Austin, our Ambassador at the United Nations, was at his home in Burlington, Vermont. Asked for a recommendation, Hickerson suggested a meeting of the UN Security Council the next morning (Sunday) to call for a cease-fire, and urgent requests to our civilian and military missions in Korea for continuing information.

I approved, and authorized Ernest Gross, Ambassador Austin's deputy, to ask Secretary General Trygve Lie to call the Security Council. Overnight Hickerson, Rusk, and Jessup were to work with the Pentagon through Frank Pace to get up such orders as the President might wish to issue should he decide to take further action, military or otherwise. Meanwhile I would telephone the President, who was spending the weekend at his home in Independence, Missouri. Any changes he wished to make in my instructions could easily overtake them.

Independence time was two hours earlier than ours. The President had just finished a family dinner when he came to the telephone and learned the situation and the instructions given. He approved and suggested his immediate return to Washington. I dissuaded him from adding the unnecessary risk of a hurriedly arranged night flight and urged instead a further report from me next morning, when our information should be more complete, and his return to Washington later in the day. He agreed and asked whether he could do anything to help us overnight. Remembering the absurd restrictions that Louis Johnson had imposed on communication between the two departments in the spring, I asked the President to let Frank Pace know that he wanted the fullest cooperation between the departments. No difficulty of any sort developed in work between them. A call of confirmation to Hickerson completed my night's work, but not his.

Sunday, June 25: The next morning at the Department the news was bad. A full-scale attack centering around a tank column was driving toward Seoul and Kimpo airport. South Korean arms were clearly outclassed. Recommendations had been prepared by the two departments for action in the light of present knowledge and a resolution drafted for presentation to the UN Security Council. A talk with the President gave him the facts, secured his approval of the resolution, and instructed me to have the available people from State and Defense meet with him at Blair House that evening. Later a message from the plane added that the group should come to Blair House, for dinner at seven-thirty. I left word at Defense for the Secretary and General Bradley, due back that afternoon, the service secretaries, and the Chiefs of Staff, and took with me Under Secretary Webb, Assistant Secretaries Hickerson and Rusk, and Ambassador Jessup.

An early draft of our resolution determined that the „armed attack on the Republic of Korea by forces from North Korea“ constituted „an unprovoked act of aggression.“ When this draft was shown to some members of the Security Council, they expressed doubt whether the information yet available established the conclusion. They were, however, prepared to say that it „constituted a breach of the peace.“ Their preference for this statement was strengthened upon learning that our representative had not yet been instructed what our course would be should the North Koreans disregard the call for an immediate cessation of hostilities and a withdrawal of their forces to the 38th parallel as provided in the resolution. To meet these views the change was made.

When the Security Council convened on Sunday afternoon, it was not known whether Malik, the Soviet Representative, who was boycotting the council because of the presence of a Nationalist Chinese and had returned to Moscow, would appear. He did not. There was no negative vote, and the resolution was declared adopted by a vote of 9-0, with Yugoslavia abstaining. I met the President with the news at the airport and drove with him to Blair House. During the afternoon I had everyone and all messages kept out of my room for an hour or two while I ruminated about the situation. „Thought“ would suggest too orderly and purposeful a process. It was rather to let various possibilities, like glass fragments in a kaleidoscope, form a series of patterns of action and then draw conclusions from them. Our recommendations for the President dealt with the next twenty-four hours or so, which was as far as we could see at the time. But what must we contemplate beyond that? One possibility was that the attack would be called off; the other, that it would not be.

For some months, as tensions had mounted again after the Berlin blockade, we had run exercises on danger spots for renewed Soviet probing of our determination. Korea was on the list but not among the favorites. Berlin, Turkey, Greece, Iran - all seemed spots where the balance of convenient operation dipped in favor of the Soviets. Korea was too near major forces and bases of ours in Japan and too far from any of theirs to offer a tempting target, though they could have judged our interest in it less than in the other places. But now the attack had come there. What was likely to happen next and how should we determine our response? It seemed close to certain that the attacke had been mounted, supplied, and instigated by the Soviet Union and that it would not be stopped by anything short of force. If Korean force proved unequal to the job, as seemed probable, only American military intervention could do it. Troops from other sources would be helpful politically and psychologically but unimporant militaryly. My two weeks in Europe left little doubt of that.

Plainly, this attack did not amount to a casus belli against the Soviet Union. Equally plainly, it was an open, undisguised challenge to our internationally accepted position as the protector of South Korea, an area of great importance to the security of American-occupied Japan. To back away from this challenge, in view of our capacity for meeting it, would be highly destructive of the power and prestige of the United States. By prestige I mean the shadow cast by power, which is of great deterrent importance. Therefore, we could not accept the conquest of this important area by a Soviet puppet under the very guns of our defensive perimeter with no more resistance than words and gestures in the Security Council. It looked as though we must steel ourselves for the use of force. That did not mean, in words used later by General Mark Clark, that we must be prepared „to shoot the works for victory," but rather to see that the attack failed.

When I set off to meet the President, I had no plan, but my mind was pretty clear on where the course we were about to recommend would lead and why it was necessary that we follow that course. The full group invited was assembled at Blair House. While waiting for dinner to be announced, Secretary Johnson asked General Bradley to read a memorandum that he had brought from General MacArthur on the strategie importance of Formosa. I recognized this as an opening gun in a diversionary argument that Johnson wished to start with me. Evidently another did also, for when General Bradley had finished, the President announced that discussion of the Far Eastern situation had better be postponed until after dinner when we would be alone. The subject was thereupon dropped and conversation, during an excellent dinner in the Blair-Lee House gotten up by the staff on a Sunday afternoon with the shortest notice, was kept to general topics. After dinner we remained at the table while the White House staff cleared it and retired.

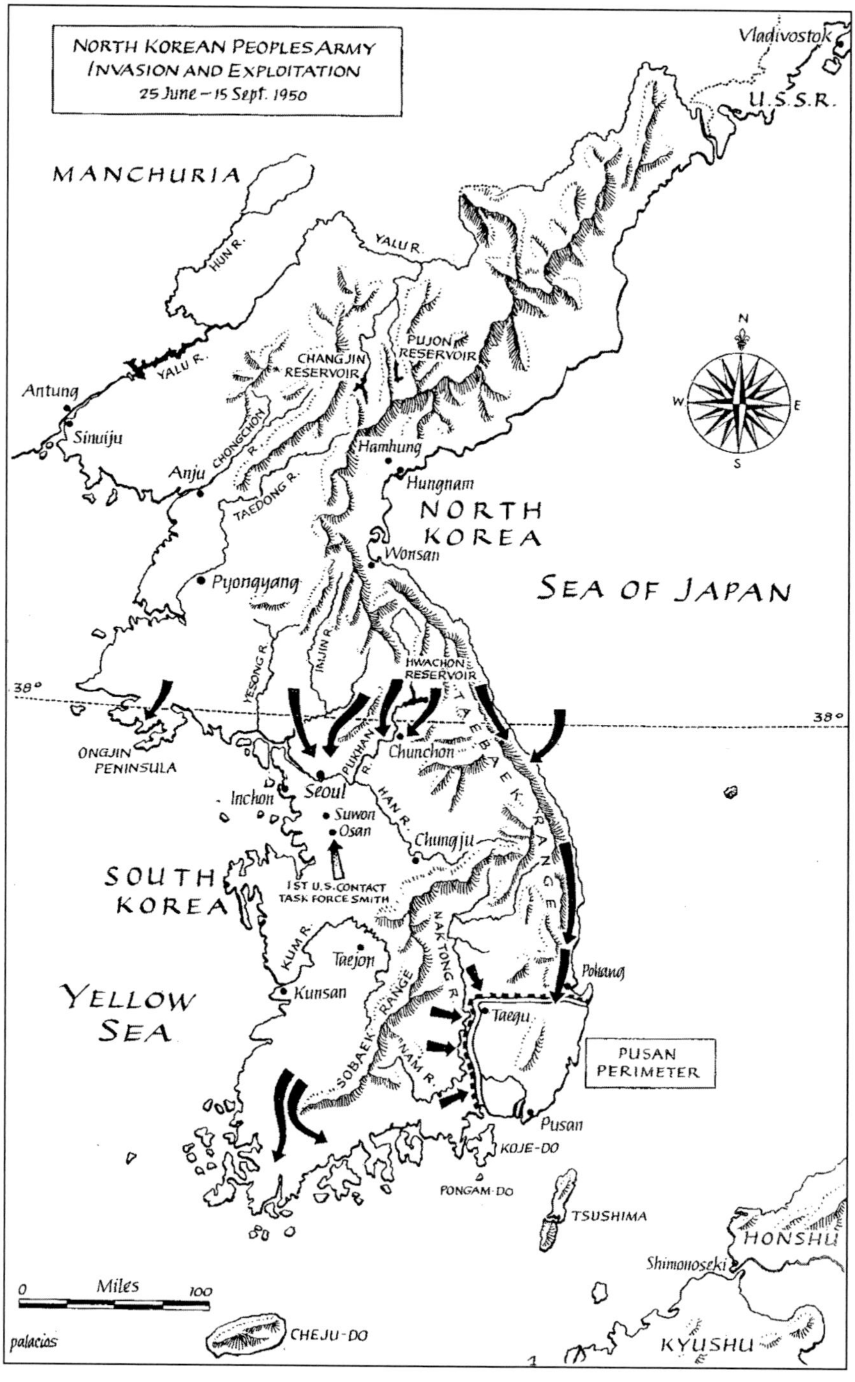
NORTH KOREAN PEOPLES ARMY
INVASION AND EXPLOITATION
25 June – 15 Sept. 1950
MANCHURIA
Vladivostok
U.S.S.R.
YALU R.
HUN R.
PUJON RESERVOIR
CHANGJIN RESERVOIR
Antung
Sinuiju
Anju
CHONGCHON R.
TAEDONG R.
Hamhung
Hungnam
NORTH KOREA
Wonsan
Pyongyang
SEA OF JAPAN
YESONG R.
IMJIN R.
HWACHON RESERVOIR
38°
ONGJIN PENINSULA
Chunchon
PUKHAN R.
Seoul
Inchon
HAN R.
Suwon
Osan
Chungju
TAEBAEK RANGE
SOUTH KOREA
1ST U.S. CONTACT TASK FORCE SMITH
KUM R.
Taejon
NAKTONG R.
Pohang
YELLOW SEA
Kunsan
SOBAEK RANGE
Taegu
NAM R.
PUSAN PERIMETER
Pusan
KOJE-DO
PONGAM-DO
TSUSHIMA
HONSHU
Shimonoseki
KYUSHU
CHEJU-DO
Miles
0
100
palacios

The President then asked me to report the latest developments and any recommendations the two departments had prepared for him. I gave a darkening report of great confusion and read three recommendations:

1. General MacArthur should be authorized and directed to supply Korea with arms and other equipment over and above that already allocated under the Military Assistance Program.
2. The U.S. Air Force should be ordered to protect Kimpo airport during the evacuation of United States dependents by attacking any North Korean ground or air forces approaching it.
3. The Seventh Fleet should be ordered to proceed from the Philippines north and to prevent any attack from China on Formosa or vice versa.

I also urged that military assistance to Indochina be stepped up.

Each person around the room was then asked for his views. The recommendations were supported with varying degrees of detail. There was quite general uniformity of view that the occasion called for prompt and vigorous action as it became clearer. The President discussed with the soldiers the likelihood of the Soviet Union's pushing the crisis to general war. The consensus was to the contrary, since the military balance was more favorable to the United States and unfavorable to the Soviet Union than it was likely to continue in the longer run. They were not in favor of using ground forces under conditions then existing. General Joseph L. Collins pressed for and obtained the President's authority to have General MacArthur send a survey team to Korea to make a firsthand appraisal and report. At the end, about eleven o'clock, the President accepted my recommendations, although reserving decision on what orders to issue to the Seventh Fleet until it should reach the Formosa Straits about thirty-six hours later and be able to carry them out.

Monday, June 26: A day of steadily worsening reports from Korea, but work went on. Assignments were made to carry out the President's instructions of the preceding evening. I went over my testimony for the Appropriations Committee, and then spent half an hour telephoning Senators Tom Connally and Alexander Wiley and Judge Kee of the House committee, repeating what was in the press; reporting our support for the United Nations, whose representatives were busy in Korea; and asking that any meeting with congressional committees be held off for a day, „until we had some hard information to report." The appropriations hearing went off without too much trouble. On my return the news was much worse. More calls from and to the Capitol; finally Assistant Secretary Jack McFall went up to prepare the chairmen for what appeared a growing rout. After lunch the Korean Ambassador, distraught and weeping, called on the President with me to present President Rhee's plea for help. The President soothed him, and I gave him a statement to read as he went out which assured him that we were solidly backing the United Nations.

Returning to the Department, I conferred with those who had been working on the President's assignments. What followed is recorded in a minute by one of those present: „The Secretary broke off the discussions we had been having with him and said that he wanted to be alone and to dictate. We were called in about 6:30 P.M. and he read to us a paper he had produced, which was a first draft of the statement finally issued by the President, and which was not significantly changed by the time it appeared the following day." After dinner downtown and further conferences with State and Defense officers, I telephoned the President that the situation in Korea was becoming so desperate that he would wish to hear about it firsthand and instruct us further. He summoned the same group to Blair House which had met there on Sunday.

It met there at nine o'clock, Deputy Under Secretary H. Freeman Matthews taking Webb's place. General Vandenberg reported that a Russian plane had been shot down by our forces and that the South Koreans were breaking all along the front under a formidable attack. In response to the President's request for suggestions, I recommended that:

1. The Air Force and Navy should give all-out support to the Korean forces, for the time being confining their efforts to south of the 38th parallel.
2. The Seventh Fleet should be ordered to prevent an attack on Formosa, the Nationalists told not to attack the mainland, and the Fleet told to prevent their doing so, if necessary.
3. U.S. forces in the Philippines should be strengthened and aid to Philippine forces accelerated.
4. Aid to Indochina should be increased and we should propose to the French that we send a strong military mission.
5. If the President approved the foregoing, he should issue the statement I had prepared as directed and which included actions recommended.
6. At the Security Council meeting called for the next morning we should propose a new resolution (which Hickerson read) calling on UN members to give Korea such help as might be needed to repel the armed attack and restore peace in the area. If Malik returned to the Security Council and vetoed the resolution, we would have to carry on under the existing one. If he did not return, it would pass without opposition.

We had speculated a great deal about the probable Soviet move. The uncertainty about it added one more element of chance to the puzzle before us. Charles Bohlen and George Kennan, who spoke with most experience on-the subject, believed that the cumbersome Soviet bureaucracy was simply not equipped to make quick decisions. It would take some time, they thought, far Moscow to figure out the correlation of forces involved. The betting was against the presence of a Russian at the meeting on the morrow. The recommendations met with general favor, including Louis Johnson's, and were approved by the President. The Army officers present doubted whether naval and air support could save the Korean forces, though the Navy and Air Force view was mare optimistic. If it became necessary to commit ground forces in Korea, they thought same degree of mobilization might become necessary. The President asked that this be given immediate study. He then raised the question of consultation with congressional leaders.

Tuesday, June 27: At the President's meeting with the congressional leaders, Assistant Secretaries Matthews, Rusk, and Hickerson and Ambassador Jessup accompanied me. The Chiefs of Staff and service secretaries came with Secretary Johnson. The meeting was held in the Cabinet Room, Johnson and I flanking the President, with the legislators around the table and the others behind them. The President asked me to summarize the situation, and then stressed the prompt action of the Security Council, read the statement, later published, of the orders he had already issued, and reported out efforts to communicate with the Soviet Government. He then asked for views. Various questions about military dispositions were asked and answered by the Chiefs, including the fact that no ground forces had yet been committed. Senator Wiley seemed to express the consensus by saying that it was enough for him to know that we were in there with force and that the President thought the force adequate. Senator Tydings reported that his committee had that morning recommended an extension of the draft act and presidential authority to call out thc National Guard.

Questions having turned to the political field, the President stated that our actions were taken in support of the United Nations efforts to restore peace in the area. In regard to Formosa, however, his orders were ancillary, aimed at preventing any new outbreak of fighting. I discussed the proposed Security Council resolution, ventured the opinion that Malik would not attend the meeting, and pointed out that since the USSR had not yet publicly committed itself we were careful not to engage Soviet prestige at this time. Congressman Eaton inquired whether the United States was now committed to defend South Korea. The President answered yes, as a member of the United Nations and in response to the Security Council's resolutions. Asked about help from other nations, I replied that not much could be expected since others either had their hands full, like the French, or had little to spare. After assurance that Congress would be kept currently informed of developments and general agreement that release of the President's statement would make separate comments unnecessary, the meeting broke up.

While we were talking the Security Council met, without Malik, and adopted the United States resolution, with Yugoslavia dissenting and Egypt and India abstaining. President Truman's statement referring to the continuance of the North Korean attack despite the UN call for its cessation said: „In these circumstances, I have ordered United States air and sea forces to give the Korean Government troops cover and support." It added that an attack on Formosa under these circumstances would be a direct threat to the security of the Pacific area and to United States forces performing their lawful and necessary functions there. „Accordingly," the President's statement continued, „I have ordered the Seventh Fleet to prevent any attack on Formosa. As a corollary of this action, I am calling upon the Chinese Government on Formosa to cease all air and sea operations against the mainland. The Seventh Fleet will see that this is done."

The statement also recited the other actions that had been taken. Later the same day we told the press of our note to the Soviet Union. In view of their

Secretary of State Dean Acheson (left), Ambassdor Philip Jessup and Assistent Secretary of State Dean Rusk leaving the White House conference at which it was decided to go all out to defend South Korea.

Representative's refusal to attend the Security Council's meeting and of their close relations with the North Korean authorities, we were approaching them directly, we said, to ask their disavowal of responsibility for the attack and the use of their influence with the North Koreans „for withdrawal of the invading forces and cessation of hostilities." On the twenty-ninth they replied that the attack had been made by the South Koreans and responsibility for its consequences rested upon them „and upon those who stand behind their back." On Tuesday Governor Dewey of New York read to me over the telephone a statement giving his support to the Administration's action on Korea and asked for suggestions. I welcomed it with warmest appreciation and gratitude. He released it at once.

Wednesday, June 28 : Immediately following Governor Dewey's support, Senator Taft opened up in the Senate. His speech was typical - bitterly partisan and ungracious, but basically honest. The Administration was responsible, he said, for the trouble that had overtaken it. The division of Korea, failure to arm the South sufficiently, the „loss of China" to the Communists, my „invitation to attack" in the January 12 speech, had all made attack inevitable. Even now the President had done the right thing in the wrong way. The Senator would have approved a congressional resolution authorizing intervention but doubted the constitutionality of the President's executive action. The ground Senator Taft chose was typical senatorial legalistic ground for differing with the President, as we have seen earlier in the case of Senator Vandenberg. As a result, discussion in Congress of these differences is singularly lacking in understanding of substantive issues. When it escapes the shackles of the separation of powers, it is apt to bog down in the moral shortcomings of those foreign governments with whom the United States is cooperating. They are usually said to be lacking either in energetic action for the common cause or in moral fervor for democratic doctrines.

At the National Security Council meeting on the afternoon of the twenty-eighth I pointed out that we could not count on the continuance of the enthusiastic support that our staunch attitude in Korea had evoked in the country and in the world. Firm leadership would be less popular if it should involve casualties and taxes. The President, mistaking my purpose, which was to prepare for criticism and hard sledding, insisted that we could not back out of the course upon which we had started. The reply was typical of one of his most admirable traits. He was unmoved by, indeed unmindful of, the effect upon his or his party's political fortunes of action that he thought was right and in the best interest of the country, broadly conceived. A doctrine that later became fashionable with presidents, called „keeping all options open" (apparently by avoiding decision), did not appeal to Harry S. Truman.

Thursday, June 29: Wednesday had been a day of pause in the rush of decisions. On Thursday it picked up again. Brigadier General John Church, who had been sent to Korea by General MacArthur to report the situation, had signaled that the status quo ante could not be restored without the commitment of United States troops, and by Thursday morning the news was much worse. All attempts to halt the South Korean retreat at the Han River south of Seoul failed. By noon the gloom deepened. The President called a meeting of the „Blair House Group" for five o'clock.

Decisions at this meeting increased the involvement of our air and naval forces to include military targets in North Korea, but not beyond, and authorized the use of ground forces to secure the port, airfield, and communications facilities at Pusan, considerably south of the combat zone. Meanwhile General MacArthur had gone by plane from Tokyo to make his own reconnaisance at the scene of the fighting. He was told that should Soviet forces intervene he was to provide for the security of his own troops and report at once to Washington. However, as I have already suggested, it was State's view that while the Chinese might intervene, the Russians would not. Shortly after this meeting I returned to the White House with an offer by Generalissimo Chiang Kai-shek to contribute thirty-three thousand troops to the Korean action, to be transported and supplied by the United States. The President seemed to look with favor on this idea, which I argued against on the ground that these troops would be more useful defending Formosa than Korea. He directed me to bring it up the next day before the full group, when he could hear all views.

Friday, June 30 : General MacArthur, back in Tokyo after a hazardous expedition to the front in Korea, telegraphed General Collins, Chief of Staff of the Army, that the Korean retreat was a rout and that American combat troops were necessary to stop it. He asked for authority to send from Japan at once a regimental combat team as the spearhead of a two-division buildup as soon as possible afterward. This message came to Collins at three o'clock Friday morning and was immediately followed by a telecon discussion by General Collins, Secretary of the Army Pace, and Assistant Secretary of State Rusk at the Pentagon with General MacArthur in Tokyo. (A telecon is a secure device by which a typewriter operated at one end records both there and through a similar machine at the other end.) General MacArthur elaborated his telegraphed report, underlining the urgent need for American military help at the front. Secretary Pace telephoned the President at five o'clock, finding him up and dressing for his morning walk. The President immediately granted authority to move the augmented regiment, promised a further reply in a few hours, and ordered a meeting of the Blair House Group at the White House at eight-thirty that morning. Rusk filled me in on the way to the meeting. The request from the front and the President's response came as no surprise to me.

At the White House the President informed us of what he had already done and asked for advice regarding the next step. He spoke favorably of Chiang's offer of troops immediately available. I opposed the latter on the ground that the net result might well be the reverse of helpful by bringing Chinese Communist intervention, either in Korea or Formosa or both. The Chiefs of Staff sided with me, saying that the transport could better be used for our own troops and supplies, since Chiang's best troops were not likely to be of much help against the North Korean armor. The unanimous advice of the group was to follow the force already authorized with the two divisions from Japan. The President so decided and approved the necessary orders. The decision not to accept the Generalissimo's offer brought from General MacArthur the suggestion that he go to Formosa to explain it. Instinct told us what experience later proved - to fear General MacArthur bearing explanations. Furthermore, better uses for the theater commander at this juncture came to mind, so a State Department officer was sent from Tokyo to Formosa with the explanation.

At eleven o'clock I returned to the White House for a meeting with congressional leaders, taking Foster Dulles, just back from Tokyo, with me. The congressional group was perhaps twice as large as the one at the Tuesday meeting. The President reported the situation in Korea, reviewed the actions previously taken by the United Nations Security Council and the United States Government, and the orders he had issued that morning. A general chorus of approval was interrupted by, I think, Senator Kenneth Wherry questioning the legal authority of the executive to take this action. Senator Alexander Smith suggested a congressional resolution approving the President's action. The President said that he would consider Smith's suggestion and asked me to prepare a recommendation. The meeting ended with Representative Dewey Short stating that Congress was practically unanimous in its appreciation of the President's leadership. Short was a Republican from the President's home state of Missouri and ranking minority member of the Armed Services Committee. Friday's decisions were the culminating ones of a momentous week. We were then fully committed in Korea.«

AVIATOR MASTERS FIRST TRANS-ATLANTIC NONSTOP FLIGHT

by Charles A. Lindbergh

The internationally famous aviator was born on February 4, 1902, in Detroit, Michigan, and died on August 26, 1974, on Hawaii. Charles Augustus Lindbergh Jr. was educated at the University of Wisconsin and entered the Nebraska Aircraft Corporation Flying School in 1922. Two years later he enrolled as a flying cadet in the United States Air Service Reserve.

When his training was completed, he was commissioned a second lieutenant and subsequently became a captain. In 1925 he became a first lieutenant in the Missouri National Guard and later was advanced to a colonel. After several „barnstorming“ trips, Lindbergh worked as an Air Mail Service pilot. On May 20, 1927 he started on the first successful flight across the Atlantic in his Ryan monoplane „Spirit of St. Louis,“ covering the estimated 3,610 miles in some thirty-three hours. This pioneer achievement brought the flier the honors of official governmental receptions in Brussels, London and Paris, where he was decorated as chevalier of the Legion of Honor. In Washington, D.C., Lindbergh was awarded the Distinguished Flying Cross and promoted to colonel in the Air Corps Reserve.

Lindbergh became associated with the Transcontinental Air Transport Company and also served as technical adviser to Pan American Airways - positions in which he explored air-routes to Asia and Europe. In the 1930's Lindbergh went to Europe to work with the scientist Alexis Carrel. At the suggestion of the U.S. military attaché in Berlin, Lindbergh made surveys of air power in Germany, France, the U.S.S.R., and England. Having returned to the U.S. in 1939, he served as a civilian technician in World War II.

Lindbergh was a consultant for the Ford Motor Company and the U.S. War Department, 1939-1944, and the United Aircraft Corporation in Connecticut and the Pacific War Theatre. After the war, he worked on his autobiography. The book, called after his famous aircraft „The Spirit of S. Louis“, was published in 1953 and soon became a bestseller. When the work came to the attention of the Pulitzer Prize jurors in the „Biography or Autobiography“ award category, Lindbergh's memoirs, according to the jury report of March 24, 1954, did not become the favorite of the committee. But the Advisory Board of the Pulitzer Prizes on its session of April 23, 1954, overruled the jury's proposals for the prize and made Charles A. Lindbergh the 1954 Pulitzer

Prize laureate for his inspiring account of the nonstop transatlantic solo flight. Following now are some pages from the award-winning book, covering the final hours of Lindbergh's flight from New York, when approaching the Paris region on May 21, 1927:

»Almost thirty-five hundred miles from New York and 33 hours across the Atlantic: I've broken the world's distance record for a nonstop airplane flight. The fuselage tank must be almost empty; and now there's no need to run it dry. I turn on the right wing-tank. In one hour more I should see the lights of Paris. The sea is calm. Southward, just out of gliding range, lies the dusk-touched coast of Normandy. Little boats sail in toward shore, apparently motionless on the surface, leaving only their wakes as signs of movement to an airman's eye. A faint point of land, far ahead on my left, marks the location of Le Havre. The expanse of water, extending on eastward below it, is the estuary of the Seine.

I cross the coast again exactly on course, over Deauville. All the east foreshadows night. Day now belongs only to the western sky, still red with sunset. What more I see of France, before I land, will be in this long twilight of late spring. I nose the *Spirit of St. Louis* lower, while I study the farms and villages - the signs I can't read, the narrow, shop-lined streets, the walled-in barnyards. Fields are well groomed, fertile, and peaceful - larger than those of England. It's not hard to see how French farmers make a living; and there are plenty of places where I could land in emergency without cracking up.

People come running out as I skim low over their houses - blue-jeaned peasants, white-aproned wives, children scrambling between them, all bare-headed and looking as though they'd jumped up from the supper table to search for the noise above their roofs. Four-twenty on the clock. That's nine-twenty here. Why, it's past suppertime! I hold the stick with my knees, untwist the neck of the paper bag, and pull out a sandwich - my first food since take-off. The *Spirit of St. Louis* noses up. I push the stick forward, clamp it between my knees again, and uncork the canteen. I can drink all the water I want, now - plenty more below if I should be forced down between here and Paris.

But how flat the sandwich tastes! Bread and meat never touched my tongue like this before. It's an effort even to swallow. I'm hungry, because I go on eating, but I have to wash each mouthful down with water. One sandwich is enough. I brush the crumbs off my lap. I start to throw the wrapping through the window - no, these fields are so clean and fresh it's a shame to scatter them with paper. I crunch it up and stuff it back in the brown bag. I don't want the litter from a sandwich to symbolize my first contact with France.

All details on the ground are masking out in night. Color is gone. Only shades remain - woods darker than fields; hedgerows, lines of black. Lights

Lindbergh in front of his plane „Spirit of St. Louis"

twinkle in villages and blink in farmhouse windows. My instruments are luminous again. The rest of the flight will be in darkness. But I can't miss Paris, even if I find no other check point on my route. I'm too close. The sky's too clear. The city's too large.

I ease back on the stick and climb - - - to five hundred - - - to a thousand - - - to two thousand feet. A light flashes from the darkness, miles ahead. Could it be - - - I stare at the area from which it came, and wait. On our mail route at home, you count eleven between flashes - - - Another flash. Yes, it's an air beacon! And there are two more, blinking dimly in the distance, to the left. It must be the airway between London and Paris! Nobody told me it had lights.

From now on everything will be as simple as flying in to Chicago on a clear night. That line of beacons is converging with my course. Where the two lines meet - the beacons and my course - less than a hundred miles ahead - lies Paris. I can project them over the horizon, into the night, and already see the city in my mind's eye. Within half an hour, its glow will lighten the south-eastern sky.

Down under my left wing, angling in from the north, winding through fields submerged in night, comes the Seine, shimmering back to the sky the faint remaining light of evening. With my position known and my compass set, with the air clear and a river and an airway to lead me in, nothing but engine failure can keep me now from reaching Paris. The engine is running perfectly - I check the switches again.

The *Spirit of St. Louis* is a wonderful plane. It's like a living creature, gliding along smoothly, happily, as though a successful flight means as much to it as to me, as though we shared our experiences together, each feeling beauty, life, and death as keenly, each dependent on the other's loyalty. We have made this flight across the ocean, not I or it.

I throw my flashlight on the engine instruments. Every needle is in place. For almost thirty-three hours, not one of them has varied from its normal reading - except when the nose tank ran dry. For every minute I've flown there have been more than seven thousand explosions in the cylinders, yet not a single one has missed.

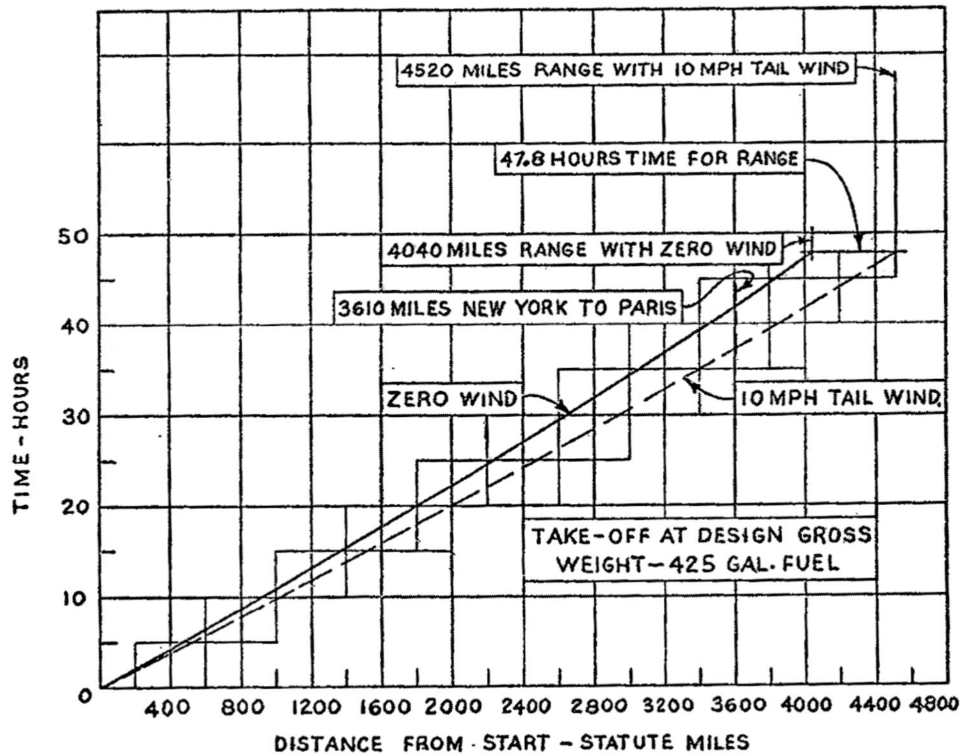

I'm leveled off at four thousand feet, watehing for the luminosity in the sky ahead that will mark the city of Paris. Within the hour, I'll land. The dot on my map will become Paris itself, with its airport, hangars, and floodlights, and mechanics running out to guide me in. All over the ground below there are clusters of lights. Large clusters are cities; small ones, towns and villages; pin points are buildings on a farm. I can image that I'm looking through the earth to the heavens on the other side. Paris will be a great galaxy lighting up the night.

Within the hour I'll land, and strangely enough I'm in no hurry to have it pass. I haven't the slightest desire to sleep, My eyes are no longer salted stones. There's not an ache in my body. The night is cool and safe. I want to sit quietly in this cockpit and let the realization of my completed flight sink in. Europe is below; Paris, just over the earth's curve in the night ahead - a few minutes more of flight. It's like struggling up a mountain after a rare flower, and then, when you have it within arm's reach, realizing that satisfaction and happiness lie more in the finding than the plucking. Plucking and withering are inseparable. I want to prolong this culminating experience of my flight. I almost wish Paris were a few more hours away. It's a shame to land with the night so clear and so much fuel in my tanks.

I'm still flying at four thousand feet when I see it, that scarcely perceptible glow, as though the moon had rushed ahead of schedule. Paris is rising over the edge of the earth. It's almost thirty-three hours from my take-off on Long Island. As minutes pass, myriad pin points of light emerge, a patch of starlit earth under a starlit sky - the lamps of Paris - straight lines of lights, curving lines of lights, squares of lights, black spaces in between. Gradually avenues, parks, and buildings take outline form; and there, far below, a Iittle offset from the center, is a column of lights pointing upward, changing angles as I fly - the Eiffel Tower. I circle once above it, and turn northeastward toward Le Bourget.

Four fifty-two on the clock. That's 9:52, Paris time. Le Bourget isn't shown on my map. No one I talked to back home had more than a general idea of its location. „It's a big airport," I was told. „You can't miss it. Just fly northeast from the city." So I penciled a circle on my map, about where Le Bourget ought to be; and now the *Spirit of St. Louis* is over the outskirts of Paris, pointed toward the center of that circle.

I look ahead. A beacon should be flashing on such a large and important airport. But the nearest beacon I see is fully twenty miles away, and west instead of east of Paris. I bank slightly, so I can search the earth directly ahead. There's no flash, But I'm flying at four thousand feet. The beacon may be sweeping the horizon. I'm probably far above its beam. It's probably like the beacons on our mail route, set low to guide pilots wedging underneath clouds and storm, not for those who fly high through starlit nights. From my altitude, I shouldn't be hunting for a beacon, but for a darkened patch of ground, bordered by straight-lined, regularly spaced points of light, with a few green and red points among the yellow; that's how a landing field should look from four thousand feet.

Yes, there's a black patch to my left, large enough to be an airport. And there are lights all around it. But they're neither straight nor regularly spaced, and some are strangely crowded together. But if that's not Le Bourget, where else can it be? There's no other suitable grouping of lights - unless the location I've marked on my map is entirely wrong. I bank left to pass overhead. Are those floodlights, in one corner of the dark area? If they are, they're awfully weak. They're hardly bright enough to be for landing aircraft. But don't I see the ends of hangars over at one side? Or are they just the buildings of some factory?

It looks like an airport. But why would an airport be placed in such a congested section? There are thousands of lights along one side. They probably come from a large factory. Surely Le Bourget wouldn't have a factory that size right next to it. I'm almost overhead now. I can see no warning lights, no approach lights, and no revolving beacon. Looking straight down on a beacon, one can see the diffused light from its beam sweeping the ground under the tower. But those are floodlights, and they show the edge of a field. Maybe the French turn out their beacons when no planes are due, like that air-mail field at Cleveland. And even the people who think I have a chance of reaching Paris won't expect me here so soon. But why leave floodlights burning, and not the boundary lights and beacon? Of course I must remember I'm over Europe, where customs are strange.

This is right in the direction where Le Bourget ought to be; but I expected to find it farther out from the city. I'll fly on northeast a few miles more. Then, if I see nothing else that looks like an airport, I'll come back and circle at lower altitude. Five minutes have passed. Only the lights of small towns and country homes break the blackness of the earth. I turn back on my course, throttle down slightly, and begin a slow descent. The altimeter shows two thousand feet when I approach the lights again. Close to a large city in an unknown country, it's best not to fly too low. There may be hills with high radio towers on top of them. There are bound to be radio towers somewhere around Paris. I point my pocket flashlight toward the ground, and key out a message. There's no response.

I circle. Yes, it's definitely an airport. I see part of a concrete apron in front of a large, halfopen door. But is it Le Bourget? Well, at least it's a Paris airport.

That's the important thing. It's Paris I set out for. If I land on the wrong field, it won't be too serious an error - as long as I land safely. I look around once more for other floodlights or a beacon. There are none - nothing even worth flying over to investigate. I spiral lower, left wing down, keeping close to the edge of the field. There aren't likely to be any radio towers nearby. I'll give those lights along the southern border a wide berth when I come in to land. There maybe high faetory chimneys rising among them.

From each changed angle, as I bank, new details emerge from night and shadow. I see the corners of big hangars, now outlined vaguely, near the floodlights - a line of them. And now, from the far side of the field, I see that all those smaller lights are automobiles, not factory windows. They seem to be blocked in traffic, on a road behind the hangars. It's a huge airport. The floodlights show only a small corner. It must be Le Bourget.

I'll drag the field from low altitude to make sure its surface is clear - that no hay-making machinery, cattle, sheep, or obstruction flags are in the way. After that, everyone down therc will know I want to land. If they have any more lights, they'll switch them on. I shift fuel valves to the center wing-tank, sweep my flashlight over the instrument board in a final check, fasten my safety belt, and nose the *Spirit of St. Louis* down into a gradually descending, spiral.

I circle several times while I lose altitude, trying to penetrate the shadows from different vantage points, getting the lay of the land as well as I can in darkness. At one thousand feet I discover the wind sock, dimly lighted, on top of some building. It's bulged, but far from stiff. That means a gentle, constant wind, not over ten or fifteen miles an hour. My landing direction will be over the floodlights, angling away from the hangar line. Why circle any longer? That's a1l the information I need. No matter how hard I try, my eyes can't penetrate the blanket of night over the central portion of the field.

I straighten out my wings and let the throttled engine drag me on beyond the leeward border. Now the steep bank into wind, and the dive toward ground. But how strange it is, this descent. I'm wide awake, but the feel of my plane has not returned. Then I must hold excess speed - take no chance of stalling or of the engine loading up. My movements are mechanical, uncoordinated, as though I were coming down at the end of my first solo.

I point the nose just short of the floodlights, throttle half open, flattening out slightly as I approach. I see the whole outline of the hangars, now. Two or three planes are resting in the shadows. There's no time to look for more details. The lighted area is just ahead. It's barely large enough to land on. I nose down below the hangar roofs, so low that I can see the texture of the sod, and blades of grass on high spots. The ground is smooth and solid as far as the floodlights show its surface. I can tell nothing about the black mass beyond. But those several pin points in the distance look as though they mark the far border.

Since Le Bourget is a major airport, the area between is probably also clear - I'll have to take a chance on that; if I land short, I may stop rolling before I reach it. I open the throttle and start a climbing turn. I don't dare pull the nose up steeply. I don't dare chandelle around the hangars to celebrate my arrival, as I often do coming in with the night mail at Chicago. I must handle the *Spirit of St. Louis* as I'd teach a student to fly.

I climb to a thousand feet. There are the lamps of Paris again, like a lake of stars. There's the dark area below, just as it was before. No one has turned on more lights. I level off for the downwind stretch. The wind sock hasn't changed - still bulged and angling across the line of hangars. The motorcars are still jammed in traffic. There's no sign of movement on the ground.

I'm a quarter-mile downwind now - - - Back on throttle - - - Bank around for final glide. Is my nose down far enough? Yes, the air speed's at ninety miles an hour. I'll overshoot if I keep on at this rate - - - Stick back - - - trim the stabilizer back another notch - - -- close the throttle - - - I can hardly hear the engine idling - is it too slow? - It mustn't stop now - The silence is like vacuum in my ears. I open the throttle for a quick burst - But I'm going much too fast.

In spite of my speed, the *Spirit of St. Louis* seems about to stall. My lack of feel alarms me. I've never tried to land a plane without feel before. I want to open the throttle wider, to glide faster, to tauten the controls still more. But - I glance at the dial - the needle points to eighty miles an hour. The *Spirit of St. Louis* is lightly loaded, with most of its fuel gone. Even at this speed I'll overshoot the lighted area before my tail skid strikes the ground. No, I'll have to pull the nose higher instead of pushing it down. I'll have to depend on the needle, on judgment more than instinct. I kick rudder and push the stick to one side, just to be sure - yes, controls are taut, there's plenty of speed. And feeling is not completely gone. I still have a little left. 1 can feel the skid and slip. But the edge of perception is dull, very dull. It's better to come in fast, even if I roll into that black area after I land. And it's better to come in high - there may be poles or chimneys at the field's edge - Never depend on obstruction lights - especially when you don't see any.

It's only a hundred yards to the hangars now - solid forms emerging from the night. I'm too high - too fast. Drop wing - left rudder - sideslip - - - Careful - mustn't get anywhere near the stall. I've never landed the *Spirit of St. Louis* at night before. It would be better to come in straight. But if I don't sideslip, I'll

7 CENTS PATRO MORE

Chicago Sunday Tribune

FINAL EDITION

LINDBERGH LANDS IN PARIS

"Am I Here," He Asks, as City Goes Wild with Frenzy of Joy

AFTONBLADET

Pris 20 öre

ockholm Söndagen den 22 Maj 1927 — Söndagsnummer — Årg. 97 — Nr 138

Flygfältet i Paris stormades.

KONUNGEN LYCKÖNSKAR LINDBERGH.

Dödshopp från 3:e våningen.

INTERVIEW WITH CAPTAIN LINDBERGH IN PARIS

San Francisco Chronicle

LEADING NEWSPAPER of the PACIFIC COAST

INDBERGH SAFELY IN PARIS $2\frac{1}{2}$ HOURS AHEAD OF SCHEDULE

The Sunday Star.

WASHINGTON, D. C. SUNDAY MORNING, MAY 22, 1927 — FIVE CENTS.

PARIS WILDLY ACCLAIMS LINDBERGH

LA PRENSA

BUENOS AIRES, DOMINGO 22 DE MAYO DE 1927 — Dirección y Administración

El aviador norteamericano Lindbergh realizó ayer la travesía aérea del Atlántico en un vuelo directo entre Nueva York y París – Resuelve el piloto estadounidense con esta hazaña uno de los problemas más arduos de las comunicaciones por el aire y sobre los mares – Lindbergh fué recibido en París con un entusiasmo indescriptible.

THE POST IS THE ONLY DENVER NEWSPAPER IN WHICH YOU GET ASSOCIATED PRESS NEW

LINDBERGH LANDS IN PARIS

GREAT OVATION GREETS AIR HERO

GIGANTIC CROWD RUSHES ON FIELD AND PULLS HAGGARD FLYER FROM HIS AIRPLANE

'WELL HERE WE ARE,' HE EXCLAIMS, EMERGING FROM 'DEATH CHAMBER'

YOUNG AMERICAN MAKES 3,600-MILE FLIGHT FROM NEW YORK IN THIRTY-

The Paid Circulation of THE DENVER POST Last Sunday Was 267,373

THE DENVER POST

HOME EDITION

THE BEST NEWSPAPER IN THE U. S. A.

DENVER, COLO., SUNDAY, MAY 22, 1927

be too high over the boundary to touch my wheels in the area of light. That would mean circling again - - - Still too high. I push the stick over to a steeper slip, leaving the nose well down - - - Below the hangar roofs now - - - straighten out - - - A short burst of the engine - - - Over the lighted area - - - Sod coming up to meet me - - - Deceptive high lights and shadows - Careful - easy to bounce when you're tired - - - Still too fast - - - Tail too high - - - Hold off - - - H@ld off - - - But the lights are far behind - - - The surface dims - - - Texture of sod is gone - - - Ahead, there's nothing but night - - - Give her the gun and climb for another try? - - - The wheels touch gently - off again - No, I'll keep contact - Ease the stick forward - - - Back on the ground - Off - Back - the tail skid too - - - Not a bad landing, but I'm beyond the light -can't see anything ahead - Like flying in fog - Ground loop? - No, still rolling too fast - might blow a tire - The field *must* be clear - Uncomfortable though, jolting into blackness. - Wish I had a wing light - but too heavy on the take-off - - - Slower, now - - - slow enough to ground loop safely - left rudder - reverse it - stick over the other way - - - The *Spirit of St. Louis* swings around and stops rolling, resting on the solidness of earth, in the center of Le Bourget.

I start to taxi back toward the floodlights and hangars - - - But the entire field ahead is covered with running figures! My reception by the French people on that May 21, 1927, cannot be compressed into a final chapter of this book. After the warnings I had been given in America, I was completely unprepared for the welcome which awaited me on Le Bourget. I had no idea that my plane had been so accurately reported along its route between Ireland and the capital of France - over Dingle Bay, over Plymouth, over Cherbourg. When I circled the aerodrome it did not occur to me that any connection existed between my arrival and the cars stalled in traffic on the roads. When my wheels touched earth, I had no way of knowing that tens of thousands of men and women were breaking down fences and flooding past guards.

I had barely cut the engine switch when the first people reached my cockpit. Within seconds my open windows were blocked with faces.My name was called out over and over again, in accents strange to my ears - on this side of my plane - on that side - in front - in the distance. I could feel the *Spirit of St. Louis* tremble with the pressure of the crowd. I heard the crack of wood behind me when someone leaned too heavily against a fairing strip. Then a second strip snapped, and a third, and there was the sound of tearing fabric. That meant souvenir hunters were going wild. It was essential to get a guard stationed around my plane before more damage was done.

„Are there any mechanics here?" I asked. I couldn't understand a single word that came back in answer - from a half-dozen different mouths. „Does anyone here speak English?" I shouted. The noise and excitement made a reply impossible. There were rips of fabric every few seconds, and I could feel my tail skid inching back and forth across the ground. I was afraid the *Spirit of St. Louis* might be seriously injured. The thought entered my mind that the longerons would buckle if enough men climbed on top; and I knew the elevators wouldn't stand much of any pressure without bending. I decided to get out of the cockpit and try to find some English-speaking person who would help me organize a guard to hold back the crowd.

I opened the door, and started to put my foot down onto ground. But dozens of hands took hold of me - my legs, my arms, my body. No one heard the sentences I spoke. I found myself lying in a prostrate position, up on top of the crowd, in the center of an ocean of heads that extended as far out into the darkness as I could see. Then I started to sink down into that ocean, and was buoyed up again. Thousands of voices mingled in a roar. Men were shouting, stumbling. My head and shoulders went down, and up, and down again, and up once more. It was like drowning in a human sea. I lost sight of the *Spirit of St. Louis*. I heard several screams. I was afraid that I would be dropped under the feet of those milling, cheering people; and that after sitting in a cockpit-fixed position for close to thirty-four hours, my muscles would be too stiff to struggle up again.

I tried to sit up - - - to slip down into the crowd - - - to roll over onto my hands and knees. It was useless. I was simply wasting strength that I might need for a final effort to save myself, if my head angled beneath my feet too far. It seemed wisest to relax as much as I could, and let time pass. I realized that the men under me were determined that no matter what happened to them, I would not fall. After the lapse of minutes whose number I cannot judge, I felt my helmet jerked from my head. Firmer hands gripped on my body. I heard my name more clearly spoken. And suddenly I was standing on my feet - on European ground at last. With arms linked solidly in mine, I began moving slowly, but unnoticed, through the crowd.

In the week I spent at Paris, between ceremonies and engagements which crammed almost every hour of each day, I pieced together the story of what happened that Saturday night at Le Bourget. Regardless of the skepticism which existed about my flight, the French authorities had prepared for my reception, Extra guards were detailed to the aerodrome; and when reports of my plane being sighted over Ireland, England, and Normandy, brought automobiles pouring out from Paris by the thousands, two companies of soldiers were sent to reinforce the civil police. It was intended that, after I landed, my plane would be guided to a position near the Administration building, where I was to be met by a reception committee of French and American officials. Press photographers and reporters were assigned to appropriate position. When the crowd broke down steel fences and rushed out onto the field, all these arrangements collapsed. Police and soldiers were swept away in the rush which followed. Two French aviators - the military pilot Detroyat and the civil pilot Delage - found themselves close to me in the jam of people. Delage grabbed Detroyat's arm and cried, „Come. They will smother him!" Detroyat, being in uniform, and tall, was able to exercise some authority over the men who had me on their shoulders. Once my feet were on the ground, it was too dark for my flying suit to be very noticeable. I soon became an inconspicuous member of the crowd. Meanwhile my helmet had somehow gotten onto the head of an American reporter. Someone had pointed to him and called out, *„There is Lindbergh! There is Lindbergh!"* The crowd had taken over the reporter and left me free.

I might have had difficulty walking when I first tried to step out of the cockpit after landing, but my muscles were well limbered up by the time my feet actually touched French soil. Delage rushed away to get his little Renault car, while Detroyat maneuvered me to the outskirts of the crowd. When the car arrived, I said that before leaving I wanted to be sure a guard had been placed around the *Spirit of St. Louis*. Communication was difficult, because my ears were still deafened from the flight. I spoke no word of French; my new friends, but little English; and in the background were the noises of the crowd. My plane was being taken care of, they told me. I should not try to go back to it. They were determined about that - there was no mistaking their tones and gestures. They laughed and shook their heads as I protested, and kept pointing to the car.

We drove into a big hangar, and I was taken to a small room on one side. My friends motioned me to a chair and put out most of the lights - so I would not be discovered by the crowd. Did I need food, drink, the attention of a doctor? Would I like to lie down? they asked. I had only to tell them what I wanted. France was mine, they said. It was easier for me to understand them indoors, with everyone speaking more slowly.

I didn't feel like lying down, and I had no need whatever for a doctor; but I was greatly worried about my plane, even though I received assurances that everything possible was being done to take care of it. I suggested that we drive back out onto the field to make certain, but the two French pilots pursed their lips and shook their heads again. I then asked what customs and immigration formalities I had to go through. I was a little worried about that, since I had no visa. But I received mostly smiles and laughter in reply. I decided that the best thing for me to do was just to wait and let events develop. Was there any word of Nungesser and Coli? I asked. Faces lengthened. No, no news had come.

I remained with Delage while Detroyat went to search for an officer of higher rank. At first, he could find no one. Then, in the midst of the crowd, he came upon Major Weiss of the Bombardment Group of the 34th A.F. Regiment. The Major could not believe that I was sitting in a hangar's darkened room. „It is impossible," he told Detroyat. „Lindbergh has just been carried triumphantly to the official reception committee." Probably he had seen the reporter with my helmet, who had been taken, struggling, to the American Ambassador before the mistake in identity was finally established. But Major Weiss followed Detroyat, and on seeing me insisted that I be taken to his office on the military side of Le Bourget - about a mile away. So we climbed into the Renault again, and drove across the field. Then, it was Major Weiss's turn to go out and search for higher officers.

It must have been an hour later when I heard American voices, and someone said that the Ambassador of the United States was outside. In a moment the door opened, and I was introduced to the Honorable Myron T. Herrick, to his son Parmely, and to bis daughter-in-law Agnes. The room soon filled with people. Ambassador Herrick was an extraordinary man. He had a combination of dignity, perception, and kindness, which few in public life possess. After extending a welcome and inquiring about my welfare, which he judged through his eyes more than through my answer, he said he was going to take me back with him to the Embassy. I accepted gladly; but I asked to see the *Spirit of St. Louis* before we left the field.

Ambassador Herrick nodded. „Of course we'll take you to your plane," he said, „if we can get there." A discussion in French followed, with several people taking part. I was assured that it was unnecessary for me to think more about the *Spirit of St. Louis* that night, because it had not been badly damaged, and it had been placed in a locked hangar, under a military guard. I needed to sleep, it was suggested. There would be time enough to see the plane after that. „Well, how do you feel about it, Captain?" Ambassador Herrick asked.

I couldn't put the cracking wood and ripping fabric from my mind that easily. I was anxious to find out for myself what repairs would have to be made. I didn't know, then, that the French authorities wished to have all repairs completed before I saw my plane. I argued that I wanted to get some items from the cockpit, and to show the mechanics how to put the windows in. Inserting the windows required a special technique, I explained.

After more conversation which I could not understand, we climbed into Delage's car and drove back to the Air-Union hangar which we had left an hour earlier. In the meantime, my *Spirit of St. Louis* had been placed inside. It was a great shock to me to see my plane. The sides of the fuselage were full of gaping holes, and some souvenir hunter had pulled a lubrication fitting right off one of the rocker-arm housings on my engine. But in spite of surface appearances, careful inspection showed that no serious damage had been done. A few hours of work would make my plane airworthy again.

It was then time for me to rejoin Ambassador Herrick and drive with him to Paris. But my escorts were unable to locate the Ambassador. After hunting for a quarter-hour, they decided to take me to the American Embassy themselves - by a special route to avoid the heavy jam of traffic. So the four of us started out - Weiss, Delage, Detroyat, and I - all in the little Renault. Nobody looked twice at our car as we wound ab out through the crowd. I settled back in the seat to rest, to see what I could through the window, and to try to understand the English sentences at which my escorts laughed and struggled.

We traveled over bumpy side roads, toward the outskirts of Paris, stopping once to ask our way. We passed Dugny, Stains, Saint Denis, and entered through the Saint Ouen gate. Soon we were driving between rows of close-packed brick and stone houses - with no yards between. It was tremendously different from America. Then came the heart of the city - „Place de l'Opera," Detroyat said. When we reached the end of a long avenue, Delage parked at the curb of a circular area in the center of which was a great stone arch. The surfaces of the arch were sculptured and softly lighted. My friends took me through the arch, and I found myself standing silently with them at the tomb of France's Unknown Soldier, with its ever-burning flame. They wanted my first stop in Paris to be at the Are de Triomphe, they said.

We arrived at the American Embassy far ahead of Ambassador Herrick. He had searched for me all over Le Bourget. And then his car had become involved in the traffic jam between aerodrome and city. Neither his driver nor his escort of motorcycle police knew about the side roads the French pilots took me over. It was three o'clock when the Ambassador reached his home at No. 2 Avenue d'Iena. I was waiting for him, after eating a supper which his staff very considerately provided in spite of the early hour. By that time a small crowd - mostly newspapermen - had assembled in the street outside. At Herrick's suggestion they were invited in, and I spent a few minutes answering questions and telling them about my flight. Paris clocks marked 4:15 in the morning before I went to bed. It was sixty-three hours since I had slept.

I woke that afternoon, a little stiff but well rested, into a life which could hardly have been more amazing if I had landed on another planet instead of at Paris. The welcome I received at Le Bourget was only a forerunner to the wel come extended by France, by Belgium, by England - and, by all of Europe.«

DIPLOMAT TAKES CARE OF POSTWAR WESTERN GERMANY

by *George F. Kennan*

The Diplomat was born on February 16, 1904, in Milwaukee, Wisconsin, he died at age 101 on March 17, 2005, in Princeton, New Jersey. At the age of eight, George Frost Kennan went to Germany to stay with his stepmother in order to learn German. He then attended St. John' s Military Academy in Delafield, Wisconsin, and arrived at Princeton University in the second half of 1921. Unaccustomed to the elite atmosphere of the Ivy League, the shy and introverted Kennan found his undergraduate years difficult and lonely.

After receiving his bachelor's degree in History in 1925, Kennan considered applying to law school, but decided it was too expensive and instead opted to apply to the newly formed United States Foreign Service. He passed the qualifying examination and after seven months of study at the Foreign Service School in Washington he gained his first job as vice consul in Geneva, Switzerland. Within a year he was transferred to a post in Hamburg , Germany. During 1928 Kennan considered quitting the Foreign Service to attend college. Instead, he was selected for a linguist training program that would give him three years of graduate-tevel study without having to quit the service.

In 1929 George Kennan began his program on history, politics, culture, and the Russian language at the University of Berlin's Oriental Institute. In doing so, he would follow in the footsteps of his grandfather's younger cousin, George Kennan (1845- 1924), a major 19th century expert on Imperial Russia and author of 'Sibiria and the Exile System', a well-received 1891 account of fhe Czarist prison system. During the course of his diplomatic career, Kennan would master a number of other languages.

In 1931 Kennan was stationed at the legation in Riga, Latvia, where, as third secretary, he worked on Soviet economic affairs. When the United States began formal diplomacy with the Soviet government during 1933 after the election of President Franklin D. Roosevelt, Kennan accompanied the American ambassador to Moscow. By the mid-1930s Kennan was among the professionally trained Russian experts of the staff of the U.S. embassy in Moscow. Meanwhile, Kennan studied Stalin's Great Purge, which would affect his opinion of the internal dynamics of the Soviet régime for the rest of his life.

Kennan found himself in strong disagreement with a new ambassador to the Soviet Union, who defended the Great Purge and other aspects of Stalin's rule. So the ambassador suggested that Kennan be transferred out of Moscow to work at the Russian desk at the State Department in Washington. During that period, Kennan began writing the first draft of his memoirs at the age of 34 when he was still a relatively junior diplomat. By September 1938, Kennan was reassigned to a job at the legation in Prague. After the occupation of the Czechoslovak Republic by Nazi Germany at the eve of World War II, Kennan was assigned to Berlin. He was interned in Germany for six months after Germany, followed by the other Axis states, declared war on the United States in December 1941.

In September 1942 Kennan was assigned as a counselor in Lisbon, Portugal. In January 1944 he was sent to London, where he served as counselor of the American delegation to the European Advisory Commission, which worked to prepare Allied policy in Europe. Within months of beginning the job, Kennan was appointed deputy chief of the mission in Moscow. In the Russian capital he felt that his opinions about the USSR were being ignored by President Harry S. Truman and policymakers in Washington. Kennan believed that a federation needed to be established in Western Europe to counter Soviet influence in the region and to compete against the Soviet stronghold in Eastern Europe.

Kennan served as deputy head of the mission in Moscow until April 1946. From April 1947 through December 1948, when George C. Marshall was Secretary of State, Kennen became the first Director of Policy Planning. In 1949, he suggested a plan for the reunification of Germany, stating the partition of Germany was unsustainable in the long run. In December 1951, President Truman nominated Kennan to be the next U.S. ambassador to the USSR, but in September 1952 he made a statement in Moscow that cost him his ambassadorship.

In 1953 Kennan left the Foreign Service to become member of the Institute of Advanced Studies at Princeton University. In 1956 he became professor at the School of Historical Studies. During the following years, Kennan wrote quite a number of books, one of them was called „Russia Leaves the War - Soviet-American Relations 1917-1920." When the work came to the attention of the Pulitzer Prize jurors in the „American History" award category of 1957, they placed it on first rank of their list of finalists and added in their report of February 19, 1957:

„Possibly some might object, that the Kennan volume does not deal primarily with the history of the United States ... We feel, however, that those who established the award did not have in mind that it should be narrowly interpreted ... Certainly, the changes which have occurred in the history of the world during the last half century have both broadened and deepened of content of American history greatly. The Kennan volume deals with one of these major changes which has affected and continues to affect the course of American civilization." The Advisory Board was entirely persuaded that the jury's choice was correct and awarded George F. Kennan with the 1957 Pulitzer Prize in the History category.

During the following years, Kennan step by step continued another book project he had in mind for some time, a retrospective view on the different phases of his main political activities as a diplomat in various functions. In 1967, ten years after receiving the Pulitzer decoration, he brought out the volume „Memoirs 1925-1950" that was well received by the public. When the work came to the attention of the Pulitzer Prize jurors in the „Biography or Autobiography" award category, they stated in their report of January 13, 1968: „Kennan's Memoirs is such a book as one can expect to see written only a few times in a generation. That it will speedily take its place among the great books in a great tradition seems unquestionable ..."

Then the report adds: „In combination with his extraordinarily varied experience in the foreign service of the United States, these qualities and Kennan's disciplined virtuosity as a writer have resulted in a book that brilliantly illuminates the tragedy of the Second World War and the ensuing tensions of the peace and the cold war from their roots in the Twenties and Thirties of this century. At the same time it is a testament and apologia, equally perceptive and moving, not untouched with humor and often touched with poetic eloquence, of one of the ablest and most deeply thoughtful public figures of our time." The Advisory Board shared the jury's praise and awarded the 1968 prize for best autobiography to George F. Kennan, who thereby got his second Pulitzer decoration after winning his first one eleven years earlier in the History category.

Following now are some pages taken from the award-winning work, dealing with George F. Kennan's various activities in Postwar Germany: »Germany was a country in which I had, by 1949, lived at various times for a total of five or six years: in the Kaiser's Germany as a child; in the Weimar Germany as a working vice consul and a student; in Hitler's Germany as administrative officer of the American embassy at Berlin. It was a country with which I was never able to identify extensively in the personal sense. I knew its language nearly as well as my own, sometimes thought in it and wrote in it, but was never in character when speaking it. I knew this. My family and friends knew it. When I took my final examinations at the Seminary for Oriental Languages, in 1931, my Russian friend, enthusiastically solicitous for my success, saw me to the door of the building and gave it to me as his final advice: „If you have any choice, speak Russian with them, not German. When you speak Russian, you are yourself; when you speak German, you are nothing at all.“

But intellectually and aesthetically, Germany had made a deep impression on me. And during the war I had felt intimately close to that portion of the German public which was itself the first victim of Hitler's madness and suffered undeservedly from the tragedy he brought down on the heads of all Germans alike. Now, in the posthostilities period, recognizing the great responsibility we had assumed for the future of the German people, I had that country constantly on my mind, considered a correct handling of our responsibilities there to be vital to the success of any policy toward Russia, winced under every evidence of superficiality and oversimplification in our public and official discussion of German matters, and suffered from the realization of my own total isolation from every form of decision-making that related to them.

If Germany could not be broken up, then the only thing to do was to thrust both Germany and Europe farther into the future: to create, that is, some sort of a united federal Europe into which the united Germany could be imbedded, and in this way to widen that horizon of aspiration and loyalty which, at its purely linguistic and national limits, had proved too narrow for the safety of Europe, too narrow for the safety of Germany herself. If Germany had to be united, then she must be a part of something larger than herself. A united Germany could be tolerable only as an integral part of a united Europe.

When stationed in Berlin during the war I had been struck with the fact that Hitler himself, albeit for the wrong reasons and, in the wrong spirit, had actually accomplished much of the technical task of the unification of Europe. He had created central authorities in a whole series of areas: in transportation, in banking, in procurement and distribution of raw materials, in the control of various forms of nationalized property. Why, I asked myself, could this situation not be usefully exploited after an Allied victory? What was needed was an Allied decision not to smash this network of central controls when the war was ended but rather to take it over, to remove the Nazi officials who had rnade it work, to appoint others (and not necessarily all non-Gerrnans) in their place, and then to supplement this physical unification with a new European federal authority. When I returned from Germany, in 1942, I tried to win understanding for this idea in the Department of State; but the effort was fruitless. The Russians, determined to exploit the economic potential of Western Germany and Western Europe and fearful of being excluded from having a voice in these regions, would not hear of anything along these lines.

No one in Washington was prepared, at that moment, to consider schemes that would clearly be in conflict with Russian wishes. The members of the anti-Nazi resistance movements and exiled governments wanted only to get home and restore the *status quo ante*. And there was FDR's well-known aversion to anything that resembled a discussion of postwar political problems while the war was on. So no serious consideration was given at that time to the problems of postwar European unification as a means of solving the problem of Germany. Instead, one staggered into the post-hostilities period with a set of concepts which envisaged nothing more than an interim period of four-power collaboration in the occupation and military government of a defeated Germany, after which that country was to be restored once more, and launched again onto the sea of international life, as a sovereign entity among others, overshadowing once again all of its neighbors in potential physical strength, and with no higher focus for the collective ideals and aspirations of its people than the framework of German nationalism itself. Whatever elements of insecurity this might involve from the standpoint of the peace of the continent were apparently supposed to be contained and counteracted by the authority of the United Nations, supported by a continued collaboration among the great powers, including Russia and China. To my own deep despair, this utterly unrealistic concept continued - despite the groving evidence of the unsubstantiality of its assumptions - to inspire American policy down to 1948. It was then modified to the extent that there was a new recognition, flowing from our preoccupstion with the problems of European recovery, that Germany's prosperity was vital to the prosperity of Western Europe. But there was little understanding, as yet, of the need for European unification as the only conceivable solution for the problem of Germany's relation to the rest of Europe.

Up to the summer of 1948, U.S. policy with relation to Germany remained, after the pattern in the case of Japan, largely the province of the War Departrnent and the military-occupational establishment in Germany. There being no German government with which we could maintain diplornatic relations, the State Department - to my recollection - did not even have a German division at the political level - only an office of sorts for maintenance of liaison with the Pentagon on matters relating to „occupied areas." But the repeated meetings of the Council of Foreign Ministers (CFM) compelled the Department of State to occupy itself increasingly with the German problem and to take under critical scrutiny the policies that had found their formal adoption at Potsdam. And with the breakdown of the CFM talks at the end of 1947, a new state of affairs was created, in which the responsibility of the Department of State could not fail to become prominently engaged. The demonstration that one could not hope to govern Germany successfully in collaboration with the Russians forced an three of the major Western countries to undertake a reexamination of their concepts and policies. It helped to remove the remaining French inhibitions against association with the British and Americans in the approach to the problem of economic recovery in Germany. And to the British and Americans it carried the connotation that one could no longer delay in proceeding to the establishment in Western Germany of some sort of a German political authority that could share the responsibility for economic recovery and provide a channel, if only initially a limited one, for the reenlistment of a sense of participation and responsibility on the part of the German population of that area. The first moves in this direction took place in the form of British-French-American exploratory discussions held at London in February and March, 1948.

There can be no doubt that, coming as it did on top of the European recovery program and the final elaboration and acceptance of the Atlantic alliance, the move toward establishment of a separate government in Western Germany aroused keen alarm among the Soviet leaders. It was no less than natural that they should do all in their power to frustrate this undertaking and to bring the three Western powers back to the negotiating table in order that Russia might continue to have a voice in all-German affairs. Their effort to do this took the form of the blockade of the Western sectors of Berlin. The first steps in this direction were instituted as early as March 1948, immediately after the first exploratory discussions among the Western powers. And when then, in June, a final round of further London discussions produced a publicly announced agreement - the so-called London Program - on the modalities of procedure looking to the establishment of a separate West German government, and when the Western powers proceeded, as a first step, to set up a separate currency for Western Germany, the Russian response was to make the blockade complete, except of course for the narrowly limited air channels which the Western powers by four-power agreement had the right to use.

The formal pretext for the blockade was the currency question; but actually it was conceived by its Russian authors as a species of squeeze play, designed to place the Western powers before an inescapable choice: either to abandon the great German capital to Communist political control, thus clearly weakening the competitive political attraction of the new régime they were about to set up in Western Germany, or to abandon the London Program in favor of a new round of talks in the CFM and the limitation of further action on Germany to whatever could command Russian agreement. Obviously, the Russians would hold out at any such CFM meeting for arrangements that would place them in a favorable position either to block German recovery or, if it could not be blocked, to assure that ir operated to their benefit and not to the benefit of European recovery generally.

The Berlin Airlift countered the Soviet Blockade of the city.

It was clear frorn the start that the Western powers might at some point find it necessary or expedient to agree to another meeting of the CFM in the interests of the removal of the blockade. (This was, indeed, what finally occurred in the spring of 1949.) It was impossible to know at the outset when such a development might occur; it could come at any time. There was thus urgent need for preparation of a new American negotiating position on the German problem, to be put forward if and when another CFM took place. The old one, plainly, would no longer do. At the end of 1947, at the last CFM meeting, the ministers had still been talking in terms of the conclusion of a treaty of peace with Germany and the establishment of an all-German government under Allied control, which would then sign the treaty and gradually take over responsibility for the conduct of German life. But now, by midsummer 1948, things had changed. The West Germans were already well launched on preparations for the election of the constituent assembly which, under the new London Program, was to devise the political framework for a purely West German government. Would we still wish, in these circum-stances, to continue to talk with the Russians about an all-German solution? Would this not disorganize the procedures now in process of implementation under the London Program? But if not, what *would* we propose? And to what extent, in formulating new proposals, would we wish to take account of the precariousness of the situation of the Western sectors of Berlin, as illustrated by the blockade now in, progress? Could we in fact, in the light of this situation, afford *not* arrive at some broad general agreement with the Russians?

In the early days of July 1948, on the heels of the imposition by the Russians of the full blockade, the Planning Staff was charged with the study of these questions. Assisted by representatives from the State Department offices and from the War Department, we struggled with this task through the hot days of Washington's midsummer. The urgency of the exercise was emphasized by the preoccupation of everyone with the immediate problems imposed by the blockade. Night after night, severaI of us gathered in the communication center of the department to receive the latest news from Germany and to exchange views with General Clay and his advisors about our next move. No one was sure, as yet, how the Russian move could be countered or whether it could be successfully countered at all.The situatien was dark, and full of danger. A tremendous premium appeared to rest on any new arrangements that would free Berlin from the virtual embrace of Russian military forces and make impossible the imposition of another blockade. To some of us on the Planning Staff, the possibilities for resolving the conflict in any satisfactory way by arrangements affecting only Berlin itself - by ones, that is, which would leave the Russians astride of Berlin's communication with theWest - appeared to be small. The best prospects for solving the problem seemed to lie along the lines of a new arrangement for Germany as a whole that would involve retirement of the Russian forces from the entire area around Berlin and make possible the establishment of normal communications between that city and the rest of Germany. Were there, then, proposals along this line that might conceivably be put forward by the United States government in the CFM - proposals that would be sound in themselves, that we could live with if accepted by others, and that offered some possibility of at least eventual acceptance by the Russians? This was our problem. The results of our preliminary inquiry suggested that there might well be such proposals, although it would take time, and further study, to work them out.

But did our government really wish to proceed along this line? An important question of principle was involved. To make a new attack on the problem of an all-German, four-power settlement would imply a readiness to suspend the London Program during negotiations, and to abandon it in the event negotiations should be successful. If, on the other hand, we abandoned the effort to achieve an all-German settlement, continued to pursue a solution to the Berlin problem only within the framework of Berlin itself, and contented ourselves otherwise with the elaboration and implementation of the London Program, the Russians would set up a rival government in Eastern Germany; the fight would be on for fair; the division of Germany, and with it the division of Europe itself, would tend to congeal and to become more difficult of removal with the passage of time. There would, furthermore, be no real and permanent solution to the Berlin problem if this alternative was adopted. In a paper presented in mid-August, I brought this question to the attention of my governmental superiors, and pointed out that we really ought to have an indication of their preference before proceeding with further planning for another CFM. No such indication was forthcoming. The query evoked, so far as its substance was concerned, only a troubled and thoughtful silence. We were encouraged, however - or permitted at least - to continue our exploration of what, hypothetically, another American proposal for an all-German solution might look like, in the event we should wish to press for a settlement of this nature. The study occupied us for some weeks. It included tapping the expertise and judgment of qualified experts within the government as well as a number of distinguished outsiders.

On November 15, we submitted the results of our work. We described the nature of the problem as we saw it. We presented a detailed „package" of proposals entitled „Plan A," to be put forward in the event we wished to push for a general German settlement. And we gave our own views as to which alternative might best be chosen. The problem, we reiterated in this paper, was whether to come forward, at an eventual new CFM, with a positive program making clear the terms on which we would be prepared to consider the establishment of an all-German government and withdrawal of Allied forces from the major part of Germany, or whether we should rest on a purely negative position, advancing no positive proposals of our own and leaving it to the Russians to make proposals which we would then presumably decline on an ad hoc basis. Plan A was conceived as a set of proposals to be put forward in the event we chose the first of these courses. It ran substantially as follows: There would first have to be agreement on a new four-power control machinery to supervise the workings of the program. Here, we would have to insist that there be no individual veto power. The entrance into operation of the new control machinery would be followed by the early election and establishment of a provisional German government.

These elections would take place under international supervision, exercised uniformly in all four zones. Simultaneously with the establishment of the provisional government, military government would cease and Allied forces would be withdrawn to garrison areas, within Germany but on its periphery. They would be so located that the lines of communication to and from them would not have to pass over German territory. It was suggested that the British area might be near Hamburg, the American near Bremen, and the Russian near Stettin, with access, in each case, to deep-water port facilities. The French area, on the other hand, would be adjacent to the French frontier and accessible directly from French territory. The territory thus liberated from Allied occupation (which would of course include most of Germany, and with it Berlin), would come under the administration of the new provisional German government. Elaborate safeguards were envisaged against any misuse of the German police by extrernist elements of either right or left in the process of transition from military government to the establishment of a central German political authority. Timing and phasing of the individual elements of the program were so adjusted as to allow no opportunity at any point for control or undue influence of the transitional process from any side by undemocratic methods. Provision was made for the continued complete demilitarization of Germany.

Out recommendation was that in the event that a new CFM meeting should take place in the near future, our government should advance something along the lines of Plan A, provided we could get a sufficient measure of agreement to it on the part of the British and the French. We saw no satisfactory alternative. Merely to ask for the extension of the London Program to all of Gerrnany, as others wished to do, did not seem to us to represent a satisfactory alternative. The London Program envisaged continuing supervision of German political life by an Allied high commission. This would scarcely be feasible on a four-power basis. The London Program also envisaged the retention of occupying forces in the various zones. But the authority of a non-Communist German government could never be effectively asserted, we thought, over an Eastern zone occupied by Soviet forces. The arrangements envisaged in the London Program were therefore simply not suitable as the basis for an all-German settlement. Something along the lines of Plan A, even if not immediately acceptable to the Russians (and we did not suppose that it would be), would at least serve to hold open the door for an eventual peaceful withdrawal of the Russians from the heart of Gerrnany. Unless this door was held open by means of some sort of positive proposals on our part along these lines, the Russians might not feel able to withdraw even if a time should come when they would like to. Our position, we explained, was deeply affected by the impression we had gained that the Western position in Berlin could never be a comfortable one, and the people of the Western sectors as well as the Western garrisons there would be living constantly on the edge of an abyss, so long as the territory around the city remained under Russian occupation and Communist authority.

It must stress again - for this was in our view a vitally important feature of the recommendations - that we envisaged that these proposals would be put forward in the CFM only after careful and confidential exploration with the French and British and only in the event the latter were willing to go along with them. I was repeatedly asked, in the weeks that followed presentation of this paper, what we would do in case the French and British would not go along. My answer was that we would then not press the project but that we would place upon the French and British governments the onus of taking the lead in devising some other Western position, we would say to them, in effect: this is our best suggestion; if you don't like it, it is up to you to name the alternative, bearing in mind the urgent and pressing need for a solution to the Berlin problem; the main responsibility is now yours.

I was also asked, of course, what we would do if the French and British accepted the idea but the Russians - as was indeed to be expected - did not. My answer was that we would then proceed to implement the London Program (always assuming, of course, that we could find some other solution to the problem of the Berlin blockade), but that we would hold the offer open. In this way, we would place upon the Russians the onus of bringing about the final split of Germany, just as we had done in the case of the Marshall Plan with relation to all of Europe. We would then at least have named the terms on which we were prepared to agree to a removal of the division of Germany; we would have made it evident that we were not averse on principle to its removal. We would avoid the misunderstanding that could arise if we put forward proposals which appeared to offer no serious possibility for overcoming the division. By this means, the door would remain open for an eventual settlement; and we would guard against the propagandistic effect of any proposals for an all-Gerrnan solution that the Russians might themselves put forward.

Over the ensuing winter of 1948-1949 the operational levels of our government were fully occupied with the mounting and maintaining of the airlift as a means of frustrating the blockade, and with the implementation of the London Program. In this last, their efforts were of course merged with those of the French and British and the Germans themselves. The West German political leaders were busy, over the winter, with the drawing up of a constitution for the new West German state. The three Allied powers were busy working out a new occupation statute, to come into effect when the West German government was established. These procedures were elaborate; the attendant negotiations were difficult and full of anguish. As the process went forward, it gained treadily in momentum and in the aura of legitimacy. People's amour propre as well as their enthusiasms became engaged. There was growing personal commitment to what was being accomplished. Increasingly, as the months and weeks went by, the undertaking assumed in many minds an irrevocable character; and the idea of suspending or jeopardizing it for the sake of wider international agreement became for these people less and less acceptable. Once again, as is so often the case in American diplomacy, what was conceived as an instrument became, little by little, an end in itself. What was supposed to have been the servant of policy became its determinant instead.

In view of this preoccupation of our senior figures with the airlift and the London Program, and in the absence, as yet, of any agreement with the Russians on the convening of a new meeting of the CFM, the question raised by the Planning Staff concerning our position at an eventual meeting of this nature was placed, over the winter, on the „back burner." No formal decision was taken as to which course we would follow. Actually, of course, our position was being determined for us, from day to day, by the steady growth in the degree and solemnity of our commitment to the London Program. I yielded to no one in my admiration for the achievement of the airlift. For the London Program, on the other hand, I could develop no interest or enthusiasm. This was partly because I recognized that it provided no basis at all for negotiation with the Russians, and meant in effect the abandonment of hope for any early removal of the division of Germany and the continent. But it was also because

George F. Kennan arrives at Berlin Airport.

this program was, intellectually and in concept, the child of our occupational establishment in Germany. It was to be implemented under supervision of that establishment. It allowed for the establishment's continued existence and authority, even after the new West German government had been set up.

In March 1949, anxious to refresh my impression of occupied Germany and to test my thought on the problems of policy, I paid a brief visit to Berlin, Frankfurt, and Hamburg. The diary notes of this visit are too voluminous to be reproduced here in full, but some of them may serve to illustrate the various factors and considerations that were at stake in the decisions of those crucial months. I arrived in Berlin - on one of the airlift planes, of course - on the evening of March 12, and was driven . . . through dark, deserted streets to the Harnack House - now an American club and guest house. The city seemed dead - a ghost of its former self. Harnack House, brightly illuminated, stood out in the darkness like a garish honkey-tonkey that has stayed open too late in a sleepy provincial town. It was Saturday night. The thumping of dancemusic oozed out with the shafts of light from the windows of the building. Cars were lined up on the street and the littie band of German chauffeurs, stamping up and down and muttering in the cold night air, seemed like an evil caricature of the bundled Russian coachmen of olden times, waiting for their masters outside the nightclubs of St. Petersburg and Moscow. Inside, the lounge had that deserted and unappreciated air of most clubrooms in the evening; but the dining room had more life. It was equipped with candles in recognition of the festivity of the occasion (Saturday night). A German band was faithfully whacking out American dance tunes which they knew by heart.

I went on to Hamburg. There I had a whole series of interviews, all interesting and revealing. Not all can be mentioned here. There was one man whom I described in my notes as „an editor, a half-Jew, who had been long in the emigration . . . a tall, thin man in whose sunken burning eyes there were the traces of long-suffering and thought.“ He spoke about the youth. He felt, like others, that it was all right. It was the older people in whom the dangerous aspects of German chauvinism still resided. Youth saw no hopes. It had no prospects. In general, it wished to emigrate. For these young people, Germany was no longer a national home; it was a national prison. But even if emigration were permitted, those who left would turn out to be the enterprising and imaginative ones, and, above all, the young men. What good could this do for a country, already staggering under a surplus of women and old people? He spoke again with a sad sort of bitterness of Allied policy. To what avail this timidity, these halfway measures? Germans would remain unrealistic until they felt the bite of real responsibility.

In particular, he pleaded for the end of denazification: for some sort of amnesty which would finish the subject once and for all. He felt the issues involved in the determination of the guilt of persons with former Nazi associations too subtle, too subjective, too little susceptible of verbal classification to be a fit subject for legal procedure. The law, he said, must deal with clear and unambiguous situations of fact, it must not work with rubber concepts. The law must have validity without exception or not at all. Had we not had enough of this misconceived evil which had now been dragging along for years and the end of which was not yet in sight? Had we not already learned that it was not even possible to treat Nazism as a question of fact before the civil courts, to say nothing of committees of laymen, unfamiliar with the law? Every effort in this direction added new injustice to old injustice, new discord to old discord. We had to get used to the fact that it was impossible to scrape together before the courts a sufficient quantity of guilt and of culprits to compensate for the enormous crime that had been committed.

My next visitor was the mayor of Hamburg, Max Brauer. I described him as a „stocky, strongly built, blond man who looked as though he might have come from my native city of Milwaukee." This American aspect, I added, was not misleading: he had indeed lived for years in the US and had at one time become an American citizen. He had come back after the war to assume this heavy and ungrateful office. He was, of course, an old Social Democrat. This alone made it possible for him to occupy this position in the socialistic city of Hamburg. The overtone of sadness and helplessness with which he spoke was ample proof to me that he was not remaining in this job for motives of personal ambition. Fifty-two percent of Hamburg's housing, he said, had been destroyed. The population had at one time been reduced to one-half but had since increased again rapidly and was now nearing the prewar level of 1,600,000. An average of 6000 refugees were reaching the citv per month, absorbing a11 the new housing that could be constructed, although building was proceeding at the peak prewar level. Every time he got something built, and a few people moved out of shacks and bunkers into houses, the shacks and bunkers were promptly filled with new arrivals from the Soviet zone.

The port was working at 32 percent of normal capacity, although it had been restored to a potential handling capacity of 50 percent. There was not much hope of increasing this figure. The hinterland was gone. 'Ship-building' was, of course, barred outside of minor exceptions. The great adjacent industrial district of Harburg had largely been laid waste by the bombings. The following day I was driven around Hamburg and given a tour, in particular, of the bombed-out areas. The spectacle was not a nice one to see, not a nice one to think about. „Here was sweeping devastation, down to the ground, mile after mile." It had all been done in three days and nights in 1943. Seventy thousand human beings had been killed in the process. More than three thousand bodies were estimated to be still in the rubble. I had experienced myself the first sixty of the British raids on Berlin, and had seen - since the end of the war - plenty of ruins; but these hit me particularly hard.

From Hamburg, I went on to Bremen. There I sat in the U.S. consul's home and talked with the president of the Bremen senate, Wilhelm Kaisen. He was a strong, simple, quiet man, with old-fashioned, drooping moustaches: a farmer by origin, and a member of the pre-1914 generation. After his original imprisonment by the Nazis, at the outset of the Hitler era, he had gone back to the country and had worked the land, silently and patiently, for twelve years, paying no attention whatsover to politics. Called back to political life after the defeat, he had dropped his tools and returned, with equal simplicity and resolution, to take the top job in the Bremen enclave. He spoke with a sad humor about the troubles of administering Bremen under our tutelege. Military government told them they had to extend the basic grade school term from four to six years. They were not objecting. They would do it. But they wanted to do it gradually. The parents of the present fourth-year class weren't used to the idea. They had started their kids out on a different understanding. He had therefore asked military government whether they might not have a transition period. The answer had been no; they had to do it all right now.

I asked the consul, who was sitting with us, just who it was in the military government who was handling these matters and giving these orders. He stated that it was the head of the educational section of the military government apparatus for the Bremen enclave. I asked what his background was. He was a high school teacher from Indiana. Was he a man of understanding and competence? The consul was taken aback by this question. He was, he replied, a good high school teacher in Indiana. The president of the senate continued his story. The gas plant had been destroyed by the bombings. There was a shortage of fuel for homes; it was important to get the plant going again. It was owned by the city and had been operated before the war as a commercial enterprise. Its financial accounts were not part of the city budget. He now wanted to rebuild it, and the postal system was willing to lend him 10 million Marks for this purpose.Eventually the debt would be amortized from profits. But military government had now vetoed this. If the plant was to be reconstructed, it had, they said, to be done out of taxes. Now the Germans were stymied. They had enough financial troubles without adding another 10 million Marks to the tax burden.

Then I returned to Berlin. The following afternoon, a friend invited me to his home, to meet Ernest Reuter, then mayor of West Berlin.We picked him up at his home out near Wannsee and drove him to my friend's house in Dahlem. I had never met him before. He was, I noted, a big man, clean-shaven and somewhat bejowled, with blue rings of fatigue under his eyes. He had just returned that afternoon from the Constituent Assembly at Bonn. We sat in the window niche of the living room and drank tea. Beyond the windows, the Scotch pines, rising tall and erect from the melting snow, presided somberly over the conversation. They were holding the line, he said, in Berlin. This was the hardest time of the year. Fresh food was at its lowest. The grippe season was upon them. But morale could be maintained as long as we Americans evidenced determination to remain. The housing shortage was not really so bad in Berlin as in the Western zones. Berlin had lost 40 percent of its housing but also 25 percent of its population.

He saw no objections to dealings with the Russians about Berlin, provided we first created the requisite bargaining power. For this, we would have to install the Western Mark as the sole currency in the Western sectors and demonstrate that the airlift could hold an average of 8000 tons a day. Only then would the Russians believe that we had a real alternative to accepting eventually their terms, and only then would they do business with us seriously. As for Western Germany, the youth was all right: it was the older people in whose minds and hearts Nazism still held sway. But youth was skeptical and suspicious about the old-line German politicians who headed the parties in Western Germany. He could not blame them. Those politicians were shortsighted and had Iearned little from experience. They were spoiled by having operated so long in the vacuum of irresponsibility. Only by having responsibility thrust upon them could they be brought down to earth; until then they would only sit around and dispure and criticize. Therefore, some form of German government was necessary, and the sooner the better. But we should not, he begged us, rearm the Germans - not under any circumstances. I assured him that we had no intention of doing so, but he remained plainly unconvinced. There was too much talk about it among our own military people in Germany.

Darkness had now fallen. Reuter left. His place was taken by dinner guests, this time from the foreign colony. I had known them before, at another post. With their arrival, talk turned to the usual foreign colony gossip and chitchat. Forgotten were the ruin and desolation outside, forgotten - the two and a half million people who lived round about in hardship and uncertainty, forgotten - the great planes whose motors could be heard overhead at exact intervals of three minutes as they swept through the rain and the gloom. I marveled at the stubborn inertia of the social habits of us Anglo-Saxons and asked myself the despairing question: How many more catastrophes would yet have to occur, how many more cities would have to be smashed, how much more horrible and insistent would have to become the visible evidences of cruelty and suffering in this world before we could be brought to stop handing each other drinks and discussing through the long evenings the price of antiques, the inadequacies of servants, and the availability of cosmetics in the PX.

After a couple of days in Berlin, I flew to Frankfurt, to attend various meetings of the High Commissioners among themselves and with senior German officials. To me, the spectacle of these latter meetings - the unlimited power of the one side and the abjectness of the other, was distasteful, but as among the various Allied officials involved, I felt a certain pride in our own. They struck me as the most serious, competent, and businesslike of the lot; and they made no effort to emphasize their position of power, or to preen themselves about it. They must, I thought, be the easiest ones for the Germans to deal with in the personal sense, though sometimes maddeningly naive.

I took occasion, while in Frankfurt, to have a long talk with an old Berlin acquaintance, now an American citizen - a man of great experience and power of discrimination, who had been observing the sessions of the German Constituent Assembly. I went out in the afternoon to the VIP guest house in the Taunus Mountains to rest. They were the same mountains where, fourteen years earlier, we internees had spent the dark hard winter of 1941-1942. Then, in the late afternoon, I drove down out of the hills to take the night train for Paris.«

PUBLISHER FACES WATERGATE AND ITS FOLLOW-UP

by *Katharine M. Graham*

The Publisher was born as Katharine Meyer in New York City on June 16, 1917, she died on July 17, 2001, in Boise, Idaho. Meyer was an alumna of The Madeira School and attended Vassar College before transferring to the University of Chicago.After graduation, she worked for a short period at a San Francisco newspaper. She began working for the *Washington Post* in 1938, after her father had bought the newspaper in 1933 at a bankrupty auction.

In June, 1940, Katharine Meyer was married to Philip Graham, a graduate of Harvard Law School. Philip Graham became publisher of the *Washington Post* in 1946, when Katharine's father handed over the newspaper to his son-in-law. Katharine later recounts, how she did not feel slighted by the fact her father gave the *Post* to Philip rather than her. In 1959, after her father's dead, Philip Graham also took the position as Chairman of the Washington Post Company.

But Philip Graham dealt with alcoholism and mental illness throughout his marriage to Katharine. He had mood swings and often belittled her. On Christmas Eve in 1962, Katharine found out her husband was having an affair with an Australian women. At a newspaper conference in Phoenix, Arizona, Philip Graham had a nervous breakdown. He was sedated, flown back to Washington, and placed in a psychiatric facility. On August 3, 1963, he committed suicide with a shotgun at the couple's estate in Virginia.

Katharine Graham assumed the reins of the Washington Post Company and of the *Post* after Philip Graham's suicide. She held the title of president and was de facto publisher of the newspaper from September 1963. She formally held the title of publisher from 1969 to 1979, and that of chairwoman of the board from 1973 to 1991. Katharine Graham hired Benjamin Bradlee as editor of the *Washington Post*.

Graham presided over the *Post* at a crucial time in its history. The newspaper played an integral role in unveiling the Watergate conspiracy which ultimately led to the resignation of President Richard M. Nixon, Graham and editor Bradlee first experienced challenges when they published the content of the Pentagon Papers. When *Post* reporters Bob Woodward and Carl Bernstein brought the Watergate story to Bradley, Graham supported their investigative reporting published in the *Washington Post* in 1972.

In 1973, the *Washington Post* earned the Pulitzer Prize in the category „Meritorious Public Service“ „for its investigation of the Watergate case.“ In 1979, Katherine Graham made her son Donald the publisher of the newspaper. So she had more time to plan and conduct a book project she had in mind for a long time: an autobiography. „From the start, I very much wanted to write this book myself, although I realized I wasn't a real professional“, she remarked when the book came out in 1997, „but because I wanted this to be a personal story, I knew I had to tell it myself .“

When Katharine Graham's memoirs „Personal History“ came to the attention of the Pulitzer Prize jurors of the „Biography or Autobiography“ award category, they stated in their report of December 29, 1997: „Her natural style allows her to tell her personal and professional histories, including her complicated love affair with her troubled husband, with remarkable candor and no hint of trendy victimization, self-pity or sensationalism. 'Personal History' goes to the heart of life in Washington ... and at the *Washington Post* as it emerged as one of the foremost heralds in the nation during critical times.“ After this kind of praise it was no question that Katharine Graham‘s book „Personal History“ earned the 1998 Pulitzer Prize decoration. Following now are some passages of the award-winning work, dealing with the coverage of the Watergate scandal right from its start until President Nixon's resignation:

»On Saturday Morning, June 17, 1972, the *Washington Post* deputy managing editor Howard Simons called to say, „You won't believe what happened last night.“ I barely believed him and listened with amusement and interest as he told me of a car that crashed into a house where two people had been making love on a sofa and went right out the other side. To top that, he related the fantastic story that five men wearing surgical gloves had been caught breaking into the headquarters of the Democratic National Committee.

Al Lewis, the *Post*'s police reporter since I935, who knew everyone in the whole department, was dispatched to begin to cover the story. As usual, he headed first to the police station to get the names of those arrested - all fictitious, as it turned out. There he serendipitously bumped into the acting chief of police, Charlie Wright, with whom he was very friendly. The two of them went off together to the Watergate, where Al just walked right in with Wright. What he saw was a hive of activity, with people from the mobile crime lab trying to get fingerprints off the front door and others removing tiles from the ceiling to look for wiretaps.

Lewis took off his jacket and stayed all day. The story of the break-in appeared on the front page of Sunday's paper, „5 Held in Plot to Bug Democrats' Office Here,“ with Lewis's byline. Contributing to the story were several staff writers, including Bob Woodward and Carl Bernstein, who also did a separate report with background information on the suspects, four of whom, Carl discovered, were from Miami, where they had been involved in anti-Castro activities.

What we were seeing, of course, was the legendary tip of the iceberg. And we might never have known the size of the iceberg had it not been for the extraordinary investigative and reporting efforts of Woodward and Bernstein, famous names now but then two young men who had never worked together, one of whom (Woodward) had not even been long at the paper. In some ways it was a natural pairing, since their qualities and skills complemented each other. Both are bright, but Woodward was conscientious, hardworking, and driven, and Bernstein messy and undisciplined. He was, however, the better writer, more imaginative and creative. In other ways the relationship was oil and water, but the end product came out right, despite - or perhaps because of - the strange mix.

From the beginning, Bob distinguished himself, and there was no question in the editors' minds whom they were going to send to court to cover the break-in. Carl Bernstein, on the other hand, had been at the *Post* since the fall of 1966 but had not distinguished himself. He was a good writer, but his poor work-habits were well known throughout the city room even then, as was his famous roving eye.

Woodward and Bernstein clearly were the key reporters on the story - so much so that we began to refer to them collectively as Woodstein - but the cast of characters at the *Post* who contributed to the story from its inception was considerable. As executive editor, Ben Bradley was the classic leader at whose desk the buck of responsibility stopped. He set the ground rules - pushing, pushing, pushing, not so subtly asking everyone to take one more step, relentlessly pursuing the story in the face of persistent accusations against us and a concerted campaign of intimidation. Howard Simons, with his semi-independent pocket of authority on the paper, helped move the story along enormously. It was Howard who carried the story in its early days.

On the editorial side, Phil Geyelin and Meg Greenfield were invaluable. Through their editorials, along with those by Roger Wilkins, they plugged away at the import of what was unfolding on our news pages. The *Post*'s editorials consistently argued the seriousness of the known facts in the first several months, well before the White House had even acknowledged special concern, and at a time when the whole matter was thought to be dead. These editorials played a great part in keeping the issues before the public and had a demonstrable impact on the way people came to think about Watergate.

An even more immediate impact was achieved by Herblock. From the cartoon that appeared a few days after the „third-rate burglary" - depicting a guard throwing one of the burglars out of the Democratic National Headquarters with Richard Nixon, Richard Kleindienst, and John Mitchell looking on, over the caption „Who Would Think of Doing Such a Thing?" - to his justly famous one of Nixon trying to hang on to the ends of two reels of tape on which the words „I am ... a crook" appear, with a clipped piece of tape with the word „not" on it in his mouth, Herblock kept up his relentless assault. He was well ahead of me and of the news side of the paper. Six days after the burglary, I was in the newsroom when he shared with me a cartoon he'd drawn showing two men investigating footsteps representing the bugging case and the Nixon fund scandals - footsteps that led right to the front door of the White House. The caption read: „Strange-They All Seem to Have Some Connection with This Place." I laughed and said, „You're not going to print that, are you?" It appeared the next day, June 23, 1972.

From the start, Woodward and Bernstein followed the trail of the Watergate burglars with alacrity and skill, and a lot of elbow grease. From the time Bob went to court and heard James McCord say „CIA," he was hooked on the story. When Carl came up with Howard Hunts address book, and the two found in it the name „Colson" and the phrase „W. House," they, like Herblock, decided there was a connection to the White House. When it was discovered that numerous calls had been made from the phone of Bernard Barker, one of the burglars, to an office shared by Gordon Liddy and another lawyer at the Committee to Re-elect the President, whose acronym, CRP, quickly turned into the unfortunate CREEP, Woodward and Bernstein were off and running.

On August 1, over a month after the break-in, the first big story appeared under the joint byline of Bernstein and Woodward, reporting on the connection of the burglars to CRP. Three weeks later, on August 22, President Nixon was renominated with grear fanfare at the Republican National Convention in Miami. The next week, apparently trying to declare the Watergate affair finished, Nixon announced that John Dean, counsel to the president, had thoroughly investigated the break-in and said, „I can state categorically that his investigation indicates that no one in the White House staff, no one in this administration, presently employed, was involved in this very bizarre incident. What really hurts is if you try to cover it up."

In October, the tempo of the whole story picked up, and the *Post* printed two articles that together brought the administration's wrath down on us. The first, which appeared October 10, described the original break-in as part of a massive, nationwide campaign of political spying and sabotage conducted in behalf of the president's re-election efforts and directed by White House and re-election-committee officials. This idea was dismissed by the main spokesman for the CRP as „not only fiction but a collection of absurdities."

Nixon's press secretary, Ron Ziegler, began his morning briefing at the White House charging that „stories are being run that are based on hearsay, innuendo, guilt by association .... [I]t goes without saying that this Administration does not condone sabotage or espionage or surveillance of individuals." That same afternoon, Clark MacGregor, who had taken over from John Mitchell as Nixon's campaign chairman, held a press conference in which he took no questions but read a prepared statement. He said that the *Post*'s „credibility has today sunk lower than that of George Mc-Govern. Using innuendo, third-person hearsay, unsubstantiated charges, anonymous sources and huge scare headlines, the *Post* has maliciously sought to give the appearance of a direct connection between the White House and the Watergate - a charge which the *Post* knows and half a dozen investigations have found to be false. The hallmark of the *Post*'s campaign is hypocrisy - and its celebrated „double standard" is today visible for all to see."

This and Ziegler's turned out to be only two of the salvos in a broadside against us. Ron Ziegler at the White House accused the *Post* of being politically motivated, and attacked Ben Bradlee for being anti-Nixon. I was feeling beleaguered. The constant attacks on us by CRP and people throughout the administration were effective and taking their toll. During these months, the pressures on the *Post* to cease and desist were intense and uncomfortable, to say the least. But, unbelievable as the revelations were, the strong evidence of their accuracy is part of what kept us going.

Many of my friends were puzzled about our reporting. Joe Alsop was pressing me all the time. And I had a distressing chance meeting with Henry Kissinger just before the election, at a big reception of some kind. „What's the matter? Don't you think we're going to be re-elected?" Henry asked me, seeming quite upset. I assured him that I could read the overwhelming polls as well as anybody and hadn't the slightest doubt that Nixon would be re-elected. Henry later told me that, although he was never part of any actual discussions that related to threats, he knew Nixon wanted to get even with a lot of people after the election. Maybe this had been his way of warning me. In any case, the implications in Henry's exclamation added to my tension.

Readers, too, were writing me, accusing the *Post* of ulterior motives, bad journalism, lack of patriotism, and all kinds of breaches of faith in our effort to get the news to the people. It was a particularly lonely moment for us at the paper. Other organizations were beginning to report the story, but we were so far ahead that they couldn't catch up; Woodward and Bernstein had most of the sources to themselves. The wire service and AP sent out our stories, but most papers didn't even run them, or buried them somewhere toward the back pages. Howard used to get on the phone to his editor friends around the country to tell them they were missing a big story. Because an exclusive story usually remained so for only about twenty-four hours before everyone jumped on it, I sometimes privately thought: If this is such a hell of a story, then where is everybody else?

Bearing the full brunt of presidential wrath is always disturbing. Sometimes I wondered if we could survive four more years of this kind of strain, of the pressures of living with an administration so completely at odds with us and determined to harm us. As I later wrote to Isaiah Berlin, „The idea of living with that gang in the White House whacking at you for four more years was depressing beyond words." I couldn't help speculating about what condition we'd all be in - including the paper - at the end of it. The best we could do while under such siege, I felt, was to keep investigating, to look everywhere for hard evidence, to get the details right, and to report accurately what we found.

To no one's surprise, President Nixon was re-elected by a landslide, with 61 percent of the vote and forty-nine out of fifty states - evidence of how little impact Watergate had had and how very powerful were these angry and vindictive men in the White House and connected with the president elsewhere. However, instead of becoming more secure with his victory in hand and working to unite the country, Nixon immediately turned to vengeance and to strengthening his hold on power. In a speech at his victory dinner with members of the administration, he mentioned *The Washington Post* several times. Right after the election, with the atmosphere between the *Post* and the president at its most poisonous, the Watergate story dried up. Our having nothing new to report fed the idea that the whole story had been political to begin with - a baseless, biased attack on the president by the *Post* for the sake of influencing the election.

That fall, after the election, partly in response to the escalating campaign we felt was being waged against the reputation of the *Post*, I began to make more speeches defending the press in general and the *Post* in particular. One of the first big ones was to the San Francisco Commonwealth Club, quite a conservative group. Meg led the team that worked on the speech, which was a strong defense of freedom of the press. I was in something of a panic about the question period to follow the speech, worrying that I would be quizzed on the minutiae of the Watergate story and not know all the players or the various events relating to it.

The Washington Post

Times Herald

SATURDAY, SEPTEMBER 9, 1972

Justice Completes Watergate Probe

By Carl Bernstein
and Bob Woodward
Washington Post Staff Writers

The Justice Department has completed its criminal investigation of the Watergate case without implicating any present officials of either the White House or the Committee to Re-elect President Nixon, acording to sources close to the investigation.

A federal grand jury is expected within 10 days to hand down indictments that will be confined to suspects actively involved in the June 17 break-in at Democratic National headquarters in the Watergate office building. Five men were arrested inside the Democrats' offices and two former White House aides have since been reported to have been inside the Watergate the same morning.

Throughout the inquiry, investigators and prosecutors were acting on strict instructions from Justice Department officials and acting FBI Director L. Patrick Gray not to consider possible violations of campaign fund reporting laws, federal sources say. Checks representing $114,000 in Nixon campaign contributions were traced to the bank account of one of the men arrested inside the Watergate.

A spokesman for the FBI declined yesterday to comment on any aspect of its Watergate investigation, including whether the inquiry has been completed.

Although the criminal investigation has ended, it is unlikely the Watergate incident — an embarrassment to the Republican campaign — will fade from public view. Two congressional committees are considering public hearings related to the incident, and the Democrats say they will continue their own investigation into the case.

Any congressional hearings are expected to focus on President Nixon's campaign funds, from which the disputed $114,000 came. In addition to this, the Democratic investigation also focuses on what the Democrats contend is an elaborate "Republican-sponsored" espionage campaign.

Meanwhile, the Justice Department is considering what action to take on 11 Nixon campaign finance violations that the General Accounting

See WATERGATE, A6, Col. 4

At the same time that the administration granted an exclusive interview to the *Washington Star*, it started a boycott of sorts on us - specifically, as an anonymous White House aide told *Time* magazine, „to screw the *Washington Post*." The thinking was, Time reported, „How can we hurt the Post the most?" We were not to have our calls answered, not to be dealt with professionally in any way; administration people were not to come to editorial lunches, and certainly not to my house for dinner. A uniquely ludicrous, petty, and rather weird form of vengeance took place when the administration excluded our charming, much-respected, and even loved senior society reporter, Dorothy McCardle, then sixty-eight years old, from covering parties and made her sit alone cooling her heels in the pressroom, barring her from one social event after another.

In April 1973 it was announced that *The Washington Post* had won the Pulitzer Prize for meritorious service for its Watergate reporting. Woodward and Bernstein were cited, and Herblock and Roger Wilkins were specially mentioned. The winning of the Pulitzer with its attendant confirmation of our reporting, the whole Watergate affair was far from over. The continuing efforts of the *Post*, and, finally, other newspapers and other media as well and the Congress and the courts helped expose the size of the iceberg.

There began a steady stream of revelations, with more and more evidence of scheming and political chicanery coming to light. Wiretaps of several journalists were revealed. We were told by many people that the *Post*'s building was bugged and even that I was being followed. Some of this was clearly an overreaction in an environment rife with paranoia. We did a sweep of our phones throughout the building and in my office and the offices of key editors, but turned up nothing. I'm fairly sure that my phones were never tapped, nor do I believe I was ever followcd, but the atmosphere was so infected that this kind of suspicion didn't seem irrational at all.

Yet the *Post* remained under attack - and the attack was becoming much more public. By this time I had warmed up to a degree of toughness of which I probably wouldn't have been capable the year before. I am not a good combatant. Generally I hate fights and would like to run from them, but when there is no choice, I feel able to take action. I was much more willing to go on the offensive than to be defensively polite, particularly in my letters to readers and others who wrote complaining about our coverage. For example, whereas earlier I may have been somewhat sympathetic with readers who wrote about the sharpness of Herblock's pen, in the later stages of Watergate I had no patience with those who complained that he was being unfair to the president. To one scathing letter, I responded, „We have been heavily attacked for biased reporting by many individuals, who, when confronted with the facts, have since resigned from the government.

On February 6, 1974, memhers of the House of Representatives voted 410 to 4 to proceed with the impeachment probe and to give the Judiciary Committee broad subpoena powers. Trying to keep all his hatred of the press, and particularly of the *Post*, within the confines of the White House proved too much for the president. On May 9, the House Judiciary Committee began formal hearings on the possible impeachment of Nixon. Privately, I felt that impeachment was right, but my personal opinion didn't get mixed up in the paper's ongoing reporting. On August 8, President Nixon announced that he would resign the next day. I stayed at the paper all that day. Together, many of us watched Nixon's television appearance about his decision to resign. On August 9, the *Post* produced a twenty-two-page special section on the Nixon years. Along with a few people in my office, I watched the weird speech Nixon made before leaving the White House.

At the *Post*, we received a lot of unpleasant phone calls, many readers expressing the sentiment that they imagined we were all popping champagne corks to celebrate the result we had wanted from the beginning - in short, the „I -hope-you're-satisfied" school of thought. What I mostly felt was relief, mingled with anxiety. Until the smoking-gun tape had turned up, no thing had been certain; right up to the last few days of his presidency, it seemed possible that Nixon could hold on. Now the unease about where all of it was leading was over. More even than Nixon's resignation, this was the end of Watergate for us. By then we had been fighting this battle against venality for two years in the case of two of the challenges and two and a half in the latter two. We had paid a heavy price, not only in money but in concern, distraction, and erosion.

On December 5, I974, both Ben and I were invited to a dinner at the Ford White House, where I was seated at the table with the new president - an exciting symbol that the whole sad affair ofWatergate was over. (An amusing sidelight on Ford's elevation to the presidency came when tee shirts were printed with his picture on them, together with the caprion, „I got my job through The Washington Post," a slogan also used by our classified-ad department.) By then, Ford had granted a full, free, and absolute pardon to Nixon, which I thought premature, believing that he should have extracted at least some sort of admission of guilt for it. I suspected that more awful deeds lurked unexposed - now likely never to surface. I' sure Ford was under a lot of pressure to get the whole disastrous affair "behind us."

Earlier, in the spring of 1974, at a time when the story had advanced considerably but was still months short of its dramatic conclusion, Woodward and Bernstein had published *All the President's Men*, their first book on Watergate. The paperback rights alone sold for $ I million. Ironically, the million dollars came their way at the time of a strike by The Newspaper Guild. I vividly recall watching a news broadcast that showed the two of them Ieaving the building with their files, and I caused a stir with a rather acid remark about their being the only two people ever to have made a million dollars while on strike.

From the beginning there had been talk of a movie. Once Woodward and Bernstein sold the movie rights to All the President's Men to Robert Redford, who intended to play Bob Woodward, there was a great deal of fun and funny speculation, both in the *Post*'s newsroom and elsewhere, about who would play whom in the movie. I jokingly told a group of circulation managers at an association meeting that I had been assured by the editors „that my role will be played by Raquel Welch - assuming our measurements jibe."

I was already worried about the effect of the use of the *Post*'s name when I opened a magazine one day and read that the movie would be filmed in the *Post*'s city room. Within minutes, I was on the phone to Bob Woodward, to whom I exploded with outrage at the idea of our newsroom as a backdrop for the movie. Among all the evils I was imagining was how little work would get done under such circumstances. Bob told me he'd never heard me so angry. In the end, we didn't allow filming in the newsroom; Redford's people had arrived independently at the conclusion that it would be too disruptive for them as well. Instead, an exact duplicate of the *Post*'s newsroom, including the stickers on Ben's secretary's desk, was created in Hollywood (for a mere $450,000, it was reported), and in the interests of authenticity, several tons of assorted papers and trash from desks throughout our newsroom were shipped to California for props. We did cooperate to the extent of allowing the filmmakers to shoot the entrance to the newspaper building, elevators, and certain production faciIities, as weIl as a scene in the parking lot.

To pile one irony on another, the world premiere of the movie took place in April at the Eisenhower Theater at the Kennedy Center, next door to the Watergate, and President Ford sent me tickets for the presidential box, along with the key to the refrigerator in the box, which contained champagne for me and my guests with his compliments. The movie's effect on us at the *Post* was electric, yet a little like a bite from the apple of discord. Maybe it wasn'tjust the movie but, rather, the outcome of Watergate itself. Sometimes the gods give us too much and then exact a price. I suggest this discord because the portrayals in the movie of the roles various people had played had a negative effect on several real-life relationships. The movie gave everything to Ben,

With Ben Bradlee emerging from a Pentagon Papers hearing

With Carl Bernstein and Bob Woodward

largely because that made for a simpler story line and because he was played by Jason Robards, but of course that wasn't Ben's fault. Howard Simons was made quite bitter by the movie. He was poorly treated - all for the sake of clarity and simplicity. Much of what he had actually done throughout Watergate was divided up in the movie between Ben and Harry Rosenfeld.

As a story, Watergate was in many ways a journalist's dream - although it didn't seem that way in those first months when we were so alone. But the story had all the ingredients for major drama: suspense, embattled people on both sides, right and wrong, law and order, good and bad. Watergate - that is, all of the many illegal and improper acts that were included under that rubric - was a political scandal unlike any other. Its sheer magnitude and reach put it on a scale altogether different from past political scandals, in part because of the unparalleled involvement of so many men so close to the president and because of the large amounts of money raised, stashed, and spent in covert and illegal ways.This was indeed a new kind of corruption in government.

Even today, some people think the whole thing was a minor peccadillo, the sort of thing engaged in by lots of politicians. I believe Watergate was an unprecedented effort to subvert the political process. It was a pervasive, indiscriminate use of power and authority from an administration with a passion for secrecy and deception and an astounding lack of regard for the normal constraints of democratic politics. To my mind, the whole thing was a very real perversion of the democratic system - from firing people who were good Republicans but who might have disagreed with Nixon in the slightest, to the wiretappings, to the breaking and entering of Ellsberg's psychiatrist's office, to the myriad dirty tricks, to the attempts to discredit and curb the media. As I said in a speech at the time, „It was a conspiracy not of greed but of arrogance and fear by men who came to equate their own political well-being with the nation's very survival and security."

The role of the *Post* in all of this was simply to report the news. We set out to pursue a story that unfolded before our eyes in ways that made us as incredulous as the rest of the public. The *Post* was never out to „get" Nixon, or, as was often alleged, to „bring down the president." It always seemed to me outrageous to accuse the *Post* of pursuing the Watergate story because of the Democratic bias of the paper. A highly unusual burglary at the headquarters of a national political party is an important story, and we would have given it the same treatment regardless of which party was in power or who was running for election.

Throughout Watergate, I was amazed at the regular allegations that somehow we had created the agony of Watergate by recklessly pursuing certain stories and thereby causing the turmoil that the president was in. How could anyone make this argument in light of the fact that the stories we reported turned out to be true?

In the end, Nixon was his own worst enemy. The *Post* had no enemies list; the president did. Nixon seemed to regard the *Post* as incurably liberal and ceaselessly antiadministration. In fact, the *Post* supported a great many of his policies and programs, but his paranoia, his hatred of the press, his scheming, all contributed to bringing him down - helped along by the appropriate constitutional processes, including the grand juries, courts, and Congress. Woodward and Bernstein were critical figures in seeing that the truth was eventually told, but others were at least as important: Judge Sirica; Senator Sam Ervin and the Senate Watergate Committee; Special Prosecutors Cox and Jaworski; the House Impeachment Committee under Representative Peter Rodino. The *Post* was an important part - but only a part - of the Watergate story.

My own role throughout Watergate is both easy and hard to define. Watergate no doubt was the most important occurrence in my working life, but my involvement was basically peripheral, rarely direct. For the most part I was behind - the-scenes. I was a kind of devil's advocate, asking questions all along the way - questions about whether we were being fair, factual, and accurate. I had a constant conversation with Ben and Howard, as I did with the top two editorial writers, Phil and Meg, so I was informed in general. As was my habit before Watergate, I often attended the daily morning editorial meetings, where the issues were regularly discussed and where editorial policy was formed.

What I did primarily was stand behind the editors and reporters, in whom I believed. As time went on, I did this more publicly, defending us in speeches and remarks to groups around the country - indeed, internationally as well. My larger responsibility was to the company as a whole - beyond the paper - and to our shareholders. I have often been credited with courage for backing our editors in Watergate. The truth is that I never felt there was much choice. Courage applies when one has a choice. With Watergate, there was never one major decisive moment when I, or anyone, could have suggested that we stop reporting the story. Watergate unfolded gradually. By the time the story had grown to the point where the size of it dawned on us, we had already waded deeply into its stream.

Once I found myself in the deepest water in the middle of the current, there was no going back. It was an unbelievable two years of pressured existence, which diminished only a little as other publications joined us and as the separate investigations and the court cases spawned by Watergate began to confirm and amplify our reporting. When it was perfectly obvious that our existence as a company was at stake, we of course became embattled. Watergate threatened to ruin the paper. The *Post* and The Washington Post Company survived partly because of the great skill and tenacity that our reporters and editors and executives brought to bear throughout the crisis, and partly because of luck.

In fact, the role of luck was essential in Watergate - and luck was on our side. One has to recognize it and use it, but without luck the end result for us could have been very different. From the first incident of the guard finding the taped door at the Watergate building, to the police sending to the scene of the crime a beat-up-looking undercover car that was cruising in the area rather than a squad car that might have tipped off the burglars, to the sources willing - some even eager - to talk and help, we were lucky. We were lucky that the original burglary took place in Washington and was a local story. We were lucky that those under investigation compounded their own situation by further mistakes and misassessments. We were lucky we had the resources to pursue the story. We were lucky that both Woodward and Bernstein were young and single and therefore willing and able to work sixteen- and eighteen-hour days, seven days a week for months on end, at least with fewer repercussions than married men might have had.

We were lucky Nixon was eccentric enough to set up a taping system in the White House, without which he might have completed his term. We were also lucky that none of us went over the precipice under the staggering pressures. During the summer of 1973, the strain on Ben was so great - his responsibility for all the people under him, for being right, for being accurate - that his eyelid began to droop. A doctor told him it might be a serious symptom, indicating a brain tumor or an aneurysm. After ten days of torture from the suspense, it turned out to be a nervous condition. The calmer people look and act under extreme pressures; the more likely they are to pay the price with physical symptoms.

Watergate was a transforming event in the life of *The Washington Post* - as it was for many of us at the paper and throughout journalism. Anything as big as Watergate changes you, and I believe it changed not only the *Post* and me but journalism as a whole. There were both positive and negative effects. At the *Post*, Watergate tested our whole organization: our talents, our skills, our ability to organize and mobilize resources to handle a long-term major investigation while still covering the daily news. Ultimately, Watergate showed what could be done by reporters arduously and painstakingly pursuing investigative work, by editors remaining skeptical and demanding and as dispassionate as possible under the circumstances, and by editorial writers helping to keep the questions foremost in the minds of our readers.

More important in terms of its effect, Watergate catapulted the *Post* to true national and international prominence. The paper became known throughout the world because of it. On one level, the changed image of the *Post* was flattering; on another, it was both „disturbing and distracting to getting on with other things,“ as I wrote Denis Hamilton of the London *Sunday Times*. The positive press we began to get was heady and headturning stuff, but the world, fortunately, has a way of keeping one humble. If the world didn't do it, I was determined to remind all of us of the need, as I said in a letter to Carl and Bob, to keep „the demon pomposity“ in control: „The sound of our own voices, while listened to by us with some awe and even some admiration, is receding. And if it isn't, there are all sorts of stark realities before us to restore balance and defy hubris.“

I came to be talked about and written about more and more. I was especially bothered by being talked about as „powerful,“ often referred to in one headline or story or another as „The Most Powerful Woman in America,“ making me feel like some kind of weight-lifter or body-builder. Actually, I was amazed at this perception relating to power, and confounded by how absurd it was to be singling me out as more „powerful“ than Punch Sulzberger or Bill Paley, for example, who controlled more powerful companies but were men.

I was also concerned - for the paper and for all of us, induding myself - that if your profile gets up too high it will be a target. Someone or something will bring you down. Accordingly, I did only interviews that I thought were professional, and tried very hard to avoid the personal ones. I was fairly confident that the work of *Post* reporters and editors would withstand critical scrutiny. I once said to Truman Capote that it looked as if either I'm going to jail or they are.“ On the other hand, I have to admit that I was frightened. I was frightened of the power of a man and his minions, of a president who thought he had the power to wrap himself in the cloak of national security. I was frightened for the future of The Washington Post Company, and, particularly after Fritz died and I became chairman as well as publisher, my responsibilities weighed heavily on me.

Watergate also changed the way journalism and journalists are viewed, and in fact the way they work. During the Watergate affair, we - at the *Post* at least - had developed certain habits that were hard to break. John Anderson, an editorial writer, insightfully discussed this in some notes he made on the editorial page at the time: „We had become accustomed to a high degree of tension and drama. Morning editorial conferences had become obsessive, as we went back and forth for hours over each day's events. Quickly they came to take up the entire morning, as we sat around Phil's [Geyelin] office with the papers spread out before us. The *Post*'s triumph in Watergate is well known, but we paid a large price for it that has had little attention. When it finally ended with Nixon's resignation, life for all of us was suddenly less interesting. For a long time afterward news coverage was eccentric and spotty because half the staff particularly young Metro reporters, were off chasing mini-scandals. It was a matter of years before we got back to consistent, orderly coverage of school boards and county councils."

Young people flocked into joumalism, some for good reasons and some hoping to be Woodward or Bernstein. Certainly, Watergate provided a great deal of evidence that the national media do indeed shape events. Clearly, press reports contributed to Judge Sirica's doubts about what he was hearing in his courtroom, to congressional questions, to public concern. But we don't set out to have such a major impact. No one - least of all the press itself - thinks we are free from errors and faults or completely without bias. I never once have believed that we in the press do everything right, but we try to keep our opinions confined to the editorial page.

The natural adversarial relationship between the press and the president was subverted in the case of Watergate, and that, too, affected journalism. I was somewhat alarmed by certain tendencies toward over-involvement, which I felt we should overcome as quickly as we could. The press after Watergate had to guard against the romantic tendency to picture itself in the role of a heroic and beleaguered champion, defending all virtues against overwhelming odds. Watergate had been an aberration, and I felt we couldn't look everywhere for conspiracies and cover-ups. On the other hand, I don't believe we „over-covered" Watergate, as some Nixon supporters claimed to the last.

As astounding as Watergate was to the country and the government, it underscored the crucial role of a free, able, and energetic press. We saw how much power the government has to reveal what it wants when it wants, to give the people only the authorized version of events. We relearned the lessons of the importance of the right of a newspaper to keep its sources confidential. The credibility of the press stood the test of time against the credibility of those who spent so much time self-righteously denying their own wrongdoing and assaulting us by assailing our performance and our motives. In a speech I made in 1970 - before the Pentagon Papers and before Watergate - I said: „The cheap solutions being sought by the administration will, in the long run, turn out to be very costly." Indeed, they did.«

NOVELIST JOINS IN ANTI-VIETNAM WAR DEMONSTRATION

by *Norman K. Mailer*

He was born on January 31, 1923, in Long Branch, New Jersey, and died on November 10, 2007, in New York City. Norman Kingsley Mailer was the son of an accountant born in South Africa. Raised in Brooklyn, New York, Norman graduated from Boys High School and entered Harvard University in 1939, when he was sixteen years old. As an undergraduate, he was a member of the Signet Society. At Harvard, he majored in engineering sciences, but took the majority of his electives as writing courses. He published his first story, „The Greatest Thing in the World,“ at the age of 18, winning *Story Magazin*'s college contest in 1941.

After graduating in 1943 he was drafted into the U.S. Army in January 1944. After training at Fort Bragg, Mailer was stationed in the Philippines with the 112th Cavalry. During this time, he was first assigned to regimental headquarters as a typist, then assigned as a wire lineman. In early 1945, after volunteering for a reconnaissance platoon, he completed more than two dozen patrols in contested territory, and engaged in a few firefights and skirmishes. After the Japanese surrender, he was sent to Japan as part of the army of occupation, was promoted to sergeant, and became a first cook.

When asked about his war experiences, he said that the army was „the worst experience of his life and the best.“ After completing courses in French language and culture at the University of Paris in 1947-48, Mailer returned to the U.S. shortly after his book „The Naked and the Dead“ was published in May 1948. The work brought him early and wide renown. A *New York Times* bestseller for 62 weeks, it was the only one of Mailer's novels to reach the number one position. The book that made Mailer's reputation sold over a million copies in its first year and was hailed by many as one of the best American wartime novels.

Besides of being a novelist, Mailer also was a journalist, essayist, playwright, film-maker, actor, and liberal political activist. While principally known as a novelist and journalist, Mailer was not afraid to bend genres and venture outside his comfort zone. After he was arrested in October 1967 for his involvement in an Anti-Vietnam War Demonstration at the Pentagon, he wrote down his experiences in a nonfiction book entitled „The Armies of the Night.“ The hallmark of the book was his use of illeism, or referring to oneself in the third person, rather than the first. Mailer said he got the idea from reading „The Education of Henry Adams“, a Pulitzer Prize decorated memoirs in 1919, when he was a Harvard freshman.

Like several others of Mailer's nonfiction books, „The Armies of the Night“ was highly political and won a National Book Award. When this volume also found its way to the Pulitzer Prize jurors in the nonfiction award category, the committee was very much impressed and stated in the jury report dated January 21, 1969: „Norman Mailer's 'The Armies of the Night' clearly stands out ... above its worthy competitors. Although I have never, frankly speaking, been an admirer of Mr. Mailer or his work," one of the jury members confessed, „I am overwhelmed by the brilliance and significance of this book. My enthusiasm is not explained by his gift for words, his powerful style, or any direct emotional involvement, on my part, with his ostensible subject.“

„Rather, I am struck“, the juror continued, „by the way Mr. Mailer has used a relatively commonplace incident - one which will warrant no more than a few lines, at most, in future history - to reveal some of the deepest tensions and conflicts within American society. As a historian, I am fascinated by his imaginative feat of juxtaposing and synthesizing subjective and objective aspects of an event, by his fusion of 'the novel as history' and 'history as novel.' As a human being, I am impressed by his ability to transcend and come to terms with his own rather unlovely persona. It seems to me that 'The Armies of the Night' raised public reporting and sociological analysis to a level of high art. If the half-comical march on the Pentagon fades from view in subsequent histories of our era, I would predict that Mr. Mailer's book will be studied, say twenty-five years from now, as a profound illumination of America in the 1960s. It is therefore my personal choice for a Pulitzer Prize.“

Since the other jury members and also the Advisory Board shared that opinion, Norman Mailer received the 1969 Pulitzer Prize in the „General Nonfiction“ award category. The same year, Mailer ran an unsuccessful campaign to become the mayor of New York City. Although Mailer took stands on a wide range of issues, from opposing compulsory fluoridation of water supply to advocating the release of a Black Panther Party leader, decentralization was the overriding issue of the campaign. Mailer foresaw the city, its indepence secured, splintering into townships and neighborhoods, with their own school systems, police departments, housing programs and governing philosophies. Looking back on the campaign, journalist and historian Theodore White called it „one of the most serious campaign runs in the United States in the last five years.“ Characterizing his campaign, Mailer said: „The difference between me and other candidates is that I'm no good and I can prove it.“

Among Mailer's twelve novels written over a close to sixty year span, his 1979 published „The Executioner's Song“ was a special undertaking. The book about the life and death of murderer Gary Gilmore shook the public. Joan Didion reflected the views of many readers when she called the novel „an absolute astonishing book“ at the end of her front-page review in the *New York Times Book Review*. When the volume came to the attention of the Pulitzer Prize jurors in the „Fiction“ award category, one of the jury members stated in a report of December 13, 1979: „I think that 'The Executioner's Song' is clearly the best work of fiction published this year and perhaps for some years.“

The complete jury report dated December 19, 1979, praised the work in this way: „Norman Mailer's 'The Executioner's Song' is subtitled 'A True Life Novel.' And although the story told is about real people, and based upon a great mass of documentary material, 'The Executioner's Song' is an extraordinarily ambitious and powerful narrative, whose daring and genius expand our conceptions of the limits of history and fiction. Mailer throughout his career has been concerned with those limits, and with the central American themes of freedom and restraint, violence and civilization. In the story of 'The Executioner's Song' he has found a series of events that perfectly articulate those themes, in a summary vision of America and of his own career to date ... In this somber meditation on the moral ambiguities of American life, Mailer has created a book that challenges our notions of fiction but that, more importantly, also challenges our understanding of the moral dimensions of the life we live now.“

After these praises, it was no question that Norman Mailer earned his second Pulitzer Prize in 1980, this time in the „Fiction“ award group. In 1982, Mailer worked on a television adaption of 'The Executener's Song'. Airing by the end of November, the production received strong critical reviews and four Emmy nominations. In 1989, Mailer joined with a number of other prominent authors in publicly expressing support for collegue Salman Rushdie in the wake of the fatwa calling for Rushdie's assassination issued by Iran's Islamic government for his having authored 'The Satanic Verses'. In the year of Mailer's death, his final novel, 'The Castle in the Forest', came out, which focused on Hitler's childhood. The book reached number five on the *New York Times* bestseller list after publication in January 2007. It was as well received by the public as about four decades ago the Pulitzer Prize-winning 'The Armies of the Night,' from which following now are several short passages, written in third person style:

»On a day somewhat early in September, the year of the first March on the Pentagon, 1967, the phone rang one morning and Norman Mailer picked it up.

It had best be stated that his immediate reaction was one of woe - he did not wish to speak to the man on the other end. That man was an author named Mitchell Goodman. Mitch Goodman, as everyone called him, was a worthy fellow, and Mailer had only good things to say of him. In fact Mailer had known Goodman for twenty years.They had been, if he recollected properly, almost in the same year at Harvard (Mailer was Harvard '43 - his 25th Reunion was coming up), they were both from Brooklyn, both married young. They had met in Paris in 1947. In fact, the last time Mailer had heard of Mitch Goodman was when the latter had led a small group of protesters out of the large hotel banquet hall where Hubert Humphrey was about to address the assorted literati and book reviewers of the American writing world at the National Book award festivities in March, 1967. Mailer had not attended.

Here, therefore, was Mailer now on the phone with an old friend and lugubrious conscience whose instinct for the winning move was not - on the face - spectacular. Mailer hated to put in time with losers. Quickly, the conversation, therefore, took a harsh turn. Before it had been going two minutes, Mailer was scolding Goodman; that was predictable enough, given the request. Goodman had just finished telling Mailer that there was going to be a March on Washington in about a month, and Mailer had hardly finished saying he doubted if he would attend since he had no desire to stand in a large meadow and listen to other men make speeches. So, no he did not think he would go to Washington, when Goodman interrupted by saying, „This is going to be different, Norman. Did you read the circular from the Mobilization Committee?"

„I get many circulars, and they're all badly written," Mailer said in a cranky voice. „Well, this one is a departure," said Mitch Goodman. „Some of us are going to try to invade the corridors of the Pentagon during office hours and close down some of their operation." Mailer received such news with no particular pleasure. It sounded vaguely and uneasily like a free-for-all with students, state troopers, and Hell's Angels flying in and out of the reports - exactly the sort of operation they seemed to have every other weekend out on the Coast. He felt one little bubble of fear tilt somewhere about the solar plexus. „Yes, this sounds more interesting," he growled. „Well, I think it will be," said Goodman. „Anyway, Norman, what I'm calling you about is something else: our group called Resist. On Friday, the day before the Pentagon, we're going to have a demonstration at the Department of Justice to honor students who are turning in their draft cards.

This is about where Mailer began to scold Goodman. He wept on for a breath or two on the redundancy of these projects. When was everyone going to cutout the nonsense and get to work, do their own real work? One's own literary work was the only answer to the war in Vietnam. As he was talking, Mailer began to realize that he had not done any real writing in months - he had been making movies - but then it didn't matter, he had done as much in the way of protest about this war as anyone, his speech at Berkeley in 1965 had attacked Johnson at a time when lots of the mob now so much against the war were still singing 'Hello, Lyndon.' Mailer, filled with such righteous recollections, was therefore scolding Goodman at near to full pedal, when the organ came to a sudden stop. „All right, Mitch", he said; „I don't know what I'm arguing for, I'm sure you'll need all your strength to melt some of the real hard heads." Mitch Goodman chuckled at the other end. It was the first hint between them of memories of somewhat more idealistic days in Paris. „Mitch, I'll be there," said Mailer, „but I can't pretend I'm' happy about it."

Leading lawyer for the Mobilization's Legal Defense Committee, and an old friend from times so recent as the trial in Boston of Naked Lunch, where Mailer and he had met, was Ed. de Grazia. The difficulty, de Grazia was explaining, was that there was no center to the March. Unlike the move on Washington in 1963 for civil rights, there was now no central supervisory or coordinatting committee to which all organizations would defer, or with whom they would even promise to maintain communication. Something like fifty thousand people were going to arrive and nearly all of them would be unaffiliated or disaffiliated. Nor was the government revealing quite what they were going to do. At the thought of their august power, a vacuum was certairnly present in the center of Mailer and de Grazia's mood. Listening to de Grazia talk of the negotiations about the route of march from the Lincoln Memorial to the Pentagon, Mailer learned that first there would be a meeting at Lincoln Memorial similar to the assembly in 1963 when Martin Luther King had said, 'I have a dream,' and many had whispered that someday he would be President...

Now, for this morning meeting four years later at Lincoln Memorial no one anticipated too much trouble, but afterward tens of thousands of virtually leaderless people were going to walk over Memorial Bridge to Virginia and from there advance to the Pentagon over a road which had still not been selected, no agreement on the route of march having yet been negotiated between the government and the war protesters. There were three roads, de Grazia explained, and the government wished the marchers to use the narrowest of the three. That was one source of trouble. Another - he hesitated. Was what? Well, in discussing police arrangements, which is to say, dispositions of city police, U.S. Marshals, and National Guard, the government representative had indicated there would be other units as well. When queried, the official had given one of those delicate technological replies: he was, he said, not volunteering to indicate what the specific unit might be. 'That sounds like paratroopers,' said de Grazia. As it turned out, he was right.

The cadres of that citizens' army later to march on the Pentagon were composed of a coalition which could never have come together ten years before, and were in factheld in a kind of suspension on this occasion only through what is considered - by reasonable consensus - the extraordinary abilities of the Chairman of the National Mobilization to End the War in Vietnam, David Dellinger, editor (it may be recollected) of the anarchist-pacifist magazine *Liberation*. Yet his previous experience for such mobilizations was surprisingly not very great. Dellinger had organized the April parade, rally, and assembly in the plaza of the UN of a host of peace groups whose number was probably so high as a quarter of a million people. By *The New York Times* estimate, this support proved twice as large as a massive counter rally in May of patriotic groups who chose to support the war in Vietnam.

While *The New York Times* was not altogether confirmed in this estimate, since the *Daily News* and some radio networks chose to reverse the size of both rallies, finding the patriotic rally to be double the protest rally in numbers, the count of *The New York Times* was more generally believed, and the April March was therefore seen as a great victory. But when its size and success proved to have an absolutely discernible lack of effect on foreign policy, and the war in Vietnam escalated again, an open conference was held in Washington at the Hawthorne School on May 20 and 2I of the National Mobilization Committee. With the exception of Dellinger who was then in Hanoi, some of the figures attending were the Reverend James Bevel, one of the leading organizers of the April March and aide to Martin Luther King; Professor Sidney Peck, a co-chairman of the Mobilization and chairman of the Cleveland Area Peace Action Council; Professor Robert Greenblatt, national coordinator of the Mobilization and an early founder of the campus antiwar teach-ins; and representatives from numerous moderate peace groups, SNCC, SDS, Socialist splinter parties, even a couple of Communists.

On the rising enthusiasm which followed the New York March it was contemplated by many at this meeting to have what would probably be the greatest rally in American history. In Washington in the fall, they would attempt to gather a million people. That was the magnetic number originally discussed, and the key slogan drafted at this May meeting was 'Support Our Boys in Vietnam - Bring Them Home Now.' The date was even picked: October 21; it seemed the best conjunction of a number of factors - the weather would still be good, there would be ample time after Labor Day to get out word of the action, and yet not so late that exam schedules would keep college students away. Already there was vague talk of civil disobedience. Still, the date, October 21, was about the only detail which was to remain constant.

Under these uneasy conditions, one may wonder at the practical judgement of men who meet in Washington in May to call for a rally in October which will assemble a million people. It is not really as unsound psychologically as it seems, any more than it is mentally unsound for the head of a middle class family to announce on his best day of the year, 'Honey, I'm going to make a million yet!' Without one such fierce element of the fantastic, middle class life is insupportable. The same may be said of the old Left Wing life. The Old Left lived for their imagination; their imagination was founded on the apocalyptic moment - not for nothing had Lenin pointed out that there were ten years which passed like an uneventful day, but there was also the revolutionary day which was like ten years.

So plans for a rally to bring a million men and women to Washington were discussed, and the near to absolute impossibility of the project was cushioned by a growing sense of apocalypse in American life. If everything was altering at an un-predictable rate, so might a mass outcry against the war build over the months of the summer. But the summer of 1967 was not favorable for the building of such a vast response". The Arab-Israeli war in June divided the Old Left one more time. Many of the Old Left and many members of the liberal peace groups were Jewish, and enraptured with Israel.Then came Negro riots near a scale of war in the ghettos of at least a dozen major American cities.

For many of these reasons therefore, the projected March on Washington was in the doldrums. Money to support it was hardly dribbling in, Dellinger had been on visits to Hanoi and thus otherwise occupied; enthusiasm among peace groups was not high. At this point Dellinger called in Jerry Rubin from Berkeley to be Project Director for the March. Rubin had enormous stature among youth groups and Under-Thirties, second perhaps only to Mario Savio. Rubin had organized Vietnam Day at Berkeley (the first mass protest of the war) had led marches in Berkeley designed to block troop trains, then massive marches in Oakland, had served a thirty-day jail sentence, and had appeared at a House Un-American Activities Committee hearing in an American Revolutionary War uniform. He had also run for Mayor of Berkeley on a platform opposing war and supporting black power and the legalization of pot, collecting in the process 7,385 ballots or 22 per cent of the vote.

It was a way of announcing to the various groups in the National Mobilization that the October event in Washington was not striking out into that no-man's-land between organized acceptable dissent and incalculable acts of revolution. As will be seen shortly, some most radical possibilities were already in Dellinger's mind, but to call on Rubin was in effect to call upon the most militant, unpredictable, creative - therefore dangerous - hippie-oriented leader available on the New Left. It is to Dellinger's credit that he most probably did not do this to save the March, since there was no doubt that, doldrums or no, a peaceful demonstration of large proportions could always have been gotten together; the invitation to Rubin was rather an expression of Dellinger's faith in the possibility - a most difficult possibility which only his own untested gifts as a conciliator could have enabled him to envisage - of a combined conventional mass protest and civil disobedience which might help to unify the scat- tered elements of the peace movement.

When Rubin arrived in New York, Dellinger's project was at the time conceived as follows: there would be an assembly, then a march past the White House down Pennsylvania Avenue to the Capitol where demonstrators who wished would enter Congress and, there commit acts of civil disobedience. There was even talk of investing Congress and taking it over, establishing, if only for an hour, a People's Congress. But Rubin did not like the revolutionary aesthetics of this plan - he argued with Dellingerthat the proposal, while on the surface most attractive, was nonetheless a move at once too radical and too soft. It was too radical because the Capitol could not successfully be occupied, and the alternate plan - for demonstrators to petition their Congressmen - was pathetically soft. In Rubin's opinion, Congress was not a source but a servant of the real power in America. So Congress did not inspire the thought of real confrontations between real enemies, it did not stir the imagination to awe and dread and admiration. In fact, for good or ill, Congress was an agreeable symbol to the vast majority of Americans.

Rubin had therefore brought another idea. On the West Coast they were talking of a March on the Pentagon which would encircle it, invest it, disrupt it, and conceivably paralyze its actions for a few days. Such a move would have symbolic meaning in America and around the world, for the Pentagon was the symbol of the American military, and so was hated wherever U.S. forces were resented or despised at home or abroad. Discussions ensued.It was later to be a subject of much amusement, and an interesting sidelight into the revolutionary differences between the visionary West and the practical East that the idea of invading the Pentagon began in California, yet the knowledge was obliged to come from New York that the Pentagon was not even in Washington, D.C., but Virginia, and the bridge or bridges across the Potomac would be therefore the place where police could stop the demonstrators with no difficulty at all.

A visionary may however always defeat a practical suggestion, for he absorbs any necessary kernel of the detailed from the aura of the other debater: splendid, said Rubin, if the police should halt the March to the Pentagon on the bridge, the demon-strators could turn back and create massive disruption in the Capitol! A few days later, about the middle of August, Rubin, Robert Greenblatt, coordinator of the Mobilization, and Fred Halstead of the Socialist workers party (whose view would be not unrepresentative of the moderate peace groups) went out to the Pentagon to study its geography and suitability for a march, a rally, and the projected civil disobedience. Their report to a meeting of the Administrative Committee of the National Mobilization was not unfavorable and the committee approved the shift from the Capitol to the Pentagon. A number of such trips were yet to be made, a number of committee members were to walk through the Pentagon in the following weeks.

It was nonetheless an historic moment when these reconnoitering vanguards of the Mobilization Committee went into the Penntagon to study its vulnerability to attack, historic not for the magnitude of the events which were to derive from this visit, but historic as a paradigm of the disproportions and contradictions of the twentieth century itself. Nineteenth-century generals would not have been permitted to explore the fortress they would attack, but they would have known its store-house when they took it. Now recapitulate the problem at the Pentagon: an enormous office building in the shape of a fortress housed the military center of the most powerful nation on earth, yet there was no need for guards - the proliferation of the building itself was its own defense: assassination of any high official in the edifice could serve only to augment the power of the Pentagon; vulnerable to sabotage, that also could work only for the fortification of its interest. High church of the corporation, the Pentagon spoke exclusively of mass man and his civilization; every aspect of the building was anonymous, mono-tonous, massive, interchangeable.

For this committee of revolutionary explorers, the strangeness of their situation must have been comparable to a reconnaissance of the moon. They could enter the Pentagon without difficulty, walk wherever they pleased - although not without attracting attention quite soon, for if most of them looked like responsible executives and experts, Rubin's hair was brushed out like a Black Militant's in five inches every direction from his head; they could nonetheless explore their target debate their approach (even debate aloud if need be in these corridors filled as much with moving people as a busy subway station) they could even if they had wished probably have paid a call on the Secretary of Defense to inform him of their project. Nonetheless, they had many discussions as to which wall of the Pentagon to approach on the day.

The north wall with its Administrative Entrance was eventually chosen. It was the main approach to the Pentagon, and the most attractive.

On August 28 at the Overseas Press Club in New York, a press conference was held to announce the March and its intention to close down the Pentagon on Saturday, October 21, by locking entrances and doorways. The effort would be continued through Sunday, and if possible through Monday. At the press Conference table sat Monsignor Rice of Pittsburgh; Father Hayes of the Episcopal Peace Fellowship; Gary Rader, former member of the Green Berets, now a pacifist; Abbie Hoffman of the Diggers' Free Store in New York; David Dellinger, Jerry Rubin, and Robert Greenblatt of the Mobilization; Amy Swerdlow of Women Strike for Peace; William Pepper, executive director of the National Conference for New Politics (about to have their convention in Chicago); Carl Davidson. of SDS; Lincoln Lynch of CORE; Fred Rosen of The Resistance; Lee Webb, co-director of Vietnam Summer; Dick Gregory, and - to everyone's surprise - H. Rap Brown of SNCC.

Reverend Hayes spoke to the press for the Mobilization and announced that the giant coalition group which grew out of the Spring Mobilization „is beginning to organize a confrontation in Washington on October 21-22 which will shut down the Pentagon. We will fill the hallways and block the entrances. Thousands of people will disrupt the center of the American war machine. In the name of humanity we will call the warmakers to task. This will be a weekend of unified activities. Individuals will act on their consciences and in their own personal styles. Not all people will take part in the massive sit-in at the Pentagon, and we are not asking people to come to Washington solely to this basis. Those who do not block the Pentagon will surround it in a massive peace-in of picketing, vigiling, music, drama, and rallies. We will bring a community of protest, expressing joy and affirmation of man, to a place whose only business is wholesale murder. This confrontation will be massive, continuing, flexible, and surprising."

This press conference naturally attracted huge attention in the press, most of it critical or mocking. The snide reaction was that the demonstrators would attempt to close down the Pentagon on a day (October 21 was part of a weekend) when it was already closed down, which was not quite true, for several thousand of the Pentagon's employees were present on any normal Saturday. That reaction was less siginificant than the dismay of the moderate peace groups through the country who on reading of this press conference were left shocked, fearful, and antagonistic. But these negative reactions were whipped to a fury by the September 1 issue of the *Mobilizer*, newsletter of the Mobilizaation, which began with an editorial written in fire: „The American people today live in a country which has developed the world's most murderous military machine. We live in a society which trains its sons to be killers and which channels its immense wealth into the business of suppressing courageous men from Vietnam to Detroit who struggle for the simple human right to control their own lives and destinies. We Americans have no right to call ourselves human beings unless, personally and collectively, we stand up and say NO to the death and destruction perpetrated in our name.“

The scene now shifts to Washington, and negotiation with the government. In the beginning, any question of jurisdiction must have been moot. It is safe to assume that no particular arm of the authorities would welcome the responsibility of negotiating with the demonstrators. A call to the Chief of the Park Police in Washington, D.C., Inspector Beye, was made by the Mobilization Committee, and when it was explained what they wanted, Beye called a small meeting at which appeared a representative of the metropolitan (D.C.) Police, Beye for the Park Police (who were responsible for order at such monuments as Lincoln Memorial), a Department of the Interior representative, another from the General Services Administration {responsible for the protection and maintenance of all government buildings), and a man from the Pentagon to represent the Defense Departrnent. It was a quiet business meeting.

The next meeting, on October 6, the government would allow a rally at Lincoln Memorial, a march to the North Parking Area of the Pentagon, and a rally in the parking lot. But if the Mobilization did not relinquish all plans to break the law the government would not even allow a rally. At this point there was nothing to negotiate. The two parties were obviously not at all close to one another. Members of the Mobilization therefore left, and went back to their office, a threestorey house at 2719 Ontario Road N.W., where a number of them got on the telephone to speak to different groups around the country. The response which came back was militant, for the reaction was that the Johnson government was now entering a period of suppression. Sentiment was for having the rally anywhere in Washington or Virginia - wherever the police intervened, massive disruption would occur. The demonstrators could move out in every direction and put Washington in disorder. The response was militant even from the Southern Christian Leadership Conference. Martin Luther King was ill these days, in need of rest, and in need of time to rebuild the SCLC.

A new offer proposed that the demonstrators assemble at Lincoln Memorial, go over Arlington Memorial Bridge, proceed on a road to be determined, to a rally in the North Parking Area, and then at a certain hour, those who wished could cross over theour-lane dual Jefferson Davis Highway, enter the

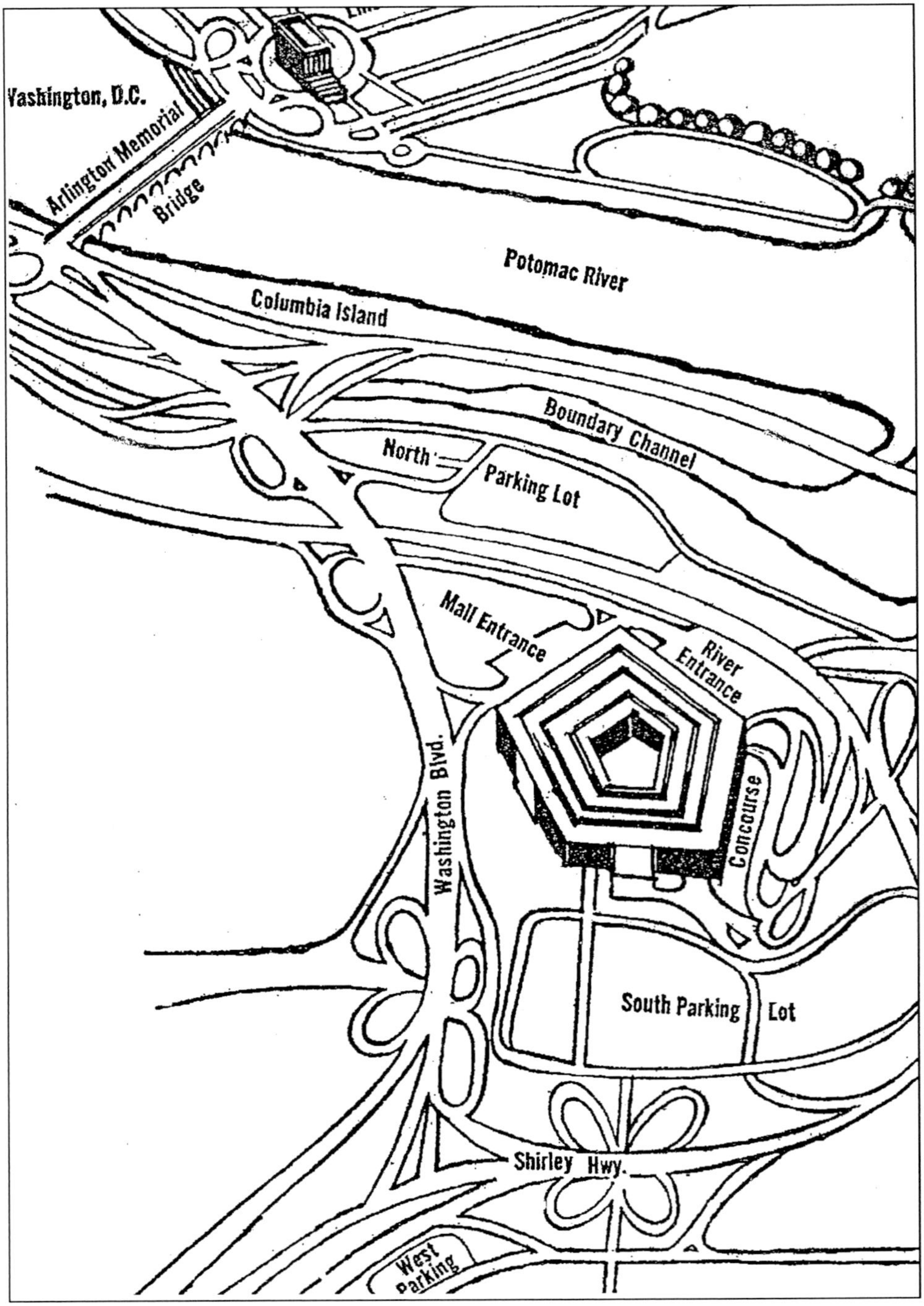
Vashington, D.C.
Arlington Memorial
Bridge
Potomac River
Columbia Island
Boundary Channel
North
Parking Lot
Mall Entrance
River
Entrance
Concourse
Washington Blvd.
South Parking
Lot
Shirley Hwy.
West
Parking

Mall in front of the Administration Entrance, and climb the first row of steps. This offer, made at the second meeting, was actually close to the final agreement drafted on the night before the March. All the essential elements, even the ground plan of the combat which ensued on October 2I, were here indicated. Debate now proceeded over the finest points - the hour of the rally at the North Parking, the specified time when demonstrators could move on to the Mall, the special regulations - those for example who left the Mall after 7 p.m. on Saturday could not come back till noon the next day. So went a host of small points. The Mobilization asked for a rally at Lincoln Memorial and were granted it, adjustments of the area on the steps above the Mall permitted to the demonstrators were made, the duration of the permit was in question, and the access road.

It was to a degree incredible, as every paradigm of the twentieth century is incredible. Originally the demonstrators were saying in effect: our country is engaged in a war so hideous that we, in the greatest numbers possible, are going to break the laws of assembly in order to protest this impossible war. The government was saying: this is a war necessary to maintain the very security of this nation, but because of our tradition of free speech and dissent, we will permit your protest, but only if it is orderly. Since these incompatible positions had produced an impasse, the compromise said in effect: we, the government, wage the war in Vietnam for our security, but will permit your protest provided it is only a little disorderly. The demonstrators: we still consider the war outrageous and will therefore break the law, but not by very much. Each side was compromised, each side was, on the face of their professed attitude, absurd. Yet each party had the most pressing practical concerns to force them into collaboration.

We can pass over the mood of Washington in the few days before the March, the sympathetic and somewhat coordinated actions of protest in other parts of the country for the week preceding October 21, we may skip over the last meetings of the government and the Mobilization Committee, the denunciations in Congress, the bill which was passed on Friday October 20 to protect the Capitol building from men carrying arms! And the scoldings and adjurations of newspaper editorials which remonstrated with the peace movement to remain peaceful. No, one we must give, it is from *The New York Times* on the day of the March: „It will be totally unnecessary for paratroopers or police or demonstrators to provoke each other, in the exercise either of duty or of self-expression today - and it will be tragic if they do. The demonstrators will be betraying their own ideals if they folllow those extremists who would deliberately turn this rally into a field of violence.“

On Friday and Saturday morning, there were front-page stories in the Washington papers on the arrival of troops. The speeches at Lincoln Memorial were done, and a mass of people, calculated by *The New York Times* as fifty thousand, walked over Arlington Memorial Bridge in the next two hours. Waiting for them at the Pentagon or engaged in police work on the route were the following forces; 1,500 Metropolitan Police, 2,500 Washington, D.C., National Guardsmen, about 200 U.S. Marshals, and unspecified numbers of Government Security Guards, and Park, White House, and Capitol police. There were also 6,000 troops from the 82nd- Airborne Division flown in from Fort Bragg, North Carolina,the same 82nd Airborne which had once parachuted into Normandy on D-Day and was now fresh from Santo Domingo and the Detroit riots. M P units had been flown in from California and Texas, the U.S. Marshals had been brought from just about everywhere - Florida, New York, Arizona, Texas, to name a few states - it was to be virtually a convention for them. In addition, 20,000 troops stationed nearby were on alert.

For the army of the demonstrators, no precise figures are available; government estimates were low and Left Wing estimates were high. The Defense Department said that it had estimated there of 35,ooo persons through military photo-interpretation techniques. At any rate, we have an army of at least 35,000 amateur soldiers consisting of doctors, dentists, faculty, veterans groups, housewives, accountants, trade unionists, Communists, Socialists, pacifists, Trotskyists, anarchists, artists, and entertainers, no, even historians may have a joke - there was no more than a smattering and a sprinkling of such professionals at the Pentagon. Present in the majority were college students from all over the East, and high school students and hippies and Diggers and bikers. And - we come to the beginning of the battle - a striking force of shock troops. There was a group which had arrived with a real idea of combat in mind. It was in fact that same advance of hundreds of men carrying placards and flags and standards whose approach on a half-run across the North Parking Area had so impressed Mailer.

A group probably composed in the main of SDS-Contingent on the plaza saw a side entrance door to the left of the main Administration Entrance guarded only by six MPs. Since only a relatively thin line of MPs were on the line to restrain them here, a small group, perhaps twentyfive, made a quick push, broke the line, broke through the MPs, and actually entered the Holy of Holies - they were in the Pentagon racing down a corridor. Not for long! Troops had been brought into the Pentagon the night before, they had slept on cots in the corridors of the building (which is not unlike laying out one's mattress in Lincoln Tunnel). Confined inside, suffering the tension of endless hours waiting

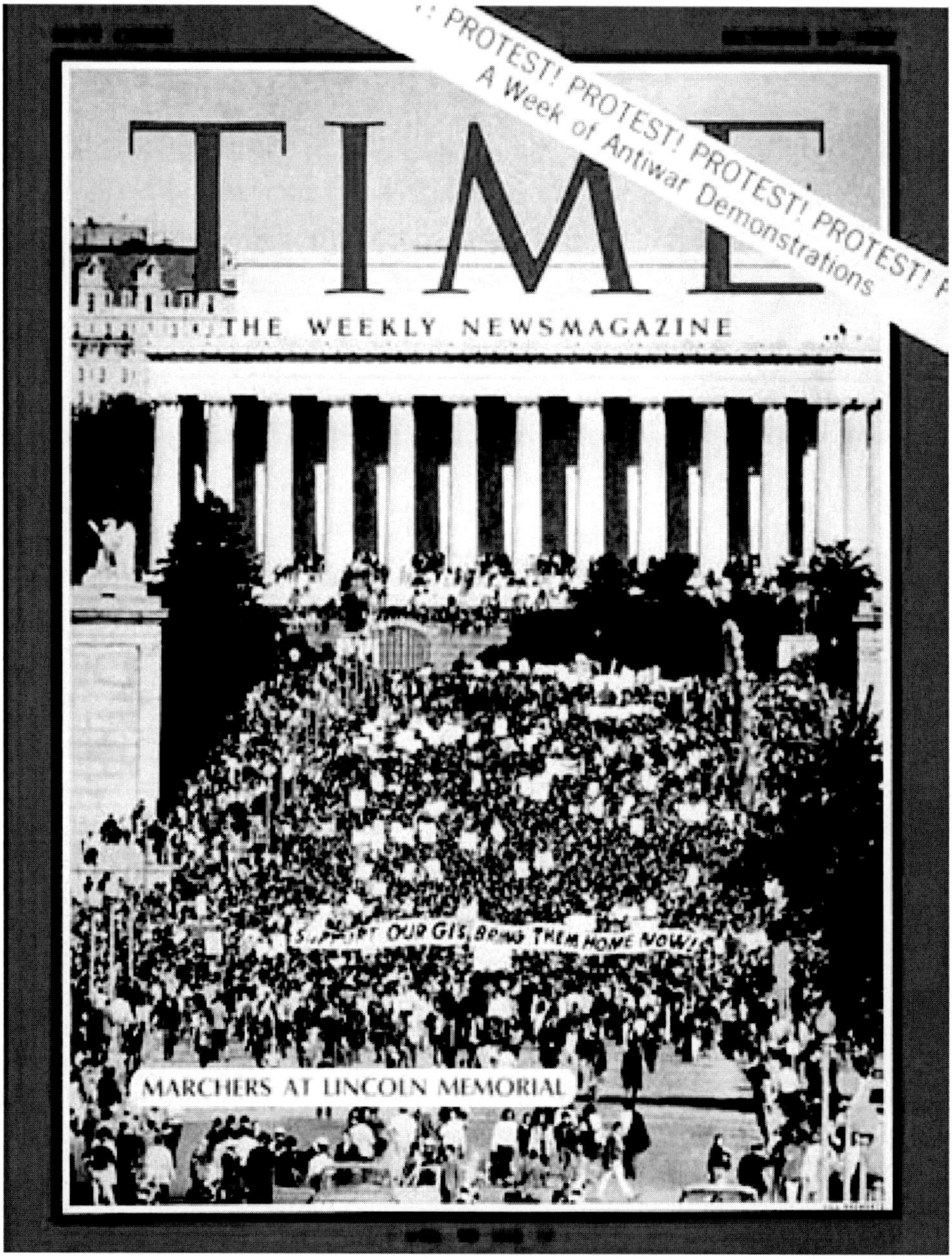

The Peace March on Washington in October 1967

for unseen anarchists, bomb-throwers, Communists, poison gassers, poison in the water, nymphomaniacs, drug addicts, insane Negroes, and common city folk to inundate them under their human wave in these drear corridors, one can only guess - unless there are films - at the unmitigated fury with which the few demonstrators were clubbed and kicked, arrested, and carried off.

It is safe to say that the beginning of this confrontation has not been without terror on each side. The demonstrators, all too conscious of what they consider the profound turpitude of the American military might in Asia, are prepared (or altogether unprepared) for any conceivable brutality here. On their side, the troops have listened for years to small-town legends about the venality, criminality, filth, corruption, perversion, addiction and unbridled appetites of that mysterious group of city Americans referred to first as hipsters, then beatniks, then hippies; now hearing they are linked with the insidious infiltrators of America's psychic life, the Reds! The troops do not know whether to expect a hairy kiss on their lips or a bomb between their knees. Each side is coming face to face with its own conception of the devil! Of course the rhetoric of the Left had been consistent in referring to these troops as innocent victims of the military machine, and there is the real possiblity that some fraction of the soldiers may have been secretly sympathetic to the demonstrators.

Minutes passed, an hour went by - these troops were more afraid of them than they were afraid of the troops! Great glory. They began to cheer. Those who were not in the first row yelled insults, taunted the soldiers, derided them - the demonstrators in the front looked into the soldiers' eyes, smiled, tried to make conversation. 'Hey, soldier, you think I'm a freak. Why am I against the war in Vietnam? Cause it's wrong. You're not defending America against Communism, you're just giving your officers a job.' Some of the dialogue was better, some was worse, some was face to face, some by bullhorn to the troops - technology land at the front. The dialogue was to change character yet, become more intimate, more awful, more excruciating for the soldiers, and the demonstrators; it was to go on for thirty-two hours of close-up dialogues across the line of confrontation, first standing, then - in response to the fear of stampede - sitting, faces inches apart, the demonstrators speaking softly; the soldiers under orders silent, some soldiers trembling - there were reports of officers coming up to say, 'Steady, soldier!' and of soldiers here and there specifically relieved, even unconfirmed stories of three soldiers who took off their helmets and joined the demonstrators.

Of course this was only the first hour of thirty-two, and involved but the first line; three or four rows back the condition was different, one was safer, more anonymous - one's abuse could have more bite for considerably less

Norman Mailer (center) at the Anti-Vietnam War Demonstration

cost. And down in the Mall a different condition existed, one of excitement, bewilderment, interest, anticipation. Cut off from the demonstration on the stairs or the plaza by the press of the crowd at the base one had only to ignore the possibility of climbing the ropes and there was no way one could not in good conscience declare one had done hishest. Of course, there were confrontations here as well. Where soldiers cut off the access roads, demonstrators from the Mall were pressing against them. Here the attitude was more ugly. Here soldiers were not cutting people of from the Pentagon, but from their own demon-strators, so the imperative to get through was more direct, the fear of being stampeded was less - there was all the Mall to run out into. Therefore the inability to mount a charge to break the soldiers' line was less excusable; closer perhaps to cowardice - hence the ugliness of the crowd.

And indeed far out in the Mall, isolated altogether from other soldiers, were very small detachments on now unknown details, three soldiers here, five there. Newspaper stories referred to them, Breslin reported they were reviled and tormented unmercifully; when it got dark a few soldiers were beaten up - so goes the story. It may be well to quote Breslin here. Taste and decency had left the scene a long time before. All that remained were these lines of troops and packs of nondescript kids who taunted the soldiers. The kids went to the bathroom on the side of the Pentagon building. They threw a couple of rocks through the first-floor windows. The soldiers faced them silently. From the steps, a captain in the Airborne kept calling out through a bullhorn: „A Company, hold your ground, A Company," his voice said. „Nobody comes and nobody goes. Just hold your ground, A Commpany." The mob on the grass in front of the soldiers began chanting. „Hold that line, hold that line."

Every time the troops moved forward to push demonstrators away from the ramps, scores, hundreds of youths would sneak behind them - up the ramp. The MPs were enveloped. People were standing with faces just inches from the barrels of M-14 semiautomatics and an occasional single barrel shotgun. The MPs executed an about-face, seeking to clear out the demonstrators who ran behind them. A youth refused to be moved. A rifle butt landed in his stomach. He grabbed the rifle. Several youths grabbed rifles. Four helmets were stolen. A demonstrator was slugged. An M P was slugged. White-helmeted federal marshals, impressed for service from the calm of courtrooms, moved forward, clubs swinging. It seemed to this observer - both in this incident and for the next 30 or so hours - that the marshals aimed particularly at women. Each time the action stopped in a particular spot, demonstrators sought to speak with the soldiers, who were under orders not to respond.

As it grew dark there was the air of carnival as well. The last few thousand Marchers to arrive from Lincoln Memorial did not even bother to go to the

North Parking Area, but turned directly to the Mall and were cheered by the isolated detachments who saw them from a ledge of the wall at the plaza. Somewhere, somebody lit his draft card, and as it began to burn he held it high. The light of the burning card traveled through the crowd until it found another draft card someone else was ready to burn and this was lit, and then another in the distance. In the gathering dark it looked like a dusting of fireflies over the great shrub of the Mall. By now, however, the way was open again to the North Parking. The chartered buses were getting ready to leave. That portion of this revolution which was Revolution on Excursion Ticket was now obliged to leave. Where once there had been thirty thousand people in the Mall, there were now suddenly twenty thousand people, ten thousand people, less.

As the buses ground through the interlocking of their gears and pulled out into a mournful wheezing acceleration along the road, so did other thousands on the Mall look at one another and decide it was probably time to catch a cab or take the long walk back to Washington - they were in fact hungry for a meal. So the Mall began to empty, and the demonstrators on the steps must have drawn a little closer. The mass assault was over. A few thousand, however, were left, and they were the best. The civil disobedience might be far from done. On the Mall, since the oncoming night was cold, bonfires were lit. The night went on. As the remaining demonstrators realized they were alone, and no longer linked to the eighty - or hundred-thousand-headed force of men and women around the reflecting pool, or the fifty thousand at the Pentagon, but were instead down to a few thousand.

The few hundred demonstrators still left in vigil on the stairs of the Pentagon in those dark hours after The Wedge and, before the dawn were being exercised in all those nerves which lead to the moral root - a physical and spiritual transaction whose emotions are, at worst, so little agreeable as the passage of the dentist's drill toward the nerve canal of a tooth. It was bitterly cold, and they slept huddled together, beggared by discomfort, even occasional acts of petty viciousnes. A sergeant went down the lines at 5 a.m. pouring cold water from his canteen on the sleeping bodies. Generally, however, there were few incidents. The Wedge had left no desire for more fight on either side. The Army had been guilty of illegal activity and knew it: the section of plaza they emptied during The Wedge had clearly belonged by the terms of the GSA contract to the area provided for demonstrators - so a few officers must now have been contemplating their actions nervously - the hippies and pacifists still remaining on the stairs could not have felt even an instant of security.

The morning came; very cold, very quiet, unexciting. Demonstrators left, all but a token force. Were there even a few hundred? The others rushed to places for a few hours' sleep, then returned. By ten in the morning, two thousand may have been back. The day was different. There was not much militancy now, but long speeches, different somehow from the speeches of the day before, because the listeners moved now on the currents of the night before and the bloodyings. Now and again draft cards were burned, and for a part of the day Gary Rader, once a member of the Green Berets, gave a speech which was thought by many to be the best hour of them all. Night was on. The demonstrators were entering the last few hours of theit march on the Pentagon. They were tired, exceptionally tired, they felt vulnerable - their aggression, their ability even to defend themselves now used up by endless calls over the hours for more adrenaline; yes the mood was pacifistic, almost saintly, but very weak.

In the night, they were all close to each other. Quietly. They were waiting. The walls of the Pentagon bulked large. Fifteen minutes before midnight, a voice boomed out of a loudspeaker in the wall. To the demonstrators it sounded like the voice of the Pentagon. Big Brother had come to be heard. 'The demonstration in which you are participating,' said the voice, ends at midnight. The two day permit which was agreed to by leaders of the demonstration and GSA expires at that time. All demonstrators must depart from the Pentagon grounds at midnight:' A silence. 'All persons who wish to leave voluntarily can board buses on the Mall.' A.pause. 'Those demonstrators who do not leave voluntarily by midnight will be arrested and taken to a federal detention center... All demonstrators are urged to abide by the permit." So the government remained to the end what it had been from the beginning: a part legalistic, a part cooperative, and a part threatening - or is it rather - a part in the area of the non-negotiable?

There was a short silence, hardly time for the demonstrators to do more than reckon with the fact that another rung in the rite of passage had been presented. But again the Voice spoke out of the Pentagon wall. 'I say again to you. The demonstration in which you are participating ...' and the same speech was read to the same conclusion. Thirty-four demonstrators accepted the offer to leave. During its last hour the demonstration seemed no menace to the helmeted legions still facing them across a single-strand rope barrier. The crowd was down to its last 200. Repeatedly, almost pleadingly, the march's leaders at that hour had reminded the soldiers and the marshals - by loudspeaker -that arrests should be made non-violently to fulfill a supposed promise. At 11:46 an amplified voice echoed across the helmeted troops and federal officers and out to the now-tense 200: 'The demonstration in which you are participating ends at midnight.' 'I say again to you. The demonstration in which ....' and on to a second full reading. 'NO,' CROWD CRIES.

This done, there was a moment of silence. Then, 'No,' a muted chorus from the demonstrators. Then, more lustily, the chant: 'Hell no, we won't go, hell no, we won't go.' Almost immediately, 57 helmeted U.S. Marshals filed out of the Pentagon, across the Mall, and behind the front line of MPs. The crowd started singing, mournfully, 'We Shall Overcome.' Most sat down, immediately in front of the first MPs. A futile attempt at 'God Bless. America,' then more 'We Shall Overcome.' And then again, from the loudspeakers : 'Attention all demonstrators. The demonstration in which ... ' It was repeated twice then, with the added notice that 'It is now 11:55 PM.' 'God Bless America' issued from the protesting remnant, their number diminished by the 34 who had accepted the ride to freedom. The announcement came again, this time with the notice: 'It is now 11:58 and a half PM. and then: 'It is now 12 PM.' A minute passed, and the second „Freedom bus" drove off. There was some shuffling about at the east end of the Marshals' line, but still no fulfillment of the arrest notice.

The closed vans, Occoquan-bound, began moving into position at two minutes after 12. And then the troops tightened around in a triangle, and the Marshals moved in on the demonstrators, now singing 'This Land Is MyLand,' and then 'Glory, Glory Hallelujah,' and finally - over and over - 'We Shall Overcome.' It was a curious last act. Almost conversational. Said a priest to a Marshal: 'Don't club that boy; this is non-violent.' And there was no clubbing. Said a bearded boy to a soldier: 'I am going limp.' He did, and the soldier obligingly lifted him. The arresting went so smoothly then that the vans could not be moved up fast enough to accept the prisoners. After six vans, two panel trucks and that one unused 'freedom bus' were loaded and driven off, it was over. 'It was over.' Jerry Rubin who had been on the steps and the Mall for twenty-eight hours of the thirty-two hours was among the last to be arrested.

When the count was made, there proved to be one thousand arrests. It was not a small number; it was not an enormous number - it was certainly a respectable number to be arrested over thirty-two hours in protest of a war. Six hundred had charges pressed. The others were taken to the back of the Pentagon, photographed, and driven away in buses to be released on the street. Of the six hundred arrested, no felony charges for assault were brought in, indeed only a dozen were charged with assault, only two went to trial, and both were acquitted. Yes, the end seemed to have come, and the immediate beneficiary of the March could be nobody other than the President of the United States. Lyndon Johnson made a point to have his picture taken Saturday sitting at a table on the White House lawn with Hubert Humphrey, Dean Rusk, and Orville Free-man. The caption informed that he had spent the day in work.

Mitch Goodman called a meeting at Town Hall. Five hundred and sixty people (including Allen Ginsberg, Noam Chomsky, and Mailer) signed statements implicating themselves legally to aid and abet draft resisters. Macdonald, Lowell, and Paul Goodman had already signed such statements. They could now all receive the same sentence. So the weekend in Washington which had begun with a phone call from Mitch Goodman gave promise of ending in Harrisburg or Leavenworth. But probably it was in Occoquan and the jail in Washington, D.C., that the March ended. In the week following, prisoners who had chosen to remain, refused in many ways to cooperate, obstructed prison work, went on strikes. Some were put in solitary. A group from the Quaker Farm in Voluntown, Connecticut, practiced noncooperation in prison. Among them were veterans of a sleep-in of twenty pacifists at the Pentagon in the spring before. Now, led by Gary Rader, Erica Enzer, Irene Johnson, and Suzanne Moore, some of them refused to eat or drink and were fed intravenously.

Several men at the D.C. jail would not wear prison clothing. Stripped of their own, naked, they were thrown in the Hole. There they lived in cells so small that not all could lie, down at once to sleep. For a day they lay naked on the floor, for many days naked with blankets and mattress on the floor. For many days they did not eat nor drink water. Dehydration brought them near to madness. Here was the last of the rite passage, 'the chinook salmon ... nosing up the impossible stone,' here was the thin source of the stream - these naked Quakers on the cold floor of a dark isolation cell in D.C. jail, wandering down the hours in the fever of dehydration, the cells of the brain contracting to the crystals of their thought, essence of one thought so close to the essence of another - all separations of water gone - that madness is near, madness can now be no more than the acceleration of thought. Did they pray, these Quakers, for forgiveness of the nation? Did they pray with tears in their eyes in those blind cells with visions of a long column of Vietnamese dead?«

WRITER REMEMBERS HIS CHILDHOOD DURING WAR TIMES

by *Russell W. Baker*

He was born on August 14, 1925, in Loudoun County, Virginia, and died on January 21, 2019, in Leesburg, Virginia. Russell Wayne Baker, at the age of eleven, decided to become a writer since he figured „what writers did couldn't even be classified as work." After leaving school, he took a scholarship to Johns Hopkins University in 1942, studying for a year before leaving to join the Navy as a trainee pilot. He left after the end of World War II in 1945, continuing his degree in English at Johns Hopkins University, graduating with a bachelor's degree in 1947.

Following his graduation, Baker took a job as reporter at the *Baltimore Sun*, working his way up to be sent to London as correspondent for the paper in 1952. Two years later, he moved to Washington, D.C., in order to take the post as the *Baltimore Sun*'s White House correspondent. Being bored with this assignment, he accepted a few months later a job offer by the *New York Times* and joined its Washington staff, covering the White House, United States Congress, and the United States Department of State for eight years.

Early in 1962 Baker was offered a thrice-weekly 'Observer' column in the *New York Times* and he accepted. For this column he wrote ironic essays on politicians and government bureaucrats, and dealt with subjects like contemporary life, children, progress and every day urban living. Initially oriented toward politics, the column began to encompass more and more other subjects when he relocated to New York City in 1974.

Russell Baker continued to write his *New York Times* columns for the next two and a half decades. When his 1978 columns came to the attention of the Pulitzer Prize jurors of the following year, according to their report dated March 7, 1979, they stated: „While famed as a humorist, he (Baker) makes incisive points with or without satire. He is one of our era's greatest social critics without many of his readers being aware of it." The Advisory Board was impressed by this praise and awarded Russel W. Baker the 1979 Pulitzer Prize in the „Commentary" category.

Besides his journalistic work, Baker also published quite a number of books like 'An American in Washington', 'Our Next President - The Incredible Story of What Happened in the 1968 Elections' and various anthologies of his columns. In 1982 Baker brought out his memoirs about his youth years, entitled

The Humble Dollar

The papers keep saying the dollar is very weak. This is nonsense. The truth is that the dollar is absolutely powerless. I sent one out for a pound of cheese the other day and it was thrown out of the shop for giving itself airs.

I used to send the dollar to the grocery with orders to bring back a pound of coffee. I figured this would teach it humility. Instead, it went into a severe depression which psychiatry couldn't cure because it has no way of treating a dollar unless accompanied by 34 others, which I didn't have at the time.

The reason I didn't have them was that one of the children had just stopped by and asked to borrow $470. The measure of how impotent the dollar has become is that children trying to cadge money no longer ask you for a quarter, but for $470. Another measure is that a parent can now borrow a dollar from a child without having to promise to take that child on the roller coaster the following Saturday.

I lent the kid the $470. His grandfather was shocked. "How do you expect children to learn the value of money?" he inquired. I was about to administer a poultice and put him to bed with a nice cup of sassafras tea and the latest list of automobile spare-parts prices when the doors caved in.

Not literally, of course. The tax people are nicer than everyone thinks. Still, they were pretty angry in their polysyllabic way and endless subordinate clauses, and you couldn't blame them.

I had sent a dollar to the newsstand for papers. The tax people naturally wanted their share of it, but it had outraced them and been battered down to a mere 35 cents by the newspaper seller before they could reach it. They were getting soft. It was the first dollar that had outrun a tax man since the South Vietnamese ruling families skipped to Switzerland with the United States Treasury.

Sample of an award-winning Commentary by Russell W. Baker, published in the *New York Times* on April 16, 1978

'Growing Up'. The New York City publishing house of Congdon & Weed on the book's dust jacket told about the work: „Every page has something wonderful - a perfect turn of phrase, a trace of quiet wisdom. 'Growing Up' is a book that will affect and delight and then, long afterward, persists in memory."

When Baker' s memoirs came to the attention of the Pulitzer Prize jurors, they praised the book this way: „A journey into the self and America's recent past that goes far beyond memoir to become a powerful work of literature and undoubtely an American classic." For the Pulitzer Prize Board it was no question that 'Growing Up' deserved the award so that Russell W. Baker earned the 1983 Pulitzer decoration in the „Biography or Autobiography" group, his second Pulitzer Prize only four years after his first one in a journalism award category. Following now are some passages from Baker's memoirs 'Growing Up':

»The United States had been at war seven months when I entered Johns Hopkins University in the summer of 1942. Through most of my childhood there had always been war. War in Ethiopia. War in Spain. War in China. Dimly, I had been aware through all those years that worlds were burning, but they seemed far away. It wasn't my world that was on fire, nor was it ever likely to be, or so I thought. Sheltered by two great oceans, America seemed impregnable. I was like a person on a summer night seeing heat lightning far out on the horizon and murmuring, „Must be a bad storm way over there someplace." It was not my storm.

I'd just turned fourteen when Hitler and Stalin signed their nonaggression pact which cleared the European stage for World War II to start, but though I delivered the papers that told the story in gigantic headlines, I was baffled when a man bought one from me, glanced at the front page, and said, „So it's war." Wasn't there always war someplace? What was special this time?

For me, World War II began a few days later as nothing more than a mild dispute with my mother. We woke that morning to a radio blaring that the German army had marched into Poland. It was September 1,1939, and we were still living on Lombard Street. It was one of those rare mornings when Herb was home for breakfast. „We'll be in it before long, mark my words," he said to my mother. "This is England's war. Let England fight it," she said.

Still four years shy of eighteen, I quickly calculated that the war would be over before it could take me. If it was a world war, I figured it would last four years. The First World War had lasted four years, hadn't it? I had the idea that four years was the standard length of world wars. My mother interrupted these calculations to talk business.

My ignorance of the world beyond schoolroom, baseball diamond, and family circle was remarkable even for a fourteen-year-old. Except for the previous year's experience at City College I had spent my childhood in the blue-collar world where there was neither money, leisure, nor stimulus to cultivate an intelligent world view. I had never been exposed to art, nor attended a concert, nor listened to a symphony even on records. A phonograph would have been an impossible luxury for my mother. The fierce political passions of the 1930s, the clash of ideas about communism, fascism, socialism, were very remote from the gray depths we inhabited. The debates that engaged the intellectual world filtered down to us in refracted and weakened distortions, like sunlight groping toward the ocean bed.

I knew about Benito Mussolini and Adolf Hitler. They were bad guys. I thought of the world in terms of bad guys and good guys, and I knew Hitler and Mussolini were bad guys, though I didn't know why. Franklin Roosevelt was a good guy of legendary proportions. All Americans were good guys, and America was invincible because it was on the good side of whatever the issue might be. Though Hitler and Mussolini were bad guys, they were also funny comic-opera figures, not only because they looked funny - Hitler with his silly mustache, Mussolini with his strut and bulbous jaw - but also because they acted as if they thought they could whip America. That was silly. Nobody could whip America.

What I knew of the world's turmoil came mostly from „War Cards" which, like baseball cards, came packed with penny bubble gum. These depicted Japanese atrocities in China, Italian atrocities in Ethiopia, and slaughters of women and children in the Spanish Civil War. From these I knew that Japan was bad and China good, that Italy was bad and Ethiopia good. The lesson on Spain was confusing. One side murdered nuns and the other bombed helpless villages, but I was uncertain which side was which, and hadn't a guess what the Spanish war was about. The passionate quarrels in intellectual circles about Nazi and Soviet intervention in Spain, and its meaning, and what decent Americans should-do about it - only the slightest sense of all this seeped down to the working-class world of southwest Baltimore, where we lived on Lombard Street.

On Lombard Street the great menace of the 1930s was the Depression, not fascism or communism.When I entered City College, where most of my classmates came from more sophisticated families, I was surprised to find boys my own age who worried about Hitler, Stalin, and the future of Europe. Many of my classmates were Jewish, and some talked about relatives in Germany and what was happening to them under Hitler. A few had refugee relatives from Germany living in their homes. One, I was startled to discover, called himself a communist and believed communism was mankind's only hope. When he

Russell at Johns Hopkins University.

told me this I decided he was a crackpot, but went on enjoying his friendship. After all, he was a musician. I'd learned on Lombard Street that longhairs were supposed to be a little nutty.

My innocence of modern politics lasted until I went to Hopkins. As a senior in high school I was called for an interview before the Honor Society, a group composed of the school's intellectual elite. Someone had put me up for membership. The interview turned out to be a trial, with the group's president acting as prosecutor. After a few questions about my academic history, he asked, „What's your opinion about the split between Stalin and Trotsky?" I had no opinion. „Why not?" „I haven't heard about it." My interrogator stared at me. Though he was about my age, he had prematurely thinning hair, a gray complexion, and a gaunt ascetic face, which made him seem much older. He wasn't in my class and we'd never spoken before, but I'd heard of his brain-power. „You must know there was a struggle for power in Russia between the Trotskyists and Stalinists," he said.

I confessed I didn't. Eyebrows were raised in the jury box. The prosecutor looked at his colleagues and committed a little shrug, as though to say, „Need we waste more time on this clod? Very impressive," sniffed the prosecutor in a tone that conveyed how unimpressed he was. „Now tell us about Stalin. Have you ever heard of Stalin?" He's the dictator of communist Russia." „Well," said the prosecutor, looking at the jury and feigning a smile, „he does know something. He's heard of Stalin." Then turning to me: „You've probably heard of Adolf Hitler, too." The United States was now at war with Hitler. I understood what I was being told. Though ignorant, I wasn't dumb, and I refused to compound my own disgrace by dignifying his last remark with a reply. They convicted me very quickly, and not without justice, since my ignorance of the modern world hardly qualified me to join the elite.

Lombard Street society would have seemed barbaric to my prosecutor and probably to most of the boys I admired at City College. To them, 1938 was the year of Munieh, when Neville Chamberlain sold Czechoslavakia to Hitler for „peace for our time." In Lombard Street, however, it was the year the dignity of the white race hung in the balance scales of history. While uptown Baltimore debated war and the future of civilization, the men of Lombard Street sat on their stoops in shirt-sleeves, puffed their pipes, and pondered a cruel theological mystery. It could best be stated as a question: to wit, why had God permitted Joe Louis to become the heavyweight champion of the world?

The racial doctrine of our neighborhood was „separate and unequal." Black people were considered unworthy and inconsequential. There was „a place" for black people, and they were tolerable so long as they knew their „place" and stayed in it. Unfortunately, some became „uppity," didn't know their „place," didn't stay in it, wanted to walk right into the fancy downtown stores - Huntzler's and Hochschild, Kohn's - and try on clothes from the rack, clothes that white people might later want to try on. Most stores, of course, didn't put up with that. They didn't refuse to sell to blacks - "niggers," as everybody in my neighborhood called them - but most refused to let them try on garments before buying.

The blacks' place in our neighborhood was Lemmon Street, the back alley between Lombard and Pratt. There they lived in ancient brick dilapidations, tiny row houses two stories high and two windows wide with views overlooking the garbage cans of the whites. There they were tolerated so long as they didn't make an unsightly show of themselves around on Pratt or Lombard where whites presided. This social organization had been in place so long, it seemed to have been divinely ordained. The superiority of the white man, the unworthiness of the black - these were assumptions at the very foundation of society. And yet, if this order had been divinely ordained, why, oh why had God permitted Joe Louis to become heavyweight champion of the world?

How could faith in the universal order be justified so long as Joe Louis, a black man, was allowed to pound white men senseless with so little exertion? Joe Louis was a living, breathing mockery of the natural order of things. He had won his title in 1937. Before then and since, he had agreeably stepped into the ring with every white hope willing to have his brains scrambled. Now at the peak of his art, Louis dispatched all corners with such finality that his challengers were called „The Bum-of-the-Month-Club." The ease with which he did the job, often in a round or two without working up a sweat, was gall in the white supremacist's soul.

Louis's exercises were broadcast on the radio and eagerly listened to by the whole community. You heard those awesome words booming out of the speaker from faraway New York: „In this corner - wearing purple trunks - weighing 197 pounds - the Brown Bomber from Detroit -" And then the monstrous roar of that faraway crowd, the gong, the crackling voice of Clem McCarthy: „- Louis measures him - a left to the jaw, a right to the body -" And then it was all over, for Louis was not a man to dawdle at his work.

And then, always, up from dismal Lemmon Street, which lay beneath our open kitchen window, I'd hear shouts, cheering, clapping, a tumult of joyous celebration issuing from the houses where the blacks lived. Out front in Lombard Street, the silence of the tomb. Once again Joe Louis had offended the white neighborhood by giving Lemmon Street a good time.

Lemmon Street people never made much fuss outside their houses. In black districts of Baltimore, celebrators poured out of houses and bars, filling the streets and whooping with pleasure each time Louis finished one of his executions, but there was none of this in white neighborhoods where blacks lived in the alleys. People in Lemmon Street obviously thought too much celebration would be indiscreet. As I discovered in 1938, though, their spirit was not completely lifeless. That summer I witnessed a spectacular development in racial affairs.

For months we had been occupied with the most momentous encounter in the history of sport: Joe Louis had signed to fight Max Schmeling for a second time. Schmeling was the only man who had ever beaten Louis, and he hadn't just beaten him, he had battered him mercilessly, then knocked him out in the twelfth round. This triumph for the white cause had occurred in 1936. Afterwards, Schmeling published a gloating article in the *Saturday Evening Post* explaining how he had found Louis's fatal weakness. Schmeling was a white man. A German, admittedly, and officially approved by Adolf Hitler at a time when Germans were not terribly popular, but, above all, he was a white man. White pulses pounded with anticipation as the second fight approached, and black pulses, for all I know, may have pounded with dread. The white neighborhood awaited the second fight with fevered hopes. Perhaps God had raised Joe Louis so high only to humble him at the fists of the great German white hope.

At last the night of the titanic battle arrived, and I settled by my radio to attend upon the pivotal point of the modern age. What occurred was not the turning of the tide at Gettysburg nor the stand of the Spartans at Thermopylae, but hardly more than a fly-swatting. At the bell Louis left his corner, appraised Schmeling the way a butcher eyes a side of beef - we all saw it over and over again in movie newsreels later - then punched him senseless in two minutes and nine seconds. Paralyzing in its brutal suddenness, it was the ultimate anticlimax for the white race.

From Lemmon Street I heard the customary whooping and cheering rise into the sour Baltimore night. I went to the kitchen window. Doors were being flung open down there. People were streaming out into the alley, pounding each other delightedly on the back, and roaring with exultation. Then I saw someone start to move up the alley, out toward white territory, and the rest of the group, seized by an instinct to defy destiny, falling in behind him and moving en masse.

I watched them march out of the alley and turn the corner, then ran to the front of the apartment to see if they were coming into Lombard Street. They were. They seemed to have been joined by other groups pouring out of other neighborhood alleys, for there was a large throng now coming around into

Lombard Street, marehing right out in the middle of the street as though it was their street, too. Men in shirt-sleeves, women, boys and girls, mothers carrying babies - they moved down Lombard Street almost silently except for a low murmur of conversation and an occasional laugh. Nervous laughter, most likely.

Joe Louis had given them the courage to assert their right to use a public thoroughfare, and there wasn't a white person down there to dispute it. It was the first civil rights demonstration I ever saw, and it was completely spontaneous, ignited by the finality with which Joe Louis had destroyed the theory of white superiority. The march lasted maybe five minutes, only as long as it took the entire throng to move slowly down the full length of the block. Then they turned the corner and went back into the alleys and, I guess, felt better than most of them had felt for a long time.

On Lombard Street enlightenment was hard to come by. When war began I followed the news as melodrama. Another encounter between the white hats (us) and the black hats (them). I was shocked by the speed with which the Nazis crushed Europe and occupied Paris and planted the swastika at the English Channel. That fall, carrying newspapers with gigantic headlines that told of the blitz on London, I marveled at the destruction of a civilization I'd thought eternal. Like many military thinkers, I guess, I'd expected are run of

Baker in his office at the New York Times

World War I and was surprised to find the script entirely new. Still, it never occurred to me that the Nazis could win. They were the bad guys.

I was flabbergasted when the Japanese attack at Pearl Harbor brought us into the war at the end of 1941. Though by then sixteen, I was still so innocent of the world around me that American involvement had seemed impossible. And Japan! Why in the world had Japan attacked us? 1 didn't know Japan had anything against us. Sitting by the small radio in the kitchen at Marydell Road that Sunday night, listening to the bulletins from Washington, I thought the Japanese attack was ridiculous. A tiny country like that, nothing more than a few specks on the map, a country whose products were synonymous with junk, a pipsqueak country on the far side of the earth - it was grotesque that such a country should take on mighty America. Settling their hash would be as easy as squashing an ant. „It'll take about two weeks to finish them off," I told my mother.

She was less confident. „I hope it's over before you're old enough to go," she said. I laughed. 1 was still two years shy of military age. In two years we would have forgotten that Japan ever existed. By the time I entered Hopkins in the summer of 1942 I knew better. Boys I'd known in high school were already in uniform. Others were registering for the draft. Responding to the speeded-up pace of wartime America, Hopkins was operating on a year-round schedule with no summer vacation. I attended classes there the day after graduating from high school. By my seventeenth birthday that August it was obvious the war would not end in the coming year and probably not in the year after that. My mother had been right to worry. Obviously I was going to have to go. I began to look forward to it with pleasurable excitement.

I had been in love with the romance of flying since first hearing as a small boy about Charles A. Lindbergh, the Lone Eagle, Lucky Lindy, who'd flown all the way to France by the seat of his pants. The pinups over my bed had been Captain Eddie Rickenbacker, Wrong-Way Corrigan, Roscoe Turner, Wiley Post, and Amelia Earhart. Enchanted by the glamour of flight, I cut out magazine pictures of the latest warplanes and pinned them up alongside Captain Eddie and Roscoe Turner. In my fantasies I flew over the trenches on the dawn patrol, white scarf streaming behind me in the wind as I adjusted my goggles and maneuvered the Fokker of Baron von Richthofen into my gun sights. Now the war offered a chance to make those dreams come true. The country needed flyers, thousands and thousands of them. While my mother, worried about my going to war, I worried too. It wasn't easy to qualify for flight training. I was afraid of being rejected and losing my shot at glory.

There wasn't much glory in college life. I still rode the trolley to school and carried lunch in a brown paper bag. Most of my friends did, too. The people I gravitated to were town boys, different from the tweedy fraternity-house crowd who wore saddle shoes and cared about lacrosse games and campus dances. We were a raffish bunch of overgrown streetwise kids sprawled in the cafeteria, chomping homemade sandwiches, arguing noisily about politics, literature, history, and economics, seething with intellectual contempt for the smooth fraternity crowd and filled with secret envy for the fraternity boys' social polish and devil-may-care ways with women.

Though I'd been an academic whiz in high school, these new companions quickly made me feel like a dolt. They were at ease in organic chemistry and integral calculus, understood the treason of Alcibiades, could argue the merits of logical positivism, debated whether Eugene O'Neill or George Bernard Shaw was the greater playwright, explained why Thomas Wolfe was a romantic sentimentalist who would never rank among the great writers. I struggled comically to catch up to them.

I took physics and calculus, thinking they would improve my chances of getting into flight training. After the first semester the calculus professor offered to erase my „Fail“ mark if I dropped the course. Discovering that this was a way out, I dropped physics, too, and concentrated on literature, history, and economics, known on campus as „bullshit courses“ because their examinations usually posed essay questions permitting a glib writer to bluff his way through. Sometimes I succeeded, sometimes not. The history professor returned my first test paper with the gentleman's C which Hopkins granted everyone not obviously an idiot and the scrawled, „You find it so easy to be smart that you don't bother to work very hard.“ How hard did he want me to work? I was laboring doggedly, yet after six weeks of college I was already six months behind most of my peers. I began looking toward military service as a vacation.

In the spring of 1943, in anticipation of my eighteenth birthday, I applied for enlistment in the Navy Air Corps. It seemed more glamorous than the Army Air Corps. Everybody was enlisting in the Army Air Corps, but the Navy Air Corps was different. It was more dangerous, I thought, therefore more glamorous. Flying off carriers - so hard, so dangerous. Flying over the vast watery desert of the Pacific. So easy to get lost out there, so hard to find a carrier to come back to in that trackless expanse. It took daring, the Navy Air Corps. It took the kind of man who had always wanted to test himself against the great von Richthofen.

I told my mother I was going to enlist. She hid her dread. The training would take fifteen months. She looked for the silver lining. „At least it'll keep you out of the war for fifteen months,“ she said. „But why don't you try to get into the Army Air Corps if you want to fly?“ “The Navy is better,“ I said. „You can't even swim, Buddy." This was true. I' d spent four years standing in the shallow end of the City College swimming pool without even learning to float. I was mortally afraid of deep water, but in my zeal for adventure I also wanted to challenge that terror. This had been another reason for choosing the Navy. "Does the Navy take people who can't swim?" my mother asked. They guarantee they'll teach you to swim," I said.

The examination was held in Washington and took a full day. I was so fearful of failing the physical that my blood pressure went up. The corpsman who took it said it was too high to suit the Navy. „Have you been eating a lot of potatoes?" he asked. I ate potatoes every night. Why? „Sometimes potatoes will drive your blood pressure up," he said. "I had potatoes for supper last night," I said. He pondered that. „Tell you what," he said. „Come back here again three days from now and we'll recheck your blood pressure. But lay off the potatoes until then." Three days later, with potatoes out of my bloodstream, I went back to Washington and was enlisted in the United States Navy under orders to report home and await my eighteenth birthday. My only other physical problem was weight. Stripped bare, I now stood six feet two inches tall and weighed 139 pounds. The Navy doctor noting these figures on the record looked up and said, „You're three pounds overweight." To weigh three pounds less I would have had to peel off my skin and get down to bare skeleton. But the doctor didn't look like a man making a joke. „I've always thought I was underweight," I said. He winked. „Young man," he said, „we're going to put thirtyfive pounds on you." They did, too, but it took a year.

Orders arrived a few days after my eighteenth birthday. I was to report to Washington with a toothbrush and a razor for transfer to a training base. Most of my friends at Hopkins had already left for war. Charlie Sussman, who'd helped me get there, was being drafted into the Army and was raring to go. „It's going to be a great educational experience," he told me, grinning happily the day we shook hands and said good-bye.

My mother had never been in an airplane - neither had I - and thought of airplanes as infernal machines which none but a fool or a wild man would step into. She knew that training promised to keep me away from enemy gunfire for fifteen months, but felt that flying an airplane was almost as dangerous as being shot at. Throughout my last weeks at home she did her best to keep a cheerful countenance, but I caught her several times looking at me gravely and hungrily, trying to press her memory indelibly with the image of someone she might never see again.

I left the house before dawn on an October morning. Our good-byes were said at the door. It was as it almost always was between us in moments of deep emotion. No tears, no clasping in each other's arms, all emotion thoroughly under control, everything correctly repressed to insure against messy outbursts. She looked up at me and with a quick, tight smile said, „Well, you'd better get going if you're going to catch that train," and I leaned down and kissed her briefly on the lips.

„Write me as soon as you get there," she said, and waved me off up Marydell Road to catch the streetcar. I knew she was worried, but didn't realize how badly, and didn't think about it for long. I was too exultant. Boarding the streetcar I had no sense of putting my life at risk. Not a bit. I felt an intoxicating sense of being free for the first time in my life. Adventure. Flight. Freedom. Now at last, all were going to be mine. By mid-morning I was in Washington and homesick, missing her so much that I telephoned home long-distance, an outrageous use of money in that time. She was so flustered at hearing my voice that she hung up in confusion before we exchanged more than ten words. Late that afternoon 1 wrote her from the train carrying us south.

„You hung up the telephone so soon I didn't get to tell you anything. The 6:30 train from Penn Station turned out to be a local and I was lucky to get to the Cadet Board on the stroke of 8. They kept us sitting around for two hours, then we ate at the expense of the Navy at a downtown restaurant. After that they whisked us to the Union Station in a truck that looked too much like the Black Maria. I called you from the station and wanted to tell you I'm headed for Pensacola, Fla., but you hung up too soon .... Please don't worry. Hold down the fort and keep things running .... After twelve hours of my adventure in freedom I was yearning for home.

For the next eighteen months, while old friends and schoolmates were discovering the face of death on battlefields from Bastogne to Okinawa, the Navy sent me on an extended tour of Dixie. After four months at Pensacola came three months at the University of South Carolina. I was in Miami living the good life at Coral Gables when Eisenhower sent the armies ashore on D-Day, and at preflight school at the University of Georgia when Patton was racing for the Rhine. I was at Memphis waiting to take off on a flight to Arkansas when a mechanic climbed onto the wing and shouted: „President Roosevelt is dead!"

Germany surrendered three weeks later and I was sent back to Pensacola. Because the Navv had overestimated the number of flyers it needed to fight Japan, flight training slowed to a crawl. The Navy had kept one of its promises - it had put thirty-five pounds on me - but its promise of glory remained unfulfilled. By the summer of 1945 we were flying out of Whiting Field. It was a broiling expanse of cleared land in the north Florida boondocks, one of those ugly, barren, temporary training bases that had been nailed together overnight. The South was strewn with them during World War II. A couple of runways and acres of stark wooden barracks surrounded by a perimeter of back-shadowed piney woods. A water tank on four steel legs. A flag hanging limp in sultry air. Pensacola was an hour away by slow bus. I made the trip to town and back several nights a week on account of Karen, an Indiana girl at the local nursing school. I was in love.

A big part of my Navy career by then had been spent in the struggle to get rid of my accursed virginity. This had been harder than learning to swim or learning to fly. The swimming had been surprisingly easy, thanks to the Navy's policy of dealing with fear by ignoring it. My fear of deep water left the Navy simply uninterested. On the first day in the pool an instructor with a voice like a bullhorn ordered fifty of us to climb a high board and jump in feet first. The board looked about two hundred feet high, though it may have been only twenty or twenty-five. A line was formed to mount the ladder and jump.

I drifted to the end of the line, then stepped out when the splashing started and introduced myself to the instructor. „I'm a nonswimmer," I said. „You want me to go to the shallow end of the pool?" At City College I'd spent four years in the shallow end of the pool. „This pool doesn't have a shallow end," the instructor said. „Well, what am I going to do?" "Get up on that platform and jump," he said.«

ATTORNEY ENDURES HEAVY VIETNAM WAR WOUNDING

by *Lewis B. Puller Jr.*

He was born on August 18, 1945 in Camp Lejeune, North Carolina, and died on May 11, 1994, by suicide in Mount Vernon, Virginia. Lewis Burwell Puller Jr. was the son of a Lt. General, the most decorated Marine in the history of the U.S. Marine Corps. He graduated high school from Christchurch School in Christchurch, Virginia, in 1963 and from the College of William and Mary in 1967.

Then he followed in his father's footsteps and became a Marine officer through its Officer Candidate Program and was subsequently commissioned as a second lieutenant. Puller received orders to South Vietnam in July, 1968, where he served as an Infantry Platoon Commander for three months. On October 11, 1968, his rifle jammed during an engagement with North Vietnamese troops.

Puller was terribly wounded when he tripped a booby-trapped howitzer round, losing his right leg at the hip, his left leg above the knee, his left hand and most of his fingers on his right hand in the explosion. The shell riddled his body with shrapnel, and he lingered near death for days with his weight dropping to 55 pounds, but he survived.

Puller later recalled the first time his father saw him in the hospital. He described how his father broke down weeping and that hurt him more than any of his physical injuries. Those who knew Puller say that it was primarily because of his iron will and his stubborn refusal to die that he survived. He was medically discharged from the Marine Corps. He was awarded the Silver Star Medal, and several others.

For years after he returned to a reasonably sound physical condition, the emotional ground underneath him remained shaky, though he earned a law degree, had two children with the woman he had married before going to Vietnam, and raised a family. He was admitted to the Virginia Bar in 1974 and began working as a lawyer for the Veteran's Administration and on Gerald Ford's clemency board.

Puller mounted a campaign for Congress in 1978 as a Democrat in Virginia but lost in a landslide with only 28% of the vote against incumbent Republican Congressman Paul Trible. Throughout the years, he battled periods of despondency and drank heavily until 1981, when he underwent treatment for alcoholism. Despite that treatment, Puller continued to suffer severe depression and occasional bouts of alcoholism.

Accordings to friends and associates, Puller spent the last months of his life in turmoil. He left his job as lawyer at the Pentagon to accept a teaching position at George Mason University. In the days leading up to his death, Puller fought a losing battle with the alcoholism that he had kept at bay for thirteen years, and struggled with a more recent addiction, to painkillers initially prescribed to dull continuing pain from his wounds.

Puller died from a self-inflicted gunshot on May 11, 1994. He and his wife Linda had separated in 1991. Puller's name is not listed on the Vietnam Veterans Memorial in Washington, which is reserved for those who died or who are listed as missing in action. However his name is listed on the nearby In Memory Memorial Plaque, which represents those veterans, like Puller, who „died after their service in the Vietnam war, but as a direct result of that service and whose names are not otherwise eligible for placement on the memorial wall." On Veterans Day 2010, „The Lewis B. Puller Jr. Benefits Clinic „at the College of William & Mary Law School was named in honor of Puller.

In addition, there is something else that will keep Puller's name in the collective memory of the American public - his award-winning autobiography „Fortunate Son - The Healing of a Vietnam Vet", published in 1991. „An extraordinary story of survival and love," the *Washington Post* had written when Puller's book came out. When the volume came to the attention of the Pulitzer Prize jurors, they stated in their report of December 29, 1991: „Lewis 'Chesty' Puller was a World War II and Korean War hero.... So it was not surprising that his son joined the Marines ..., went to Vietnam in 1968 and at his request was assigned to lead field troops ... But before his tour ended, he stepped on a land mine while fleeing the enemy. He lost his left leg above the knee, the right leg at his torso, most of his left hand and the thumb and finger of his right hand ... He spent most of the next two years in hospitals. All of this is told in gripping detail ... At the risk of a cliché, 'Fortunate Son' is a beautifully written testament to the strength of the human spirit" and was decorated with the 1992 Pulitzer Prize for Biography/Autobiography. Following now are some details from his work:

»In late January 1968, several weeks after my Basic School class had begun, the Vietnam War suddenly escalated as North Vietnamese regulars and Vietcong guerrillas began a coordinated assault on hamlets and cities throughout the provinces of South Vietnam. Up to that time the war had been characterized by more or less sporadic bursts of activity with a steady but slowly mounting escalation throughout all South Vietnam. This was different. The North Vietnamese offensive shook the foundations of Middle America, and outside the theater of war the reverberations were probably felt nowhere more strongly than at Basic School. The Tet offensive had begun, and as the ancient citadel of the city of Hue fell into Communist hands with an attendant massacre of thousands of innocent citizens, the magnitude of what we had signed on for registered ominously with my classmates.

After the Tet offensive, the media stepped up its reporting of the rising toll of weekly casualties, and the networks provided graphic footage of the firefights they were able to film; but the war, at least in my mind, was still a television war, the horror of which I was as yet unable to comprehend fully. Despite the fact that by now twenty thousand Americans had given their lives in pursuit of a foreign policy for which much of America was rapidly losing its stomach and for which there was no apparent end in sight, I still knew only one person who had been killed in the war. In addition, the OCS and Basic School classes were so self-contained that contact between marines in different classes was infrequent. As a consequence, we were spared the psychic trauma of personally knowing the dead lieutenants who had in many cases occupied our own physical space only weeks or months earlier.

Nevertheless, Tet gave the Vietnam War an immediacy that had theretofore been lacking, and my fellow marines responded to it in different ways. Some saw the stepped-up pace of the war as a challenge and in their youthful exuberance welcomed the chance to prove themselves worthy of the uniform. Others surveyed the situation with an eye toward the number of junior officers being killed or wounded each week and began scrambling about for military occupational specialties that offered insulation from combat. I began to notice, for the first time, the graffiti that had been carved into classroom desktops by anonymous students from earlier classes. „Why die? Go Supply,“ one admonished, while, another advised, „Motor T and out in three.“ A third put it simply: „What the fuck, drive a truck.“ The opposite viewpoint also was made by some gung ho student, who wrote for the more bloodthirsty of us, „War is our businessand business is good.“

Somewhat ironically, as our concern over the military occupational specialties into which we would be channeled grew with the rising casualty toll, our options became more and more limited until, for some classes at the height of the war, they were nonexistent. The Marine Corps had a duty to field combat officers, and if that duty required that every officer in a Basic School class become an 0-3 infantry officer, that is precisely what would happen.

I had joined the Marine Corps with the intention of becoming a combat platoon leader, and nothing that happened during Tet in any way altered my determination. I could not have faced my father, or lived with myself, if I had chosen an easier way. For me, therefore, there was no moral dilemma or soul-searching agony when it came time to list my preferences. My choice of specialization was infantry, my choice of duty was Vietnam, and the Marine Corps was more than happy to oblige me. Shortly before our selections were made, Basic School hosted a career-night cocktail party, during which officers from the various career branches were available to discuss our options over meatballs and shrimp cocktails. The infantry officer adviser told us with a perfectly straight face that since we had to spend a tour in Vietnam anyway, we might as well find out what the war was really about by selecting his specialty and seeing a little action. The logic of his position seemed irrefutable to me, and I happily reported to my wife Toddy that I had found a man who had been through it and still shared my views. She listened politely but made no comment.

As Basic School progressed and our technical proficiency grew, I found that there were aspects of the training that I actually enjoyed. Each of us fired every weapon in the Marine Corps arsenal from the smallest handgun to the largest artillery piece, and we assembled and disassembled most of them until their cycles of functioning became second nature. After our assignments had been made, virtually all the leadership billets for the various field problems were meted out to those of us who had been selected as infantry and artillery officers, and while the rest of the class had an easier go of it, there was considerable satisfaction in leading a patrol to a successful conclusion or coordnating a company-size helicopter assault.

Looking back, I can see now that the Marine Corps instilled in us a pride and professionalism more closely akin to a calling than an occupation and that many of us actually looked forward to our inevitable baptism by fire. There were, of course, times when we questioned our ability to master the sheer volume of information we were expected to absorb or when bone-numbing weariness would drive us to despondency, but it seemed that at each critical juncture, when the class was on the verge of mutiny, the Marine Corps would back off or offer some reward designed to boost our spirits. When all else failed and I was overcome by the feeling that the Marine Corps dictated all my choices in life, there were always Toddy's waiting arms to provide the solace that nothing else could come close to approximating.

Sometime later, when I had come to Vietnam, one day I concentrated as best I could on making certain that the two squads to my left were on line and in position to hook up with the platoon adjacent to them, but in the confusion and noise from the other helicopter around us, control was almost impossible. The skipper's position was to be atop the high bluff to our right, overlooking Viem Dong, where we had camped the night before Barton died. After I had gotten my men on line, my next assignment was to connect with his location. Watson followed closely in my tracks with the radio, but the two nearest men to us were at least twenty meters away on either side and for all intents and purposes out of hearing range. As we maneuvered, I scanned the area to my immediate front, which I had been neglecting in my effort to maintain platoon integrity.

Suddenly I saw a squad of green-uniformed North Vietnamese soldiers begin running out of the village and in my direction. They had apparently panicked when the helicopters began landing and were now probing for a way out of the noose we were drawing around them. As they advanced toward me, I was unable to get the attention of the marines near me, and it dawned on me, to my horror, that I was the only obstacle between them and freedom. I raised my rifle to my shoulder and attempted to draw a bead on the lead soldier; but my first bullet was off the mark, and when I pulled the trigger the second time, my rifle jammed. By now the North Vietnamese soldiers had spotted me, and several of them fired wildly in my direction until they abruptly altered their advance and veered off to my left. Standing alone with a malfunctioning weapon and seven enemy soldiers bearing down on me, I was at once seized by a fear that was palpable and allencompassing. My throat became as dry as parchment, and beads of perspiration popped out on my forehead before coursing down my face. I turned abruptly, with Watson in tow, and ran as fast as I could toward the safety of the bluffs above Viem Dong, where the company headquarters party was to be located.

A narrow trail led up the hill to the headquarters group, and as I approached, it never occurred to me that the thirty meters between my course and the commanders' position had not been secured. I knew only that the firepower advantage of the NVA squad I had just encountered would be neutralized if I could reach the men milling at the crest of the hill. With only a few meters left to cover in my flight, a thunderous boom suddenly rent the air, and I was propelled upward with the acrid smell of cordite in my nostrils.

When I landed a few feet up the trail from the booby-trapped howitzer round that I had detonated, I felt as if I had been airborne forever. Colors and sound became muted, and although there was now a beehive of activity around me, all movement seemed to me to be in slow motion. I thought initially that the loss of my glasses in the explosion accounted for my blurred vision, and I had no idea that the pink mist that engulfed me had been caused by the vaporization of most of my right and left legs. As shock began to numb my body, I could see through a haze of pain that my right thumb and little finger were missing, as was most of my left hand, and I could smell the charred flesh, which extended from my right wrist upward to the elbow. I knew that I had finished serving my time in the hell of Vietnam.

As I drifted in and out of consciousness, I felt elated at the prospect of relinquishing my command and going home to my wife and unborn child. I did not understand why Watson, who was the first man to reach me, kept screaming, „Pray, Lieutenant, for God's sake, pray." I could not see the jagged shards of flesh and bone that had only moments before been my legs, and I did not realize until much later that I had been forever set apart from the rest of humanity.

For the next hour a frantic group of marines awaited the medevac chopper that was my only hope of deliverance and worked at keeping me alive. Doc Ellis knelt beside my broken body and with his thumbs kept my life from pouring out into the sand, until a tourniquet fashioned from a web belt was tied around my left stump and a towel was pressed tightly into the hole where my right thigh had joined my torso. My watch and rifle were destroyed by the blast, and my flak jacket was in tatters; but I did manage to turn my undamaged maps and command, of the platoon over the Corporal Turner during one of my lucid intervals. I also gave explicit orders to all the marines and corpsmen hovering around me that my wife was not to be told of my injuries until after the baby was born. There was, of course, no possibility of compliance with my command, but the marines ministering to me assured me that my wishes would be honored.

Because we were on a company-size operation, there were six corpsmen in the immediate area around Viem Dong, and each of them carried a supply of blood expanders, which were designed to stabilize blood pressure until whole blood could be administered. As word spread of my injuries, each of the company's corpsmen passed his expanders to Doc Ellis, who used up the last of them while my men slapped at my face, tried to get me to drink water, and held cigarettes to my lips in an attempt to keep me awake. When the chopper finally arrived, I was placed on a stretcher and gently carried to its entrance, where a helmeted crew chief and medevac surgeon helped me aboard. Someone had located my left boot which still contained its bloody foot and that, too, was placed on the stretcher with me.

As the chopper began its race toward the triage of the naval support hospital in Da Nang, I was only moments from death, but I remember thinking clearly before losing consciousness that I was going to make it. I never again saw the third platoon of Golf Company, a remarkable group of young men with whom I had had the most intense male relationships of my life, and I felt guilty for years that I had abandoned them before our work was finished. I was to feel even worse that I was glad to be leaving them and that, in my mind, I had spent my last healthy moments in Vietnam running from the enemy. I came to feel that I had failed to prove myself worthy of my father's name, and broken in spirit as well as body, I was going to have to run a different gauntlet.

In the naval support hospital triage in Da Nang, located just down the road from the Seabee compound where I had feasted on frozen strawberries and ice cream only a few days earlier, the remainder of my clothes were cut away, massive transfusions were started directly into my jugular vein, and my severed foot was discarded. On arrival, my blood pressure had failed to register, but once it was restored and I was stabilized, I was wheeled into the operating room, where my left stump was debrided and left open, and the femoral artery, which was all that remained of my right leg, was clamped shut. The procedure was fairly simple because there was so little left to work with. I remember thinking, before I succumbed to the anesthesia, how clean and shiny the tiles in the operating room appeared, how cold the room was, and how worried the eyes all seemed above the green masks of the doctors and nurses who labored over me.

When I regained consciousness, I was in a clean bed with white sheets. An assortment of tubes carried liquids to and from my body, and when I reached up to remove the annoying one affixed to my nose, I found that I could not do so because both my hands were wrapped in bandages the size of boxing gloves. I understood the reason for my bandaged hands because I had seen my right hand with its missing thumb and little finger earlier, and I also knew that my left hand now retained only a thumb and half a forefinger. The word prehensile no longer applied to me. I did not yet know or knew only vaguely that I had lost my right leg at the torso and that only a six-inch stump remained of my left thigh. In addition to the damage to my extremities, I had lost massive portions of both buttocks, my scrotum had been split, I had sustained a dislocated shoulder and a ruptured eardrum, and smaller wounds from shell fragments peppered the remainder of my body. Only my face had been spared. It remarkably contained only one small blue line across my nose from a powder burn.

Back in the United States, where the attention of most Americans was occupied with the outcome of the World Series, the assistant commandant of the Marine Corps, General Lewis Walt, who had been one of my father's company commanders in World War II, called Saluda, Virginia, with the news of my wounding and followed up his conversation by coming down from Washington. A young marine officer was dispatched to Fort Belvoir to break the news to my wife. There was no one home at the Todd quarters when he arrived, but he alarmed neighbors, who alerted my father-in-law as soon as he returned home. He called and through official army channels was able to ascertain roughly what had happened.

Communications from both the army and Marine Corps were badly garbled in the first days after my wounding. My wife was at first told that I had lost only one leg and later that I had lost one leg below the knee and one above the knee. When she got the first message, she went straight to her father's pantry, poured a double shot of bourbon, and tossed it off in one motion. Already furious that she had been the last to receive the news, she spent a sleepless night after Walter Cronkite reported my injury on the „CBS Evening News.“ The next morning she traveled to Saluda to be with my parents. By the time she arrived, they had received a mate accurate assessment of my injuries, and my wife was soon to discover that if I survived, as was doubtful, I would do so with „a bilateral above the knee/hip disarticulation.“ Numb with fear and exhaustion and seven months' pregnant, she took solace from the only male Puller who was still capable of standing on his own two feet.

Sometime later that week, before I was medevacked to Yokosuka, Japan, in the first stage of a painful journey home, a marine general and old family friend, Tommy Tompkins, made a special visit to my bedside to pin a Silver Star and Purple Heart on the pillow cradling my head. For the photo opportunity that accompanied the presentation and reading of my citation, the tube was removed from my nose and the photographer was careful to frame his shots of me from the waist up. Even in my delirious state I did not feel that I had earned a Silver Star, and I expressed my reservations repeatedly to Colonel Tom McKenney, another old family friend who spent most of those first few critical days in Da Nang at my bedside. There was no such reservation about my eligibility for the Purple Heart, and while my first one may have been cheap, the second award could hardly have been paid for more dearly.

While I was still in Da Nang, a parade of young officers who had been my peers in Basic School made the obligatory trek to the hospital to see me, and the concern on each of their faces so alarmed me that I finally requested and was given a bottle of whiskey to help them through the experience. For my part, I was becoming dependent on massive injections of morphine to quell the phantom pain in my missing limbs and postpone the inevitable acceptance of my loss, so my visitors were forced to drink alone. Mike Downs, my future brother-in-law, who was on his way back to the States, rerouted his homeward path to spend a few minutes with me, and he told me years later that he had resigned himself to never seeing me alive again after he had completed his visit.

Lewis B. Puller Jr. in wheelchair talking to President James Earl Carter.

For the most part the medical personnel who attended me while I was in Da Nang, as well as those who treated me in Yokosuka, were dedicated professionals who worked tirelessly every day in a world of blood and gore that would have broken men and women of lesser stature. There were also Red Cross volunteers who spent hours at my side as I began, through a narcotic netherworld, to assimilate the magnitude of my physical loss. Several of these „doughnut dollies," as they were affectionately labeled, helped me with letters to my wife that I do not remember dictating but that she saved, along with all the other letters I had written as a virile young platoon leader, the youthful optimism of a newlywed just separated from his bride contrasting with the stark terror of a shattered war casualty who had as yet no frame of reference for life without legs.

There was one exception to the caring individuals who nurtured me in those first days as I clung precariously to life, whom I was told about by Tom McKenney a year after I had returned to the States. A young doctor who objected generally to American involvement in the war, and specifically to the fact that he had been drafted, entered the triage shortly after I was carried in and began taking pictures of me. It was assumed that he was documenting the effects of trauma on newly wounded combatants, so no effort was made to stop him until later in the week, when he announced to some of his colleagues that he had gotten some great pictures of the Puller kid that he was going to use in antiwar lectures after rotating. His pictures were confiscated immediately. I have often wondered if he was ever able to separate his views on the war from his Hippocratic obligation toward the warriors who were fighting it.

My journey home was begun against the best medical advice, but because my father, who was himself in poor health, had begun talking about flying to Japan to meet me, a decision was made to send me home early. In Yokosuka I developed a stress ulcer as a result of the shock of being wounded, and two-thirds of my stomach had to be removed. The pain was excruciating, and I was not expected to survive the operation, which exposed a second ulcer once the surgeons got inside. In my debilitated state the second ulcer was considered inoperable, but remarkably it stopped bleeding on its own, and I was again stabilized. When we got under way again, I was assigned a nurse whose sole duty was to be available in case the exposed femoral artery in my right side ruptured.

A day later my plane set down at Andrews Air Force Base outside Washington, D.C. I had, in keeping with the parable of the Spartan soldier, returned on my shield. My temperature was 105 degrees, and I had not had a dressing change since leaving Japan. I was transferred to the base hospital near the terminal, where my wife and family had gathered and had begun steeling themselves to meet me. There were no brass bands to greet me, no rousing renditions of „Stars and Stripes Forever," and no politicians to offer their support for a job well done. I was home, though, back in the United States after a splendid overseas tour that had not quite reached its third month. And I had avoided, for whatever reason, the fate of those casualties who were returning home in aluminum boxes.

By the time I had been made as presentable as possible it was late in the evening, and a nervous hospital commander, justifiably concerned that I might die on his watch, reluctantly agreed to let me receive visitors. In my precarious state it was decided that I should see only one family member at a time, and my father was the first to enter the room. He stood quietly at the foot of my bed for a few moments, surveyed the wreckage of his only son, and then, unable to maintain his stoic demeanor, began weeping silently. He moved to my side and grasped my shoulder as if that simple act of communion would stay the convulsions that now racked his stooped frame, and I in my helpless state was unable to reach out or otherwise console him. It was only the second time in my life that I had seen my father cry, and as the nurse led him from my room, I felt an aching in my heart that all but eclipsed the physical pain from my wounds.

After I had regained my own composure, my wife was allowed to see me, but having spent my emotional load with my father, my meeting with Toddy was, at least for me, less wrenching. When she bent to kiss me, the warmth of her lips against mine eased my grief, and I was mercifully unable to read the anguish and uncertainty that she hid behind a mask of grim determination. With the ice broken by the kiss and my inhibitions diminished by morphine, I asked her to raise her skirt so that I could assess the state of her pregnancy, and when she complied, we smiled at each other conspiratorially over our handiwork. Years later she told me that she had prepared herself as best she could for the sight of my mangled body, but that the nose tube that pumped secretions from my ulcerous stomach had almost unnerved her.

After I had spent a few minutes alone with my wife, my nurse and doctor decided to permit the rest of my visitors to enter as a group. I was exhausted from the long flight, the unremitting pain that was by now a constant companion, and the effort required to talk to my wife and father, so the group's visit was a quick one. I was also receiving injections of morphine every three or four hours, and my memory of the remainder of the visit as well as of the events of the next several weeks remains clouded. My mother could not bear to look at me and as a defense mechanism tried to steer the conversation to the Detroit Tigers' victory in the World Series but stopped when I made it clear that I was not interested in baseball. I did, however, manage to exact a promise from her that she would give me my grandmother's diamond engagement ring to add to the solitary band I had given Toddy when we married, and although Toddy's embarrassment was acute when I broached the subject, I must have known that for once in my life I had the upper hand in bargaining with my mother. After our reunion was concluded and my family and in-laws retired to try to assimilate the magnitude of my injuries, I was given another injection of morphine and slept fitfully until another onslaught of pain cut through the narcotic.

I had been scheduled for transport to the Philadelphia Naval Hospital by ambulance later that morning, a trip of several hours' duration, but my pain was so intense and my energy so depleted that I recoiled at the thought of the long ride and begged for a helicopter. My request was agreed to by the base commander, who wanted nothing so much as to send me on my way and relinquish the responsibility for a level of medical care that his hospital was ill equipped to provide, and by noon I was flying north toward Philadelphia with my wife and family following by car. On arrival at the Philadelphia Naval Hospital I was taken immediately to the operating room and given general anesthesia while my wounds were debrided and my dressings changed. When Toddy arrived, the procedure had been completed and I had been transferred to the hospital intensive care unit, which was my home for the next month. Because of my father's reputation, the hospital commmander made a point of welcoming my family to his facility, but he pulled no punches in conveying his assessment of my condition. According to him, my chances of survival through the critical next ten days were about 50 percent unless I contracted pneumonia, in which case I would almost certainly die. The good news was that if I survived, his surgeons would do an excellent job of putting me back together again.

In the fall of 1968 and throughout my hospitalization in Philadelphia, the government had given no thought to temporary lodging for the families of wounded servicemen, and my family checked into a motel near the hospital for that week, in what was the first of many agonizing and expensive stays. They were so concerned initially about my condition that the expense of the accommodations was simply regarded as a nuisance; but as time wore on, the economics of the situation became intolerable, and they began to double up on rooms or plan day visits from Washington. Later in my hospitalization, when I had recovered sufficiently to take an apartment near the hospital grounds, my wife remembered her early problems with costly motels and invited the wives of severely wounded patients to sleep over with us. It was bad enough to be shot to pieces in the service of your country; but it was outrageous then to be expected to sustain heavy outside costs associated with recovery, and Toddy and I were doubly sympathetic to the plight of the enlisted wives, for whom the extra costs were often an unbearable hardship.

By the end of my first two weeks in the intensive care unit, the odds favoring my survival had improved considerably, although to the unpracticed eye the reverse must have seemed the case. Several times a day my bandages had to be changed, and without morphine the ordeal was so painful that I was quickly reduced to the level of a snarling animal. For a period of time I became convinced that the staff as well as my family had entered into a conspiracy designed solely to increase my torment, and I lashed out at all who dared enter my room. Because I threw up so much of what the corpsmen tried to spoon into my mouth, I simply began to refuse food, and when my weight dropped to less than sixty pounds, orders were issued that I be fed through the tube in my nose. I was also completely immobile and had to be rotated from my back to my stomach and vice versa every three hours in a special bed that employed two thin mattresses on a circular track and resembled a sandwich board more than a resting place. Despite the constant turning, I developed bed sores from the pressure and the perspiration with which I was constantly soaked, and by the time I had completed my stay in intensive care I had open sores the size of quarters along my backbone and pelvis.

Toward the end of my stay in intensive care I was moved from the windowless room near the nurses' station to a more remote but more cheery end room that my corpsmen referred to as the solarium. I was its sole occupant, so remained as isolated in my new setting as I had been in the old room. The few visitors who came to see me in both rooms were required to don white dressing gowns to maintain a sterile environment, an unintended result of which was that for weeks I lived in a world without color. My principal contact with the outside world was through a transistor radio that played pop music from the nightstand beside my bed, and I still get goose bumps when I hear „Abraham, Martin and John“ and „Little Green Apples,“ songs that the disc jockeys in Philadelphia played over and over in the fall of 1968. Once I was in my new surroundings, a decision was made to wean me from the morphine, on which I had become psychologically, if not physically, dependent, and I begged and then screamed for my shots as the time between injections was lengthened and the dosage was decreased. Without the morphine to dull my senses, I had to face both physical pain and the reality of my loss, and for several days I was nothing more than a bundle of jagged nerve endings.

During the first month of my hospitalization I was confined to the electrically powered bed that rotated me as if on a roasting spit, and the combination of my injuries and lack of mobility left me as weak as a newborn baby. I deteriorated to the point where I could not lift my head from the pillow, and I developed a dangerous-looking bald spot on the back of my head where a bed sore was beginning to form. By the time the boxing glove-size bandages on my hands were removed at the end of the month, the muscles in my arms had atrophied to the extent that my elbows appeared huge in comparison with my forearms and biceps.

There were signs of progress, however, and a major improvement was the new freedom made possible by getting back what was left of my hands. Without the bandages I was at least able to scratch a few itches and mop my own face, although I was appalled at how badly my hands had been mangled. At first my fingers were so stiff and swollen that I could not manage a cigarette on my own, and an exasperated McMonagle, tired of catering to my need for nicotine, finally bought me an ivory roach clip that allowed me to smoke on my own but made the doctors and nurses suspect that we were smoking marijuana on the sly. He, of course, delighted in their suspicions and even increased them by introducing incense into my room to string them along further. The tube was also removed from my nose sometime during the month. That greatly cheered up Toddy and, more important, ended the staffs capacity to pump gruel into my stomach when I refused to eat.

In early November I was taken off the critical list and moved to the twelfth floor of the hospital. SOQ 12, sick officers' quarters 12, was the area of the hospital set aside for officers undergoing long-term hospitalization. The majority of its patients had been seriously wounded in Vietnam and would eventually be boarded out of the service, but there were also a few terminally ill cancer patients and the usual assortment of malingerers and misfits looking for a place to hide. McMonagle wheeled me up to my new quarters in the electric bed on which I had lain for the previous month, and it was a close call as to whether the intensive care unit personnel were more relieved to be done with the two of us or we with them. In any event, our reputation for obstreperousness had preceded us, and the head nurse, a Commander Zatzerine, met us at the entrance to her domain and made it clear that she allowed no shenanigans on her ward.

On the Monday following my transfer to SOQ 12, many of the patients who were far enough along in the recuperation process to get weekend passes returned from liberty, including my roommate, Lieutenant Paul Barents, a double above-the-knee amputee. Lieutenant Barents had been raked across the knees by automatic-weapons fire while setting up an ambush in Vietnam eighteen months earlier, and his wounds were so severe that both legs had been amputated surgically. He had made remarkable progress, however, at adjusting to the wooden prostheses with which the hospital's limb and brace shop had outfitted him, and when he walked into our room that first Monday morning with only a cane to steady his balance, I was amazed to discover that a man with so little remaining of his legs could ambulate. He was a tall, wiry man with a neatly trimmed mustache and a deep, booming voice, and when I ignored the cheerful salutation with which he greeted me, he quickly realized that I was not yet ready to talk and he did not press the issue. Instead he took a seat, slipped his stumps out of the sockets of his prostheses, and transferred himself into the wheelchair beside his bed. He then placed his legs in a corner of the room.

Because I was unable to turn myself over in bed or otherwise move around, I was particularly impressed by Paul's mobility and skill with his wheelchair. He could transfer from bed to chair in the blink of an eye, and when in the chair, he could pop wheelies, do 360-degree turns on a dime, and maneuver as if the chair were a natural extension of his body. He had also developed an extra measure of upper-body strength by using his arms to do the work of his legs, and throughout the short time that we roomed together, he was constantly challenging all comers to arm-wrestling contests and more often than not beating them. That evening Kathy, Paul's wife, dropped in to visit him, and as they discussed the operation he was to have later that week and their future plans, I was shocked to discover that they appeared to have a fairly normal relationship. Kathy was a slim, vivacious woman with delicate features and a ready smile, and as they talked, I eavesdropped and became aware that she was as dependent on Paul as he was on her.

As I watched Paul sleeping peacefully in the bed across the room from me, I wished desperately for one night's rest free of pain or discomfort. It then occurred to me that Paul must have been through the same hell I was now experiencing, and he had survived the ordeal. He had also redefined his relationship with his wife in a positive manner and in a few weeks would be putting the Marine Corps and the Vietnam War behind him and looking for a job. By the time blessed sleep finally came, I had begrudgingly come to realize that I must undergo a drastic change in attitude to avoid spending the rest of my days as a miserable, lonely freak. As Paul's roommate I was privy to many of the conversations he had with the other patients on SOQ 12, many of whom stopped by that first week to wish him luck on his operation. Their conversations turned to Dr. Nicholas Cabot, the orthopedic surgeon who would be doing Paul's stump revision and who would later help to piece me back together.

I first met the notorious Dr. Cabot the day before Paul's operation, when he dropped by to explain the procedure to Paul and to obtain his signature on the surgery consent form. The explanation was a formality since Paul had undergone numerous stump revisions in the course of his hospitalization, but after he had signed the form and returned it and the clipboard that held it in place, Dr. Cabot came over to my side of the room. He began examining my left stump, which lay open and exposed as if freshly hacked by a meat cleaver, and only after he had completed his task did he bother to introduce himself. Still trembling from the kneading that he had given my stump, I extended my mangled right hand to acknowledge his belated introduction, but he ignored the gesture and began explaining the course of treatment he had in mind. His principal concern was the closure of my stump, and toward that end he informed me that the staff would be around later that day to place what remained of the limb in traction in preparation for the surgery that he planned to undertake within the next several weeks.

While Paul was recovering from his operation, the corpsmen first tried to get me into a wheelchair. The model they selected was an enormous wooden structure with a wicker back and seat, which looked like a leftover from the Civil War. It was obviously designed more for comfort than mobility, but despite many readjustments of rubber rings and pillows to ease my pain, I could at first bear sitting in it for only a few minutes at a time. In mid-November I still had open bed sores along my spine and barely healed skin grafts across my buttocks, and I was so weak from my wounds and inactivity that the first few times I was placed in the wheelchair my head flopped over onto my shoulder as if it were connected to my torso by a Slinky. At less than sixty pounds I was so emaciated that I did not recognize myself the first time I was wheeled by a mirror, and I automatically reached for my face to make certain that it was mine. It was also difficult to move me with the weight attached to my stump.

On the Friday before Thanksgiving my father-in-law called from Fort Belvoir with the news that Toddy had given birth to our son, Lewis Burwell Puller III, whom she was already affectionately calling Lewpy. She had gone into labor the previous night, sending the Todd household into an uproar because the baby was not due until late December; but the delivery was a textbook performance, and Colonel Todd informed me proudly that mother and son were doing fine. By the time I had absorbed the news that I was a father and gotten back to my wife by phone later in the day, my flagging spirits had taken a sharp turn upward and I had completely abandoned the idea of leaving her. We were a real family, and despite the rocky start, I could tell, as I talked to my wife, that this child was God-sent and destined to solidify our marriage. I also learned in the course of the conversation that Toddy had lost fifteen pounds during what had otherwise been a routine pregnancy.

Before I got the opportunity to see my son for the first time, Thanksgiving came and went. Paul had recovered enough for outpatient status, and alone and blue I spent the holiday in the doldrums. Ten days later, on the weekend before Dr. Cabot had scheduled my surgery, Toddy and her parents made the trip up from Fort Belvoir to let me meet our son, and the hospital's commanding officer made a room available to us adjacent to his office on the first floor. I was too frail to take him in my arms, but Toddy proudly pointed out the features that she considered especially good, and I instinctively knew that I had real competition for the first time since we had begun dating. While we chatted, she nursed him, and although I was not particularly impressed by his scrawny condition, I had never seen my wife look more radiant. As the baby suckled, I felt a possessiveness toward both of them that was unlike anything I had ever felt prior to Lewis's arrival. I also felt a stirring in my loins as I watched my wife and much to my amazement realized that I was aroused and as much in need of Toddy as the baby at her breast.

Dr. Cabot closed my stump the following Wednesday in a lengthy operation that had life-threatening and unexpected consequences. The procedure seemed to go smoothly enough as he rounded off the femur, reshaped the exposed muscle and tissue, and closed the wound with a lattice of sutures that resembled the laces on a football. Unfortunately the stump ruptured later in the recovery room while I was still under the anesthesia, and I was rushed back to the operating room and stabilized with a dozen units of blood while Cabot and his team worked frantically to undo the damage. When I finally awoke two days later back in the intensive care unit, I was given Demerol intravenously to counter the excruciating pain in my stump, and Dr. Cabot actually performed the procedure himself. Once I had recovered from the effects of surgery and was released from traction, my world began to expand.

Paul's final operation was also a success, and shortly before he left the hospital for the last time, I was transferred from my electric bed to a regular hospital bed. With considerable effort and Paul's encouragement I managed to turn myself over in bed for the first time since being wounded, and I grinned proudly at my achievement while Paul centered me on the mattress. From that day forward I was able to sleep more or less regularly, and my newly found ability to turn over in bed began the healing of my bed sores. On the day that Paul was scheduled to check out of the hospital, I was wheeled back to my room from a postoperative evaluation and pushed over to my bunk, where I waited for the corpsmen to help me back into bed. To my surprise, Paul dismissed them and announced that he had a parting gift for me. He then wheeled to the foot of the bed, hoisted himself onto the mattress, and grabbed me by my pajama top. "It is time, Lew," he said, „for you to learn to do this on your own." As I got his drift, I pushed downward on the armrests of the chair while he pulled me up by my armpits.

After I learned to get in and out of bed on my own, it quickly became obvious that I needed to learn how to push myself in the wheelchair. When Cabot was told that I could transfer from bed to chair without help, he instructed the SOQ 12 staff to stop helping me around the ward, and I sulked in my room for several days rather than venture out on my own. I also complained to the nurses and corpsmen that there was no way I could navigate the bulky wooden chair I had originally been provided. Rather than argue the point, they replaced the ancient model with a standard folding chair and continued to ignore my calls for help. When I finally decided to strike out on my own, it took me fifteen minutes to propel myself the length of the hall and back.

On the morning I was first taken to physical therapy, I was apprehensive yet excited to be beginning a new phase of my hospitalization. PT and OT were located in a remote part of the hospital a considerable distance from SOQ 12, and I was pushed to the unit by one of the ward corpsmen, who returned for me later in the morning. Eventually I became strong enough to wheel the entire distance on my own, but for the first few weeks the corpsman gave me a push, or another more healthy mobile patient detailed to patient escort duty assisted me.

Occupational therapy was far less demanding for me because compared with most of the upper-extremity amputees, the damage to my hands was minor. On my left hand I still had the thumb and half a forefinger, and on my right hand, though missing most of the thumb and little finger, I still had the middle digits. Combined, they amounted to almost a whole hand, and what I could not do with one hand, I could sometimes accomplish when I put them together. The OT unit was located in a smaller room adjacent to physical therapy and, like PT, was directed by a commissioned officer who was assisted by a staff largely comprised of enlisted personnel. In the winter of 1968 there were far fewer patients on the OT service than on PT because of the enemy's use of booby traps and land mines, triggered by men walking over them. The nature of the therapy was different in OT since arms and hands perform much more delicate and complicated functions than legs and feet.

After a few days of double sessions of therapy, I began to feel as if I were on a never-ending carousel. If I was not doing push-ups for Shaughnessey or putting together jigsaw puzzles in OT, I was being shuffled back and forth between the two units or waiting for a pusher from patient escort. It was probably good that I was almost too busy to have time to think, but I resented being so completely under the control of a network of doctors and nurses to whom I often felt I was nothing but another case study. When Cabot put me on a beer ration to try to increase my weight, I drank several cans a night and topped them off with prescribed sleeping pills. My resulting incoherence so alarmed the staff that the sleeping pills were discontinued; but I continued to drink the beer, and by Christmas I had added 5 pounds to my 60-pound frame. I had weighed almost 160 pounds when I entered the Marine Corps, and although I never came close to weighing that again, I still needed to gain another 40 pounds.

The week between Christmas and New Year's seemed interminable, and because so many of the staff and patients were on leave, the hospital was half empty. I worked hard at OT and PT, which I had almost to myself, and the skeleton crew that remained on duty through the holidays was able to give me extra attention. Commander Shaughnessey taught me an exercise to strengthen my atrophied gluteal muscles by pretending that a coin was positioned between the cheeks of my buttocks and then trying to squeeze it, and as I concentrated on the exercise, I imagined Toddy doing the same thing. Within seconds I was forced to roll to my side to relieve the pressure in an area I was not even exercising, and Shaughnessey wryly noted that I was definitely making progress.

I worked hard at my rehabilitation and gradually began to get stronger. One day at PT, as I was straining against the exercise table in the push-up position, I surprised myself by pushing my entire body into the air, where I hung suspended for a second with only my hands touching the table. I collapsed onto the table almost immediately; but my nosedive was the result of lack of balance rather than lack of strength, and an excited Commander Shaughnessey hurried over to the table to congratulate me on having just completed my first real push-up. I was also getting to the point where I could hold my own against Shaughnessey in arm wrestling, and I almost drooled at the prospect of being able to slam her knuckles onto the tabletop where she had beaten me so many times. Later in that week, after a particularly exhausting workout, I daydreamed absentmindedly about moving into an apartment with my wife, while the blue-bath- robed pusher from patient escort wheeled me back to my room.

In the course of my hospitalization several other enlisted patients who had been in my company in Vietnam were admitted, including one who had been in my platoon, but none affected me as strongly as Higgins in our brief encounter. My discomfort may have been caused by the strange way he acted in not identifying himself when he first came for me or by my failure to recognize him, but I believe it was caused by our reversal of roles as much as by anything. That same reversal of roles carried over into every other aspect of my hospitalization and was at times maddening. In Vietnam I had had the power of a god, with lightning and thunder only as far away as the nearest artillery battery. My commands may have been questioned, but they were always followed; and although I came to despise the life-and-death decisions I was forced to make, I had learned to make them professionally and competently.

All that was taken from me at the moment I was wounded, and it was difficult to adjust to being totally powerless. Many times I struck out blindly and irrationally at the corpsmen and nurses who were trying to help me, and it only increased my frustration that in my weakened state I was unable to inflict any damage on them. I now had to ask for everything, and it was damnably difficult to maintain a self-image when I was still soiling my bed.

Shortly after New Year's I also had the first of many identical dreams. In it I was back in Vietnam, and my platoon and I were preparing for a combat mission. As I gathered up my gear for the engagement, I could not find some of the equipment I needed: an ammunition clip, some socks, or a helmet. The particular lost item varied with the dream and was not nearly as important as the life-or-death situation we would be facing shortly, but frustration over its loss rather than apprehension of impending danger was the dominant emotion associated with the early part of the dream. The middle sequence was hazy, but as the dream ended, we had engaged a unit of enemy soldiers, and I had become separated from my men. The soldiers chased me through the surrounding area, and as they closed in on me, I awoke, covered with perspiration and certain that I had barely avoided that last look into my soul that surely will precede my death.

I have had the dream many times since it first roiled up from my subconscious in the winter of 1969, and each time it has been as terrifying as if I were experiencing it for the first time. I am able to see now that the dream is a reenactment and playing out of the events leading up to my wounding, but my understanding of the dream's origins does not ease the terror associated with it. In fact, it serves only to remind me anew that had I chosen to confront the enemy on that now-distant battlefield where I almost died, I would perhaps have come to know myself better.«

BIBLIOGRAPHY

Unpublished Materials

Media Exhibits

Alfred A. Knopf Entry for Katharine M. Graham, 1998
Charles Scribner's Sons Entry for Edward W. Bok, 1921
Charles Scribner's Sons Entry for Michael I. Pupin, 1924
Charles Scribner's Sons Entry for Charles A. Lindbergh, 1954
Congdon and Weed Entry for Russell W. Baker, 1983
Frederick A. Stokes Entry for John J. Pershing, 1932
Grove Weidenfeld Entry for Lewis B. Puller, 1992
Houghton Mifflin Company Entry for Henry B. Adams, 1919
Little, Brown and Company Entry for George F. Kennan, 1968
The Macmillan Company Entry for William A. White, 1947
The New American Library Entry for Norman K. Mailer, 1969
W. W. Norton Company Entry for Dean G. Acheson, 1970

Jury Statements

„Biography/Autobiography“ Jury Report, February 8, 1919, 1 p.
„Biography/Autobiography“ Jury Report, April 27, 1921, 1 p.
„Biography/Autobiography“ Jury Report, February 25,1924, 1 p.
„Biography/Autobiography“ Jury Report, March 12, 1947, 4 pp.
„Biography/Autobioorаphy“ Jury Report, March 24, 1954, 1 p.
„Biography/Autobiography“ Jury Report, January 13, 1968, 3 pp.
„Biography/Autobiography“ Jury Report, March 7, 1983, 1 p.
„BiographyjAutobiography“ Jury Report, December 29, 1991, 4 pp.
„Biography/Autobiography“ Jury Report, December 29, 1997, 2 pp.
„General Nonfiction“ Jury Report, January 21, 1969, 2 pp.
„History“ Jury Report, March 22, 1932, 1 p.
„History“ Jury Report, January 6, 1970, 3 pp.

Published Materials

Acheson, Dean G., Present at the Creation - My Years in the State Department, New York 1969.

Adams, Henry B., The Education of Henry Adams, New York 1918.

Baker, Russell W., Growing Up, New York 1982.

Bates, J. Douglas, The Pulitzer Prize - The Inside Story of America's Most Prestigious Award, New York 1991.

Bok, Edward E., The Americanization of Edward Bok, New York 1920.

Brennan, Elizabeth A./Clarage, Elizabeth C., Who's Who of Pulitzer Prize Winners, Phoenix, Az., 1999.

Felsenthal, Carol, Power, Privilege and the Post - The Katharine Graham Story, New York 1993.

Fischer, Heinz-Dietrich, American Historians Describe the European Past - Pulitzer Prize Winning Works, Vienna - Zurich 2016.

Fischer, Heinz-Dietrich, Main Achievements of American Presidents - Pulitzer Prize Winning Books' Excerpts, Vienna - Zurich 2014.

Fischer, Heinz-D./Fischer, Erika J., The-Pulitzer Prize Archive, Vol. 7: American History Awards 1917-1991, Munich - London - Paris 1994.

Fischer, Heinz-D./Fischer, Erika J., The Pulitzer Prize Archive, Vol. 8, Biography / Autobiography Awards 1917-1992, Munich - London - Paris 1995.

Fischer, Heinz-D./Fischer, Erika J., The Pulitzer Prize Archive, Vol. 9, General Nonfiction Awards 1962-1993, Munich - London - Paris 1996.

Fischer, Heinz-D./Fischer, Erika J., The Pulitzer Prize Archive, Vol. 19, Chronicle of the Pulitzer Prizes for History, Munich 2005.

Fischer, Heinz-D./Fischer, Erika J., The Pulitzer Prize Archive, Vol. 20, Chronicle of the Pulitzer Prizes for Biography, Munich 2006.

Gill, Brendan, Lindbergh Allone, New York 1977.

Graham, Katherine M., Personal History, New York 1997.

Griffith, Sally F., Home Town News - William Allen White and the Emporia Gazette, New York 1989.

Hohenberg, John, The Pulitzer Diaries - Inside America's Greatest Prize, Syracuse, N.Y., 1997.

Hohenberg, John, The Pulitzer Prizes - A History of the Awards in Books, Drama, Music, and Journalism, New York - London 1974.

Johnson, Walter, William Allen White Defends America, Chicago 1945.

Kennan, George F., Memoirs 1925-1950, Boston - Toronto 1967.

Mailer, Norman A., The Armies of the Night, New York 1968.

Mayers, David, George Kennan and the Dilemmas of U.S. Foreign Policy, Oxford 1988.

McClellan, Bavid S., Dean Acheson - The State Department Years, New York 1976.

Milton, Joyce, Loss of Eden - A Biography of Charles and Anne Morrow Lindbergh, New York 1993.

Miscambe, Wilson, George F. Kennan and the Making of American Foreign Policy 1947-1950, Princeton 1992.

Lindbergh, Charles A., The Spirit of St. Louis, New York 1953.

Pershing, John J., My Experiences in the World War, New York 1931.

Puller, Lewis B., Fortunate Son - The Healing of a Vietnam Vet, New York 1991.

Pupin, Michael I., From Immigrant to Inventor, New York 1923.

Rich, Everett, William Allen White - The Man From Emporia, New York 1941.

Samuels, Ernest, Henry Adams, Cambridge, Ma., 1989.

Seitz, Don C., Joseph Pulitzer - His Life and Letters, New York 1924.

Simpson, Brooks D., The Political Education of Henry Adams, Columbia, S.C., 1996.

Steinberg, Salme H., Reformer in the Marketplace - Edward Bok and the Ladies Home Journal, Baton Rouge, La., 1979.

White, William A., The Autobiography of William Allen White, New York 1946.